IMAGES
of America

BELLINGHAM

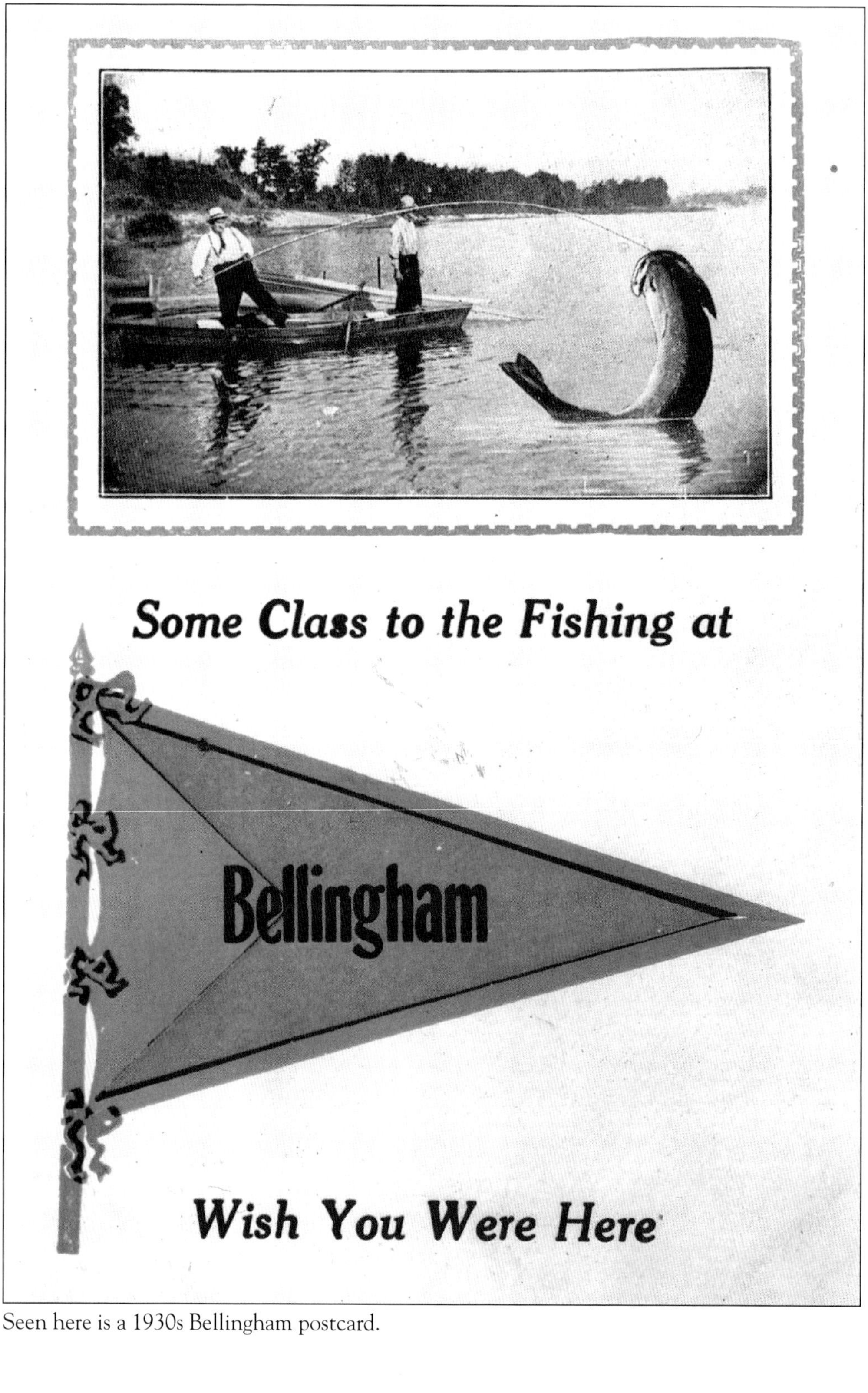

Seen here is a 1930s Bellingham postcard.

IMAGES
of America

BELLINGHAM

Ernest A. Taft

ARCADIA
PUBLISHING

ISBN 978-0-7385-1255-6

Published by Arcadia Publishing
Charleston, South Carolina

Printed in the United States of America

Library of Congress Catalog Card Number: 2003106547

For all general information contact Arcadia Publishing at:
Telephone 843-853-2070
Fax 843-853-0044
E-mail sales@arcadiapublishing.com
For customer service and orders:
Toll-Free 1-888-313-2665

Visit us on the Internet at www.arcadiapublishing.com

Contents

ACKNOWLEDGMENTS

Not one part of this book would have been possible if it was not for the hard work of the Bellingham Historic Commission. For 31 years, this commission has been collecting photographs and compiling and recording local history. Thanks go out to all those individuals who have given their photographs and stories to the commission. This project was undertaken in order to forever record the people and events of Bellingham so they may endure for all time. While examining thousands of photographs, I became aware of just how much more has to be done. Many photographs I hoped we had, we did not. So, a long process of tracking down individuals had to be undertaken. A note of thanks goes out to those individuals. Fran Donovan, Medway historian, with his contribution of Bellingham photographs certainly has made my job easier. The other photograph collection, the bicentennial collection of 1969, was from Edward J. and Cecile A. DeNault. My apologies go out to those individuals whose donated photographs do not appear in this book. Maybe a second volume will be warranted. I also thank Tammy Kraal and Anne Arcand for their long hours of typing. I am not a professional writer or historian. I am just an interested individual doing the best that I can.

Introduction

Bellingham (1719) was the last town to be incorporated in Norfolk County. Until then, the area was known only as "common or undivided land of Dedham." Mendon, on the west, was an independent town in 1667. Wrentham, on the east, was settled in 1673. The main reason for this delay in settlement was the fear of Indian attacks. On July 14, 1675, some settlers very near the Bellingham border with Mendon were massacred. The ravages of King Philip's War on all sides of the territory kept away newcomers. King Philip (*Metacomet*) claimed to own the land of the "Dedham Woods," later to become the principal part of Bellingham. During December 1675, every home in Mendon was burned. With the death of Metacomet in August 1676, the war was over. The settlers began to return to the area. As the colonists spread out, the Dedham selectman sent two men to examine this area. According to Dedham town records, on "Jan ye 4th 1692 ye land neer Mendham [Mendon] is not worth ye laying out in a Devident [for division]." Then on June 7, 1698, the proprietors of the undivided land of Dedham met with another committee and decided to draw lots of 100 acres each. Jacob Bartlat and Nicolas Cook were the first two settlers to draw lots. It has been determined that Jacob Bartlat's property would now be in Woonsocket, Rhode Island, close to the Blackstone River. The Nicolas Cook property would be in the vicinity between South Main Street and Peter's River. Bellingham's first two settlers had little to fear from wild beasts. The Dedham selectman offered a bounty of 10 to 20 shillings for every wolf killed, 6 pence for each rattlesnake, and 20 shillings for a wildcat. Soon, all of these species disappeared from the area. The only thing the early settlers, a Quaker and a Baptist, had to fear were the strict laws of Massachusetts governing religion.

Soon, the number of settlers increased, and it became necessary for them to form their own government. The town of Dedham consented and the General Court of Massachusetts was petitioned for a township. Bellingham became a town on November 17, 1719.

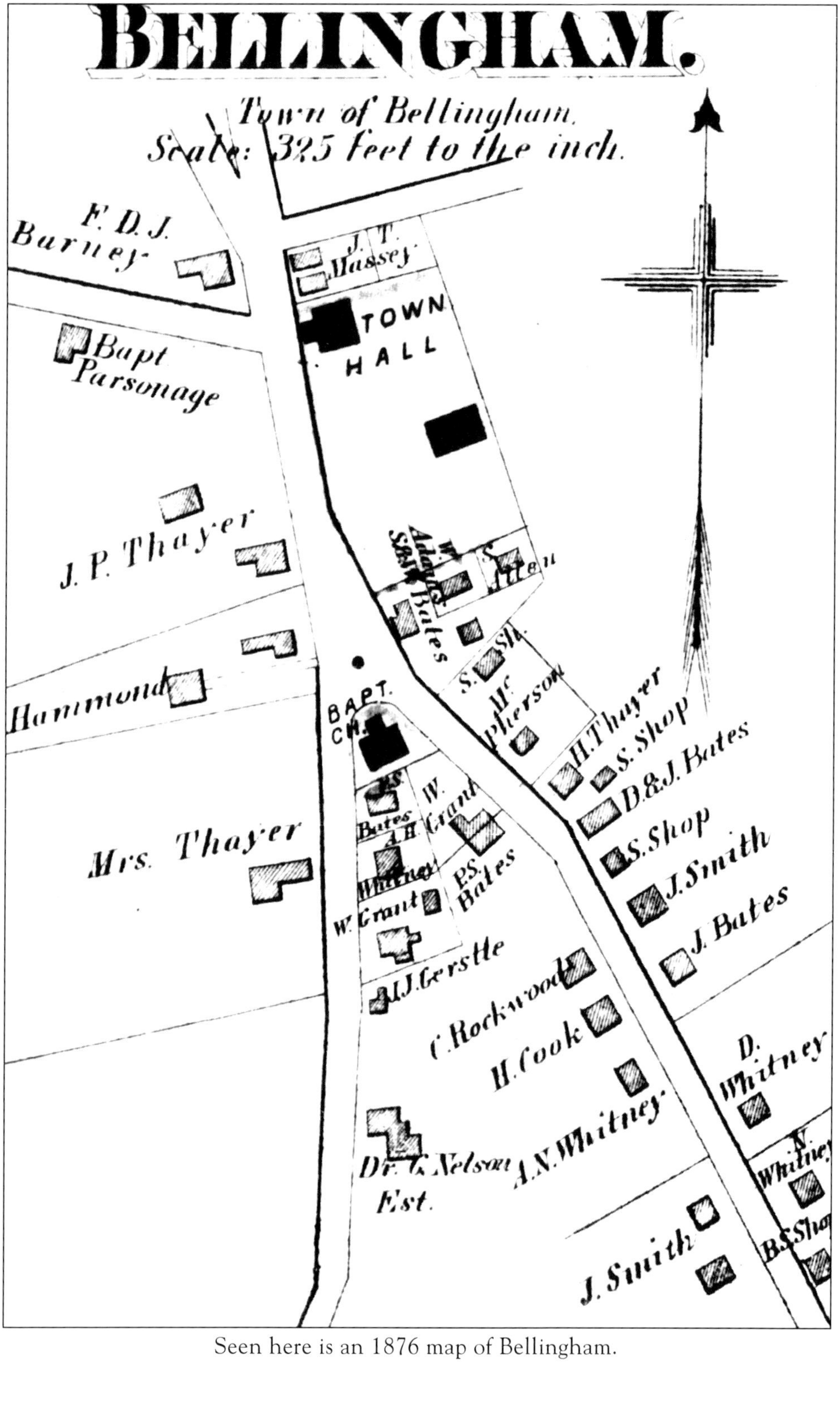

Seen here is an 1876 map of Bellingham.

One

Bellingham Center

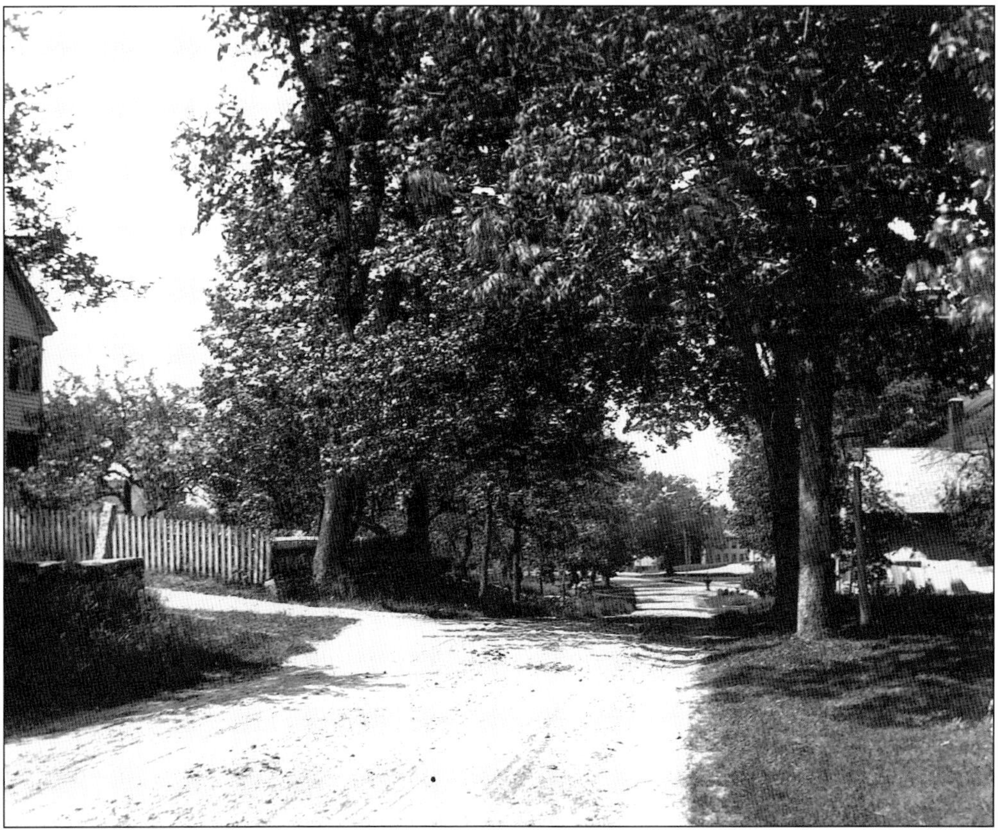

This 1906 view of South Main Street is looking toward Bellingham Center. The water fountain at the bottom of the hill can be seen.

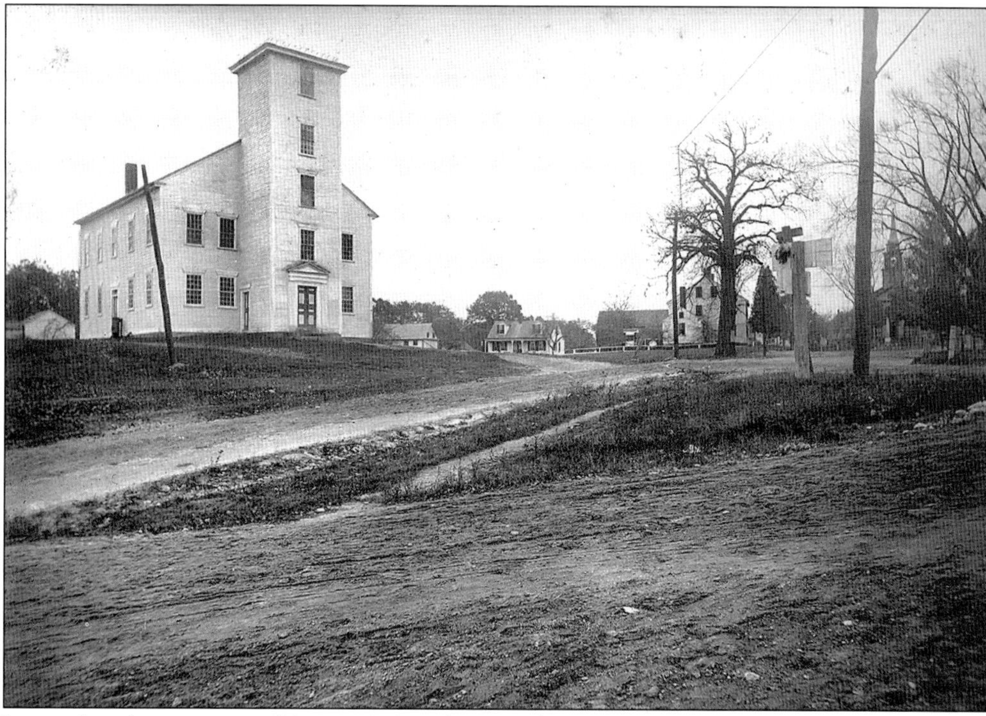

Located at the junction of Routes 140 and 126 is the town hall. Pictured in 1898, this corner was then called Barney's Corner. From left to right are the town hall, the Webber home (now the planning board), the Nash home (now a museum), Bates Tavern (now Domino's), and the Baptist church.

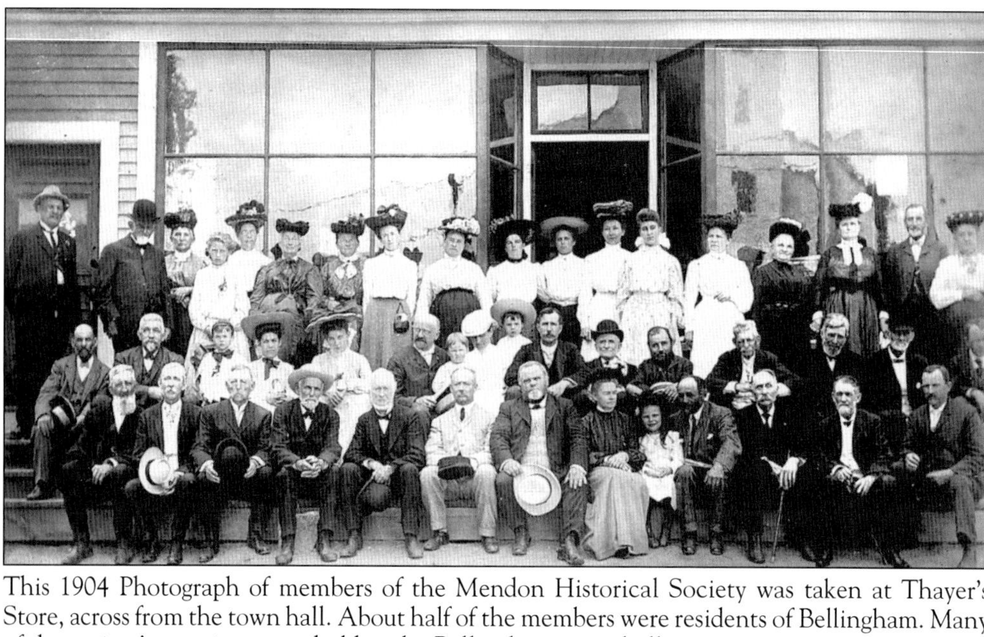

This 1904 Photograph of members of the Mendon Historical Society was taken at Thayer's Store, across from the town hall. About half of the members were residents of Bellingham. Many of the society's meetings were held at the Bellingham town hall.

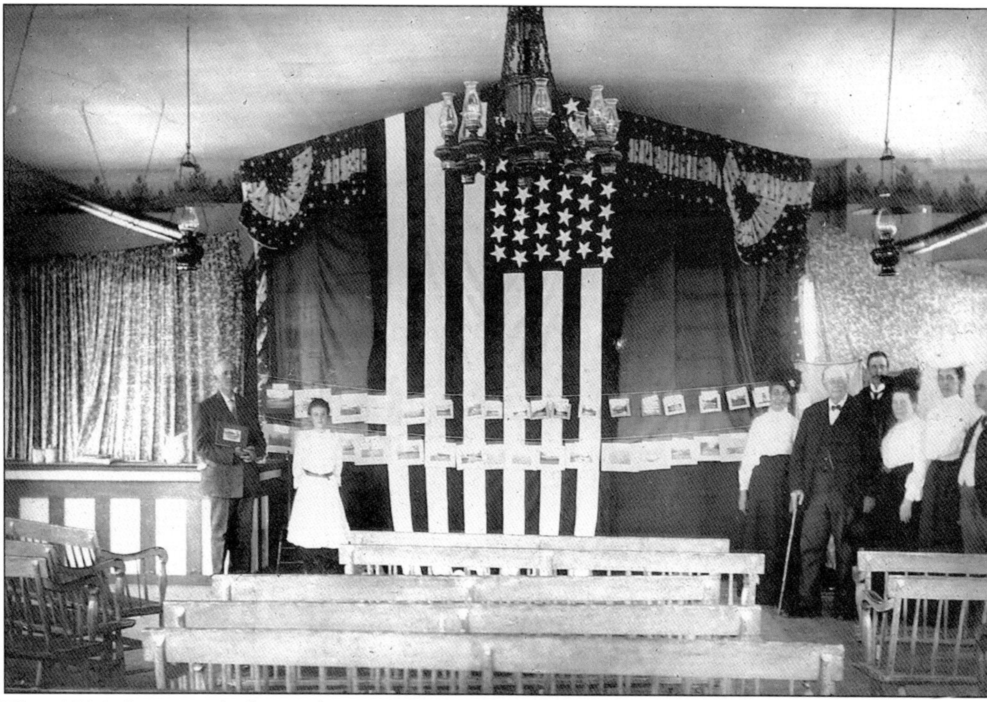

This 1896 photograph shows the upstairs interior of the town hall. Note the kerosene lamps and the wooden benches. We can identify Henry Whitney on the left, standing with an unknown student. Seen in the group on the right are, from left to right, Mrs. Capron, Burlington Briggs, two unidentified people, Lewis Clark's wife, and Lewis Clark.

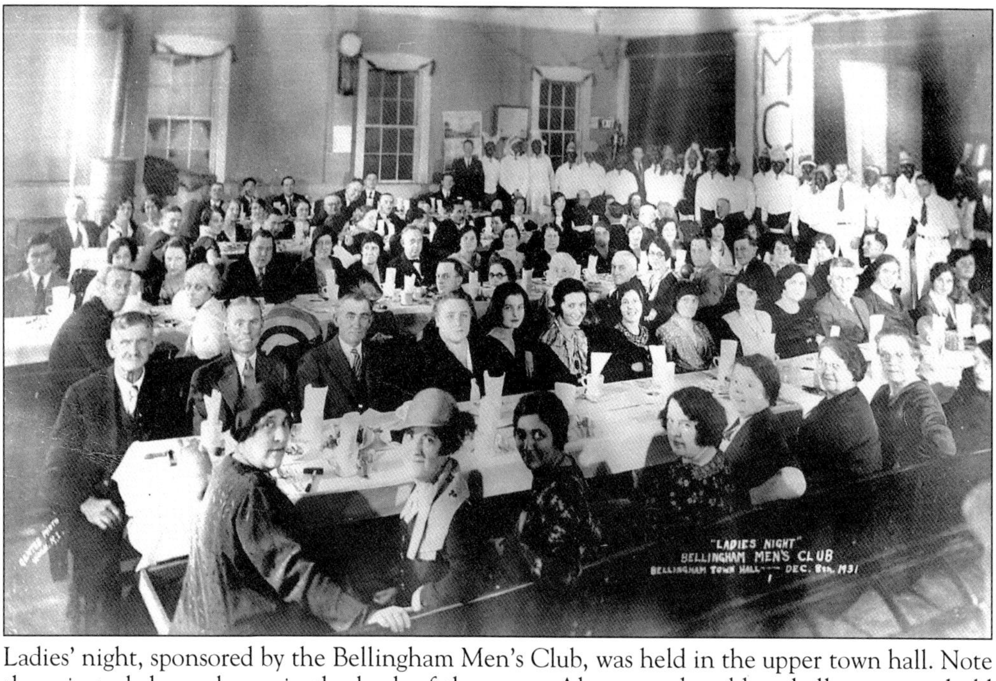

Ladies' night, sponsored by the Bellingham Men's Club, was held in the upper town hall. Note the minstrel-show players in the back of the room. Also note the old potbelly stove and old clock on the outer wall. The event took place on December 8, 1931.

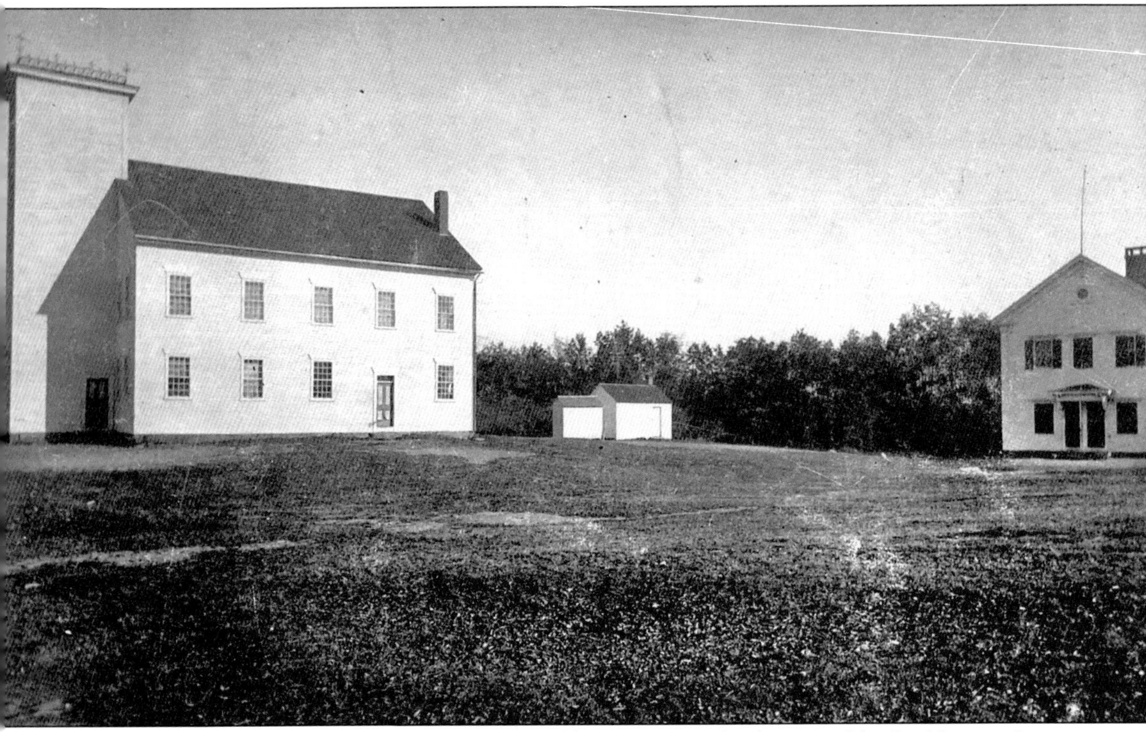

The town hall was built in 1802 at a cost of $4,000. It was built as a public building to "transact their public concerns" and "for the accommodation of said Religious Society for a House of Public Worship." The town paid $1,000, and the remaining balance was paid off from the rental of pews. Bellingham's town hall is the third oldest town hall still in use in the state. In 1840, the third floor of the tower was completed for use as an armory. At that time, there were 132 people involved in the local militia, Bellingham Rifles. In 1843, a stove was installed, and in 1853, part of the tower was rented out for a boot shop. On May 22, 1892, the Bellingham Grange, No. 190, was organized. The Grange met at the town hall for nearly 100 years. The town hall was remodeled in 1910. Tin ceilings were put in along with a kitchen, dining room, vault, and offices. The hall used kerosene lamps until 1913, when the Union Light and Power Company of Franklin first supplied electricity to this building. On October 9, 1941, a civil-defense observation post was erected on the top floor of the tower. The post was manned 24 hours a day during World War II. The post was used to report the position of spotted planes to the main office of the civil defense headquarters. Today, after 200 years, the Bellingham town hall is still the main focal point of a variety of activities. The town lockup in the center of the photograph was built in 1875. The two-room Massey School on the right was built in 1873. All of these town buildings sat upon the village green, or town common.

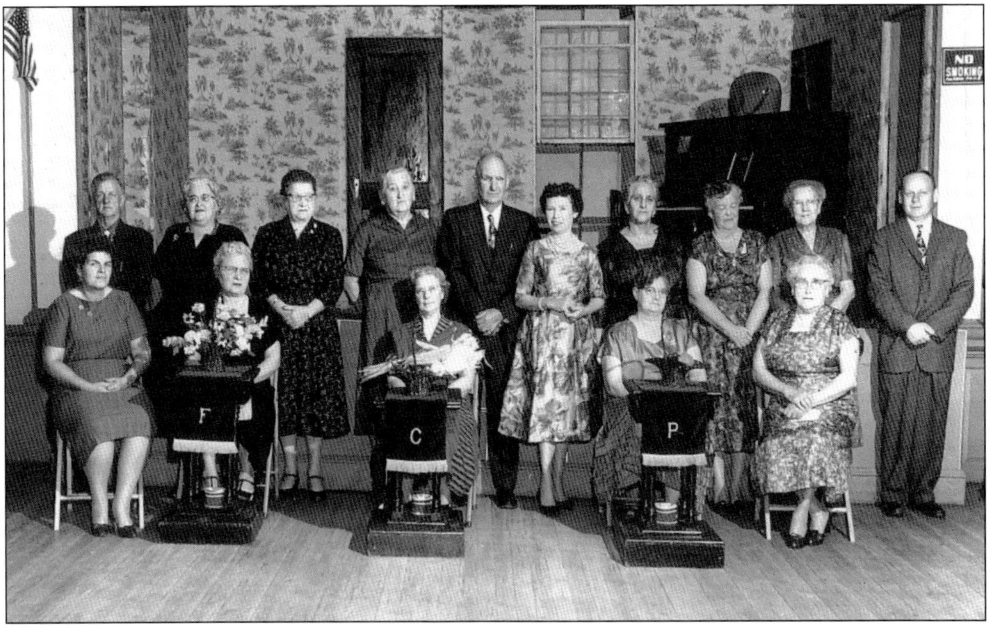

Bellingham Grangers (Patrons of Husbandry) of Grange No. 140 are pictured in the upper town hall c. the 1950s. They are, from left to right, as follows: (front row) Shirley Holmstrom, Florence Noseworthy, Edna Brown, Mae Vater, and Marie Cooke; (back row) Ray Patrick, Marion Fraser, Letitia Knott, Kathryn Gariepy, Lloyd Brown, Marion Norman, Anna Patrick, Marion Thayer, Amanda Winn, and William Shea.

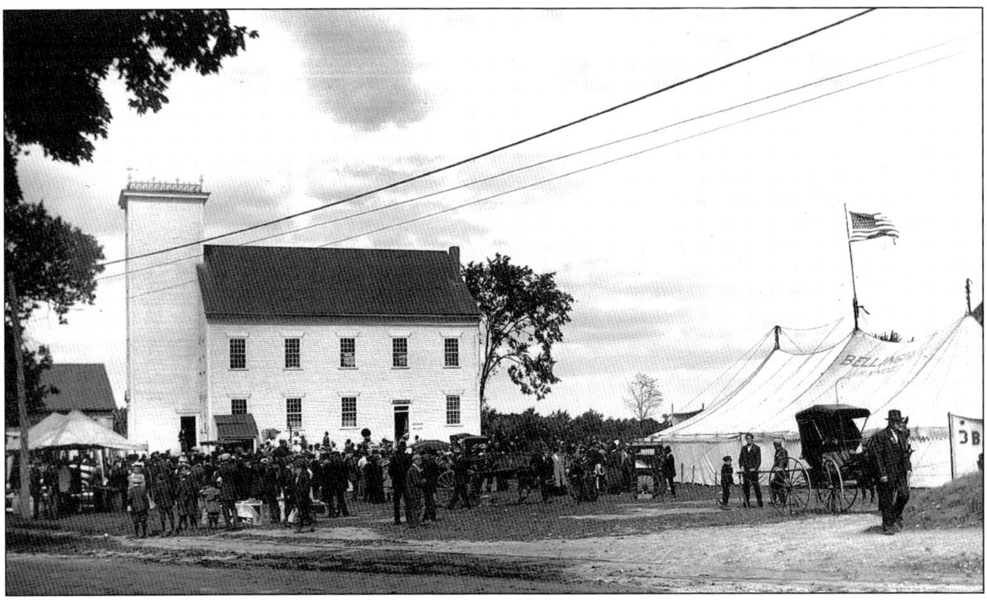

Every September, the Bellingham Grange held its Old Home Days fair, shown in this c. 1905 photograph. In one day, this fair attracted hundreds of people from neighboring towns. They would come to the town hall by horse and buggy, train, trolley, or foot for the all-day affair. The town band played, and there was always plenty of food. There were vegetables, fruit, preserves, and baking contests with ribbons awarded. Other activities included horse and oxen competitions, greased pig catching, vegetable displays, and women's foot races.

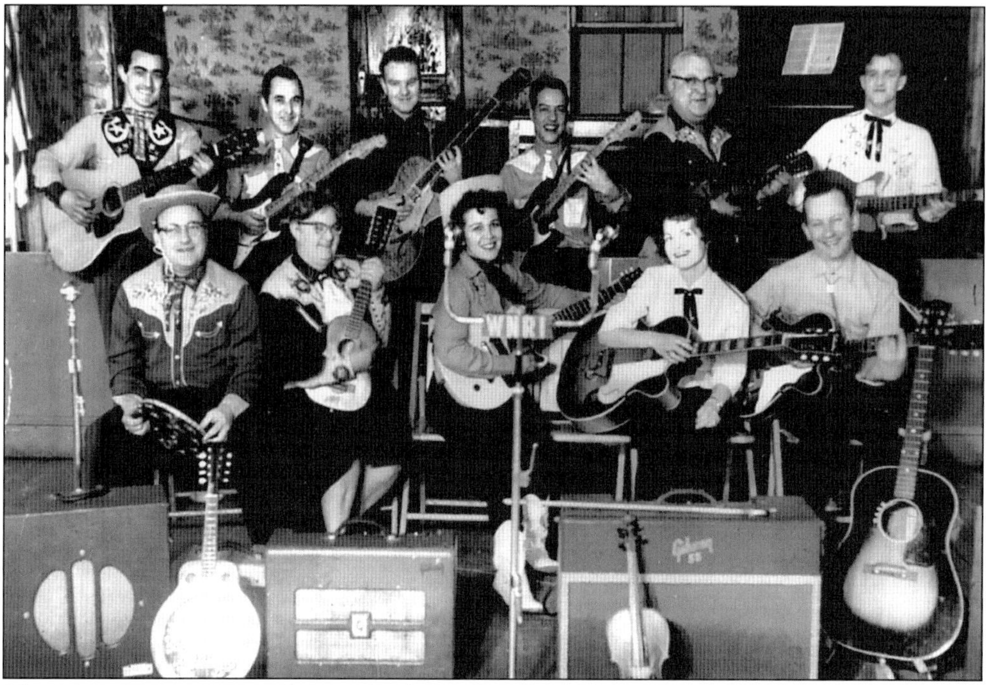

The Westones were a popular country band during the 1950s and 1960s. They played at local establishments and had a Saturday-morning country hour that could be heard on WNRI radio. Seen here are, from left to right, the following: (front row) Dave ?, Mae Vater, Cara ?, Rusty ?, and Paul Johnson; (back row) Frank ?, Dell ?, Sonny ?, Dennis ?, Jim Riley, and Hank ?.

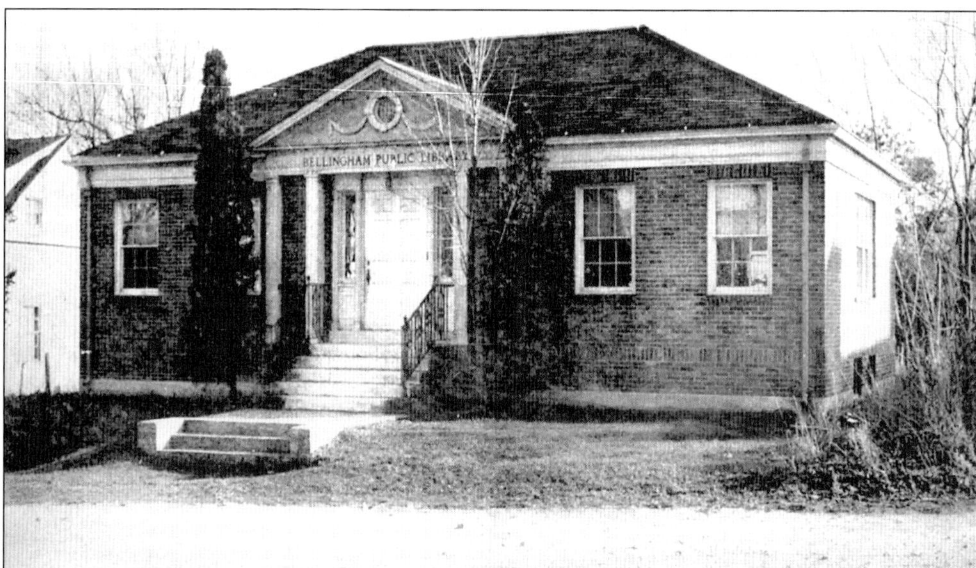

This building, located at 3 Common Street, originally opened on May 15, 1930, as a town library. In 1989, the library moved to a new location, and this building became the home of the Bellingham Historical Commission. It is now a museum and research center and houses most of Bellingham's historical artifacts.

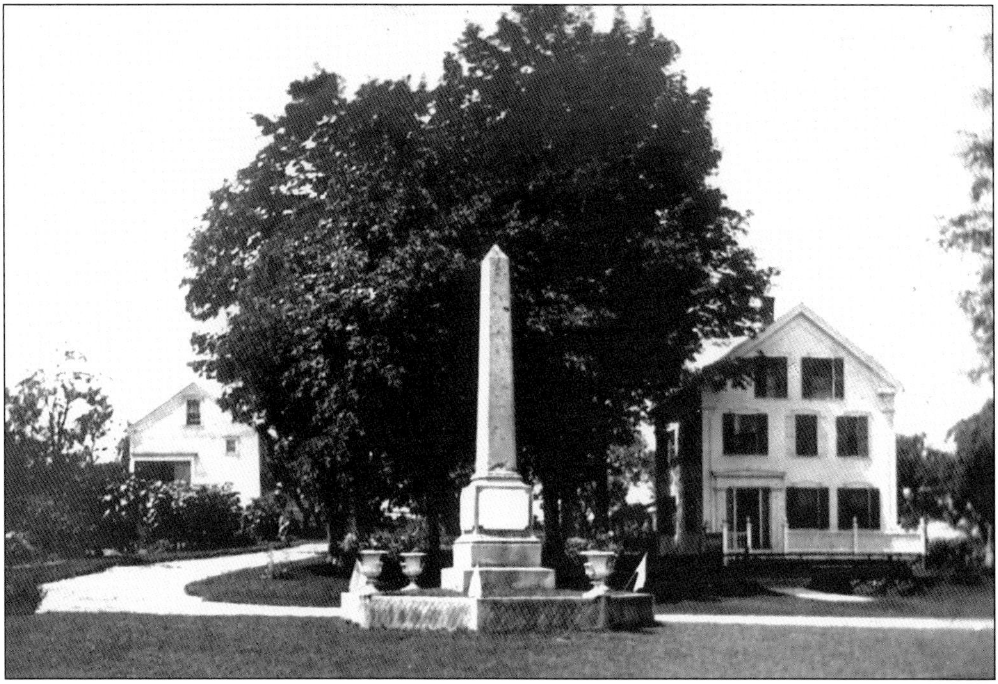

The Eldredge house located on South Main Street was the location of Bellingham's first free public library. On December 5, 1894, Sara Tufts Rockwood opened a reading program in her home, which would be used as a library.

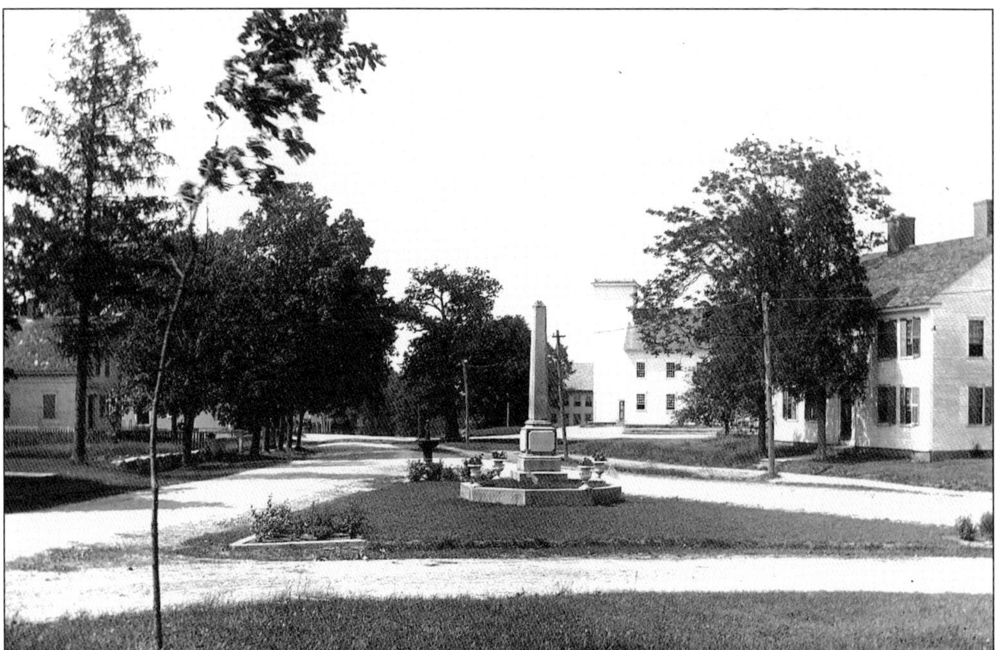

Here is a view of Bellingham Center looking north. On the right is Bate's or Sullivan Tavern. In the middle of the photograph are the water fountain and the Civil War monument. The town hall can be seen in the background.

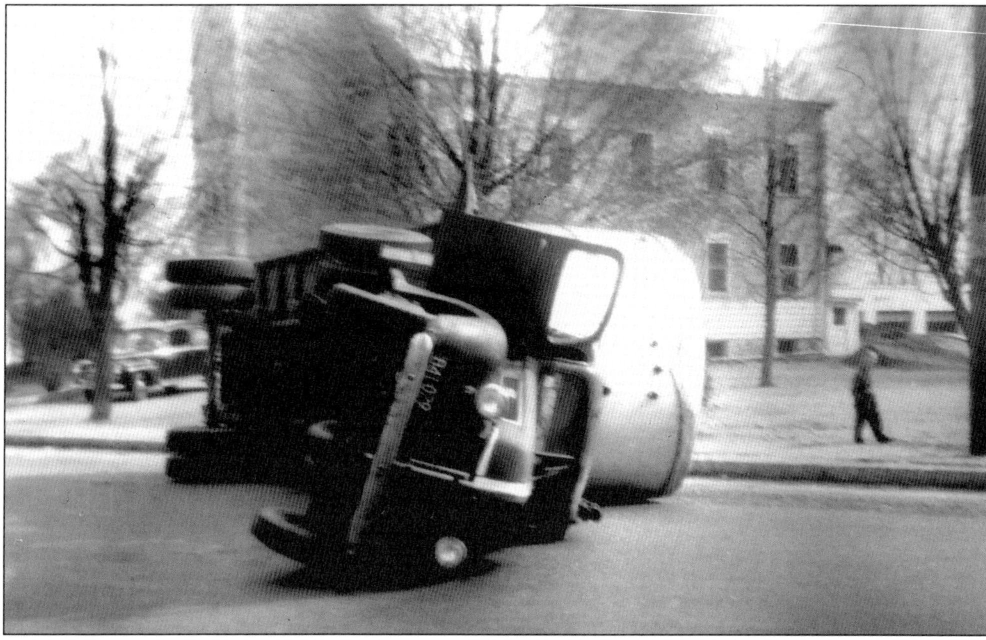

With today's traffic congestion, it is not uncommon to see an accident at Bellingham Center. But in 1941, when this tractor-trailer rig flipped over, it made front-page news at many of the state's newspapers.

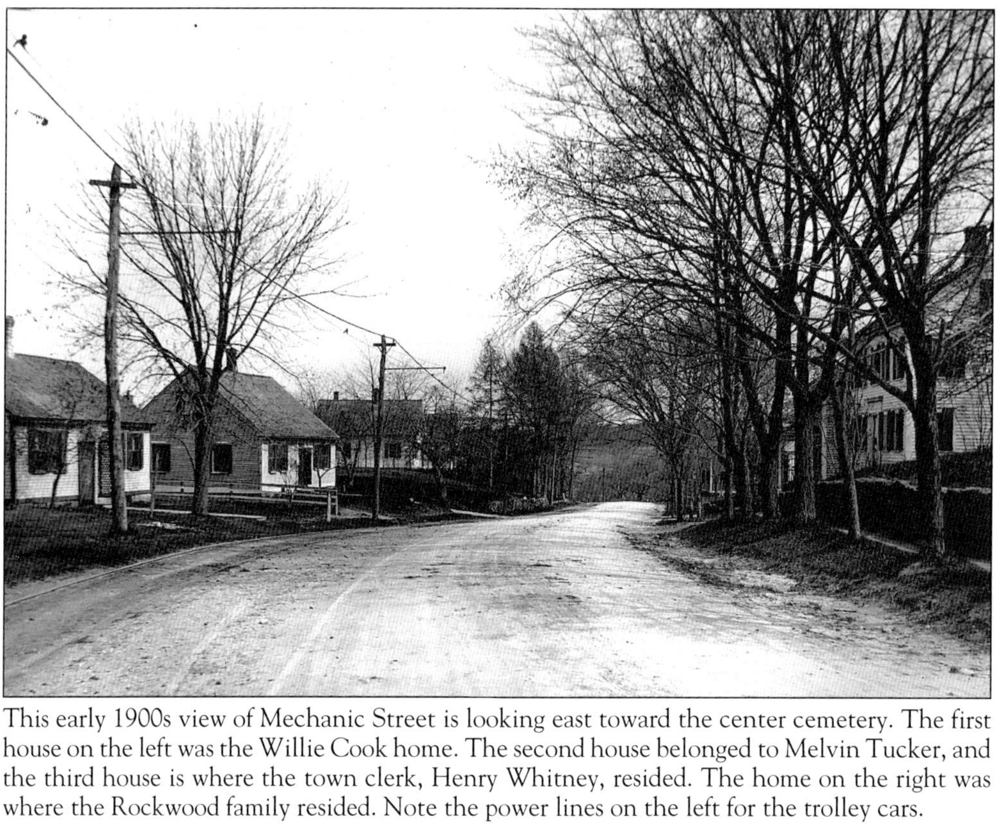

This early 1900s view of Mechanic Street is looking east toward the center cemetery. The first house on the left was the Willie Cook home. The second house belonged to Melvin Tucker, and the third house is where the town clerk, Henry Whitney, resided. The home on the right was where the Rockwood family resided. Note the power lines on the left for the trolley cars.

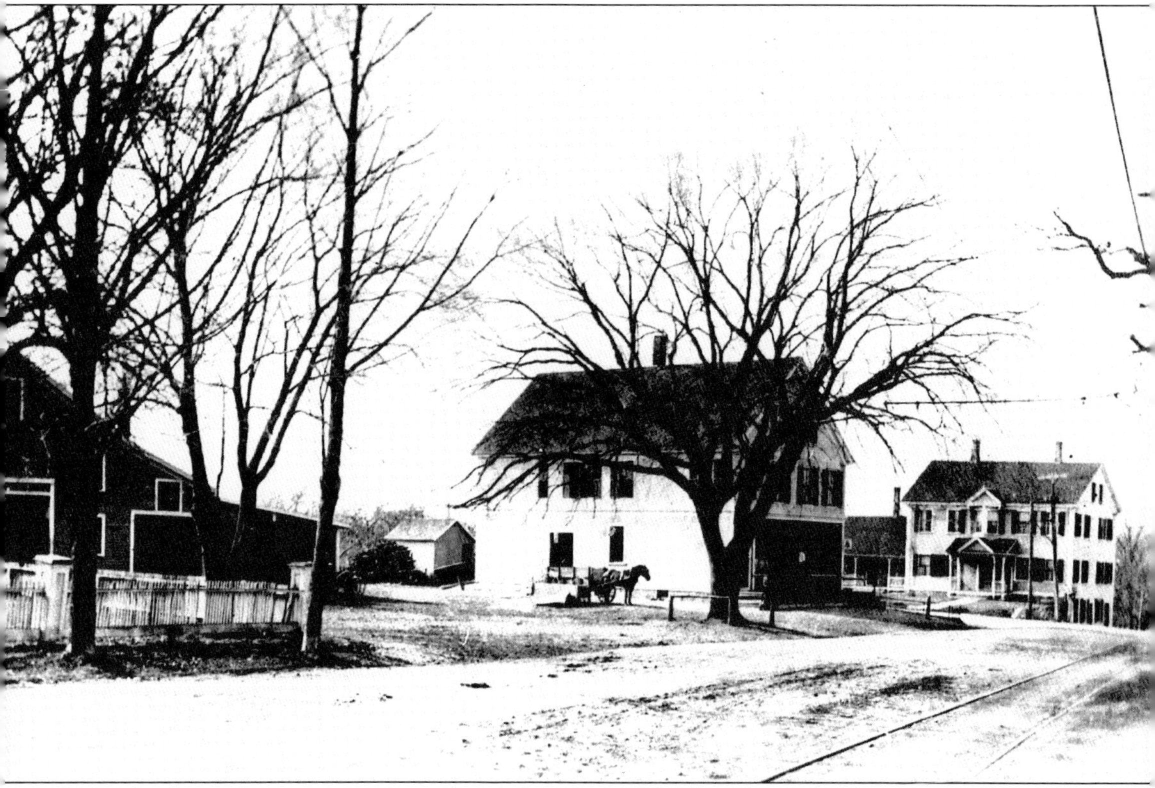

Under the large elm tree was where the Nash girls would sell duck sandwiches every Sunday. A post office was established beside the Thayer Store, with Edward E. Rockwood appointed postmaster in 1895. In 1915, Ruel S. Thayer was appointed postmaster and served for 42 years. L. Francis Thayer built and opened a store here in 1895. The store first operated as a general dry-goods store, but kerosene, coal, and grain were also available. Thayer sold Wirthmore Grain and Feed from the barn for 75 years. The Center School took water from the Thayer's horse barn, and when there was a fire in town, it was mainly the Thayer horses that were used to pull the converted fire wagon. The Thayer Store closed on December 18, 1964. This store was located directly across the street from the town hall. Currently, the site is a mini-plaza.

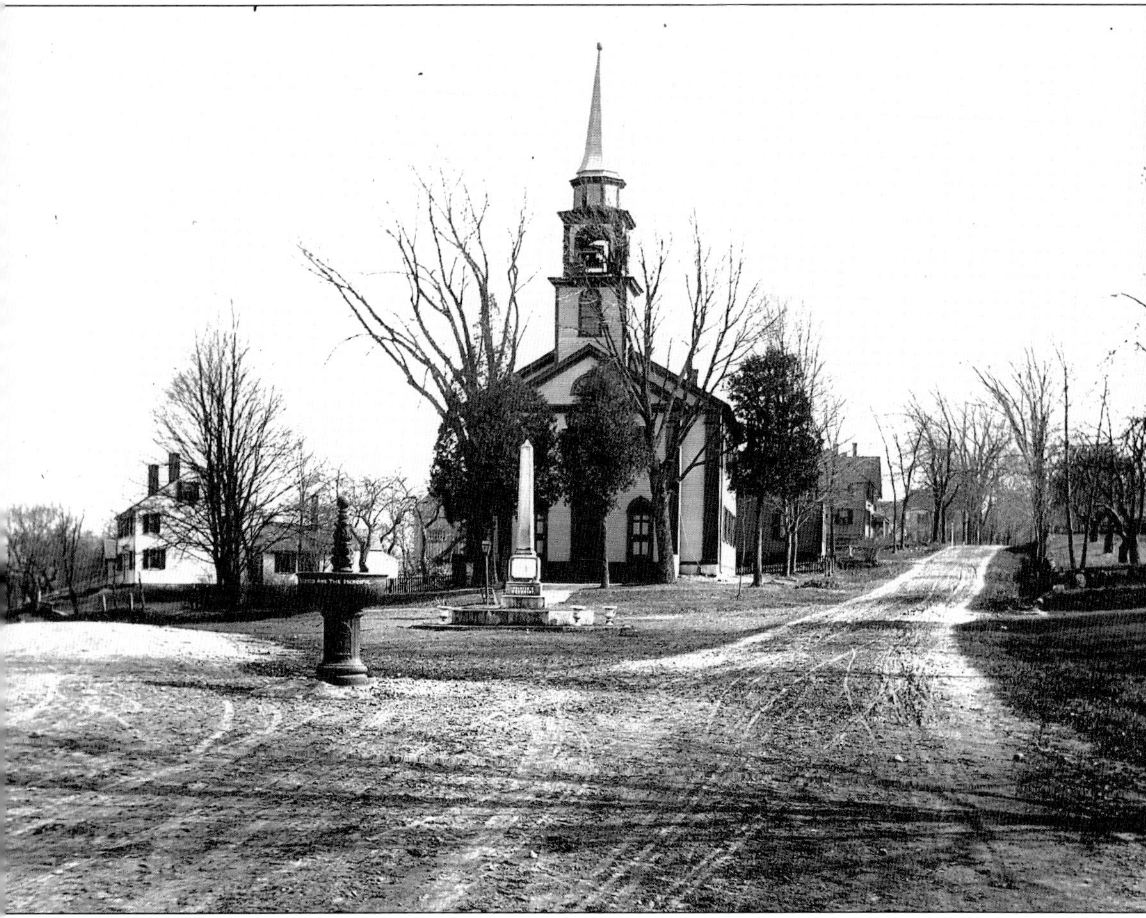

This 1906 view from Bellingham Center looks south to where the road splits at the First Baptist Church. The water trough was installed in 1904. Henry Jenks was paid $131 for the fountain, and $143.02 was paid for labor installation. The Wentworth Fund, which gave money to towns to establish drinking fountains on the condition that "Blessed are the Merciful" be inscribed on them, gave $20. James Lilly was paid $1.25 to do the lettering. The Soldier's Monument, or Civil War monument, was constructed in 1874 and dedicated to 10 Bellingham soldiers who were killed during the Civil War. The base of the monument is 12 feet wide, and the entire monument stands 16.5 feet tall from ground level. It stands in honor of the following: Thomas Carey, W. Ellis Cook, Moses Drake, C. Philip Hancock, Jos. W. Holbrook, Jairas Lawrence, Joseph Osgood, H. Perry Slocum, Calvin C. Thayer, and Lewis E. Whitney.

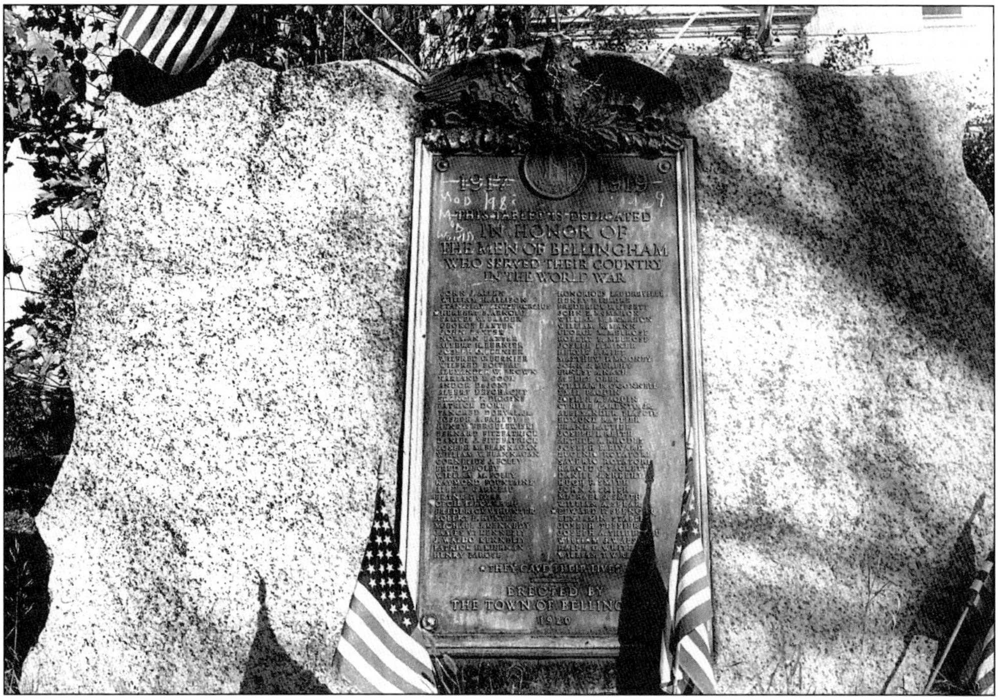

This monument was dedicated to Bellingham veterans who served during World War I. It contains the names of 75 men and was erected by the town of Bellingham in 1920. It stands directly in front of the town hall.

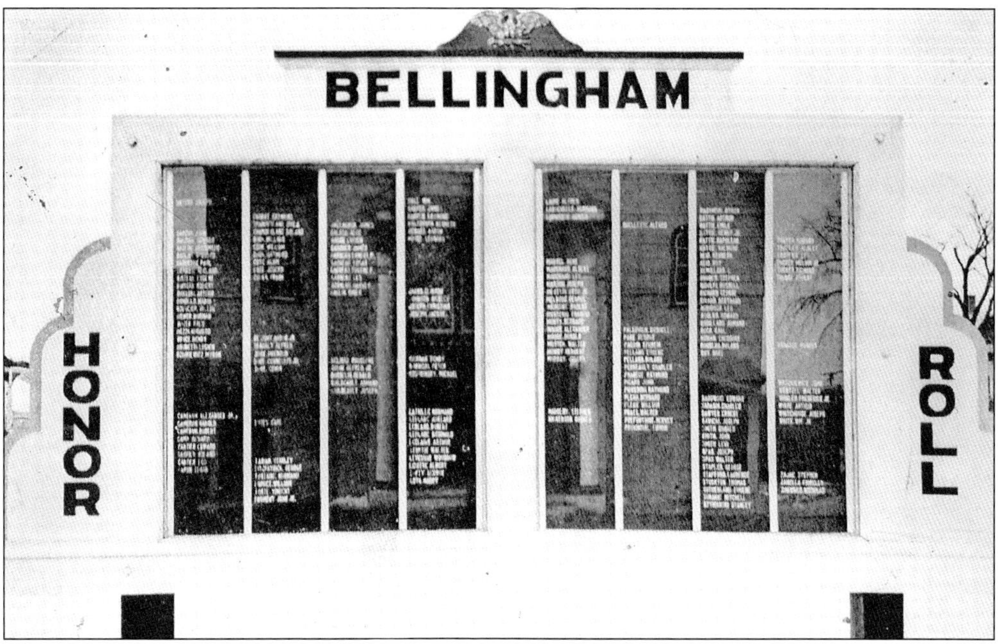

This is one of three honor rolls in town listing the names of those who served their country during World War II. This honor roll stood on the old Bellingham town common and was erected in 1942. The names were updated until the end of World War II. The wooden, glass, and plastic honor-roll boards deteriorated and, in 1963, were removed.

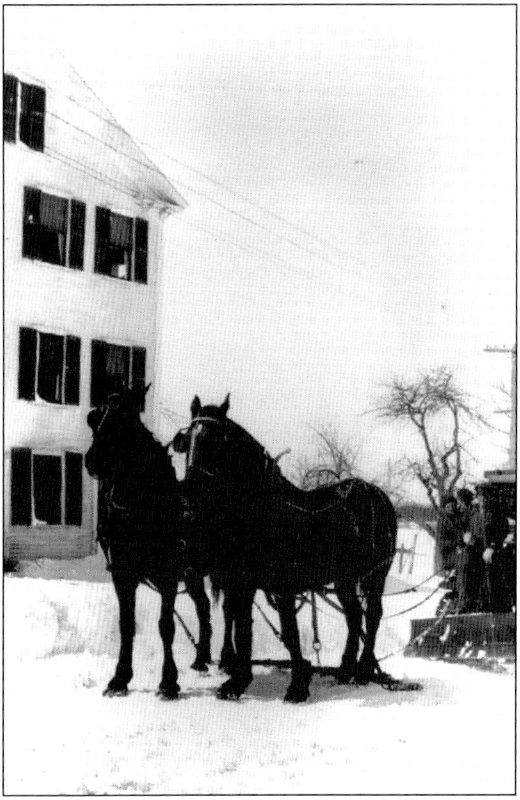

Horses are pulling a snowplow in this c. 1923–1924 photograph.

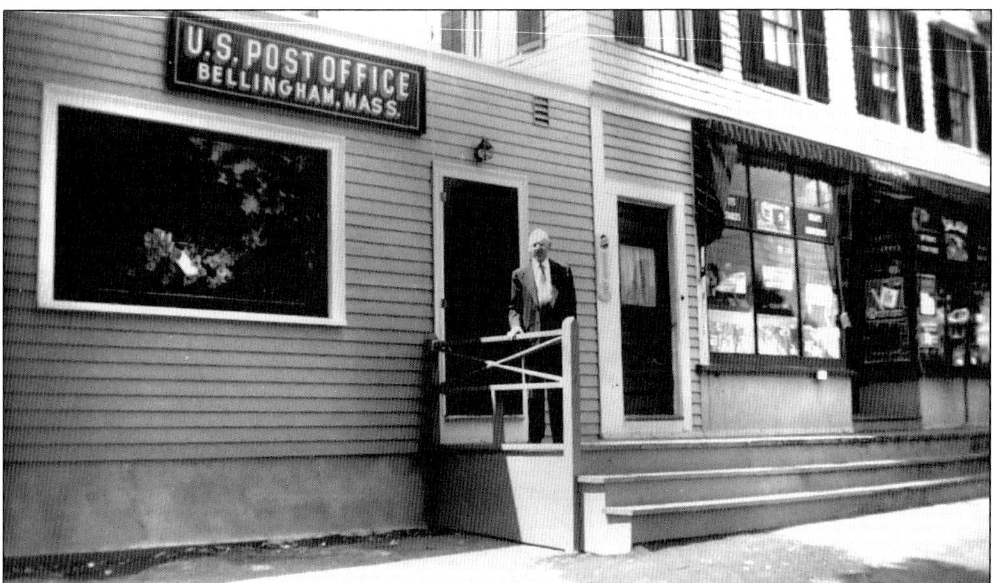

Postmaster Ruel S. Thayer is standing outside his post office at Bellingham Center.

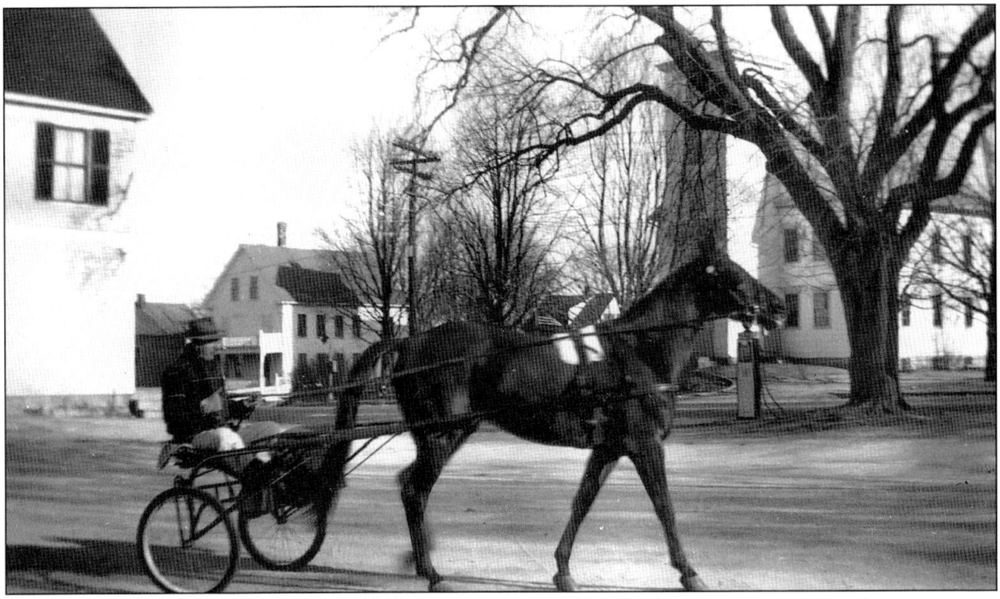

In this 1925 photograph, taken at Bellingham Center, Ruel Thayer is trotting his horse.

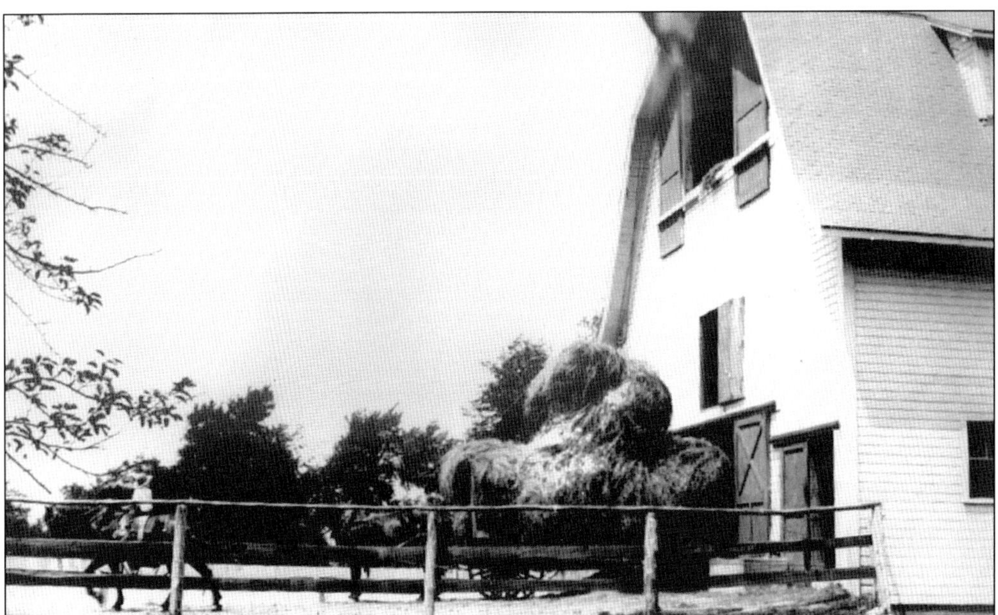

It is haying time at the L.F. Thayer barn in Bellingham Center in 1925.

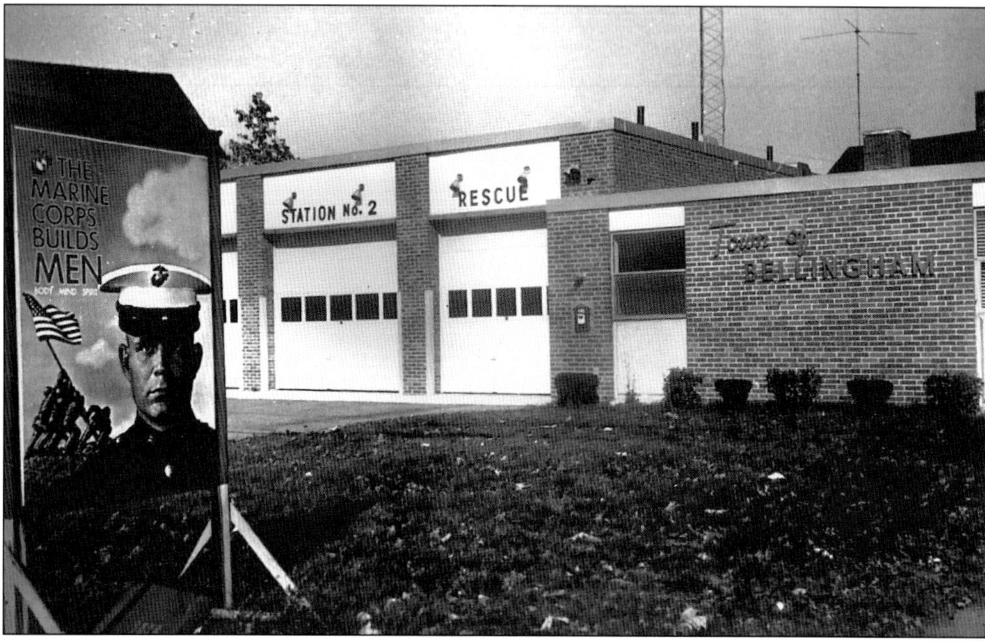

In 1965, the combination police-and-fire station was built upon the town common. The fire department shared one-half of the building and was designated as Station No. 2. In 1989, Station No. 2 was moved to a new facility on Blackstone Street. From 1989 on, this building served as Bellingham's police station, dedicated to the memory of former Police Chief Euclide E. Fleuette.

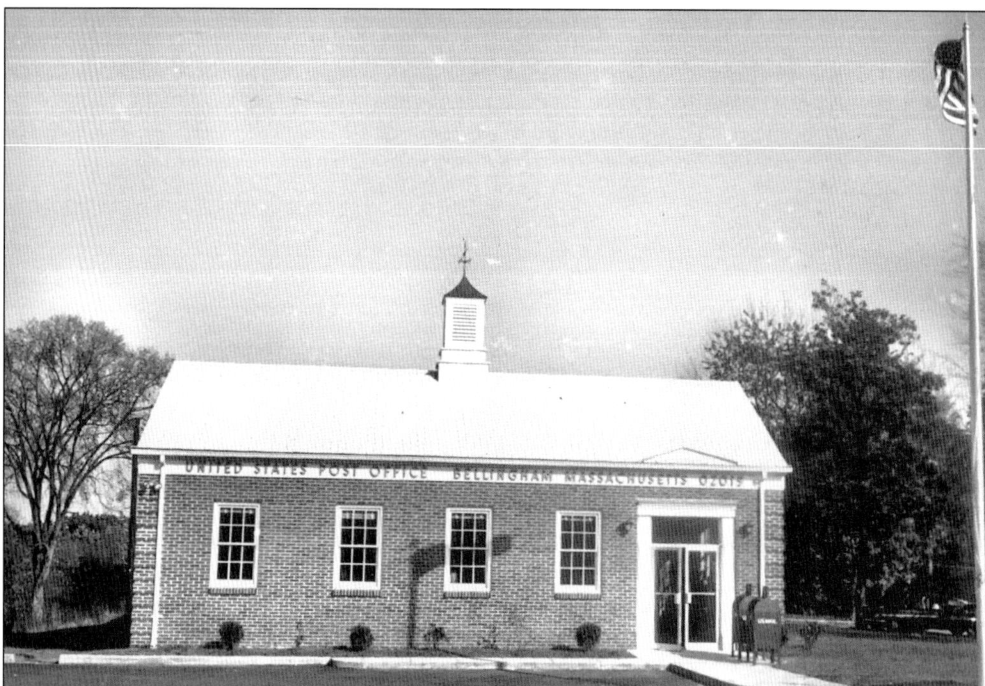

This building, located on North Main Street, served as Bellingham's post office from 1967 to 1991.

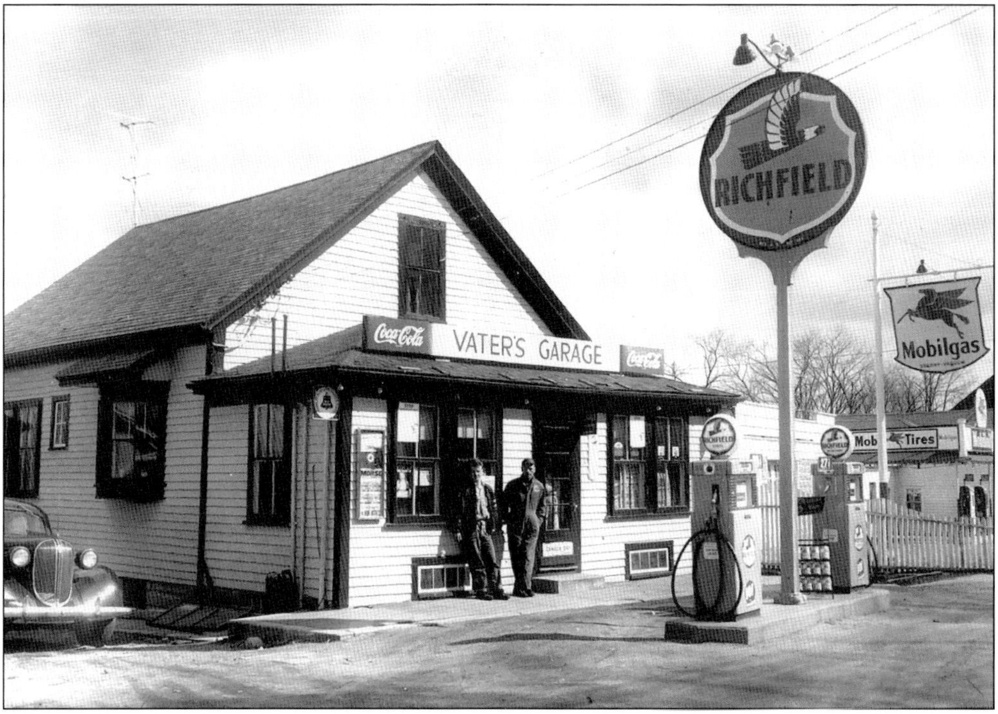

Vater's Garage, also a gas station, was located at Bellingham Center. Walter J. Vater ran this gas station from 1945 to 1970. Walter is on the right in the above photograph. His son, Walter S., is on the left.

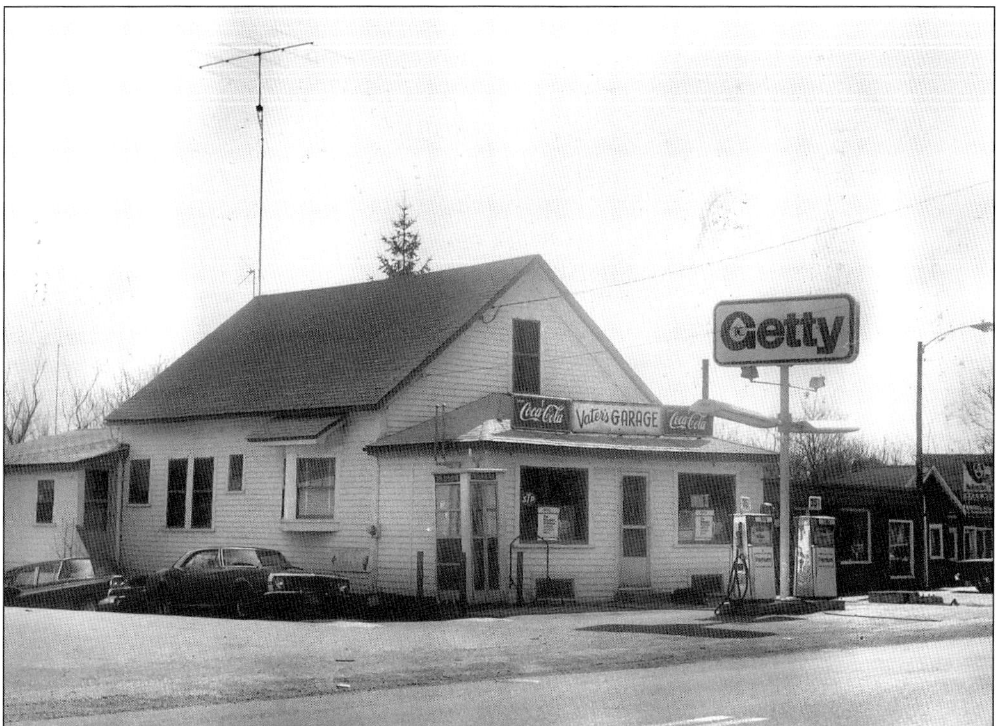

1776. 1876.

GRANDE OLDE TYME PARTIE,

In ye

Big White Painted Towne House,

With ye Weather Vane near ye Olde Chestnut Tree,

On ye Main Roade, in ye Olde Towne of

BELLINGHAME,

Tuesday nighte, ye twenty-fifth day of ye fourthe monthe, called Aprile, in ye year

1876.

☞Ye Tithing Man will collect for ye single Ticket, FIFTEEN PENNIES.

☞Sarg't Rocket will swinge open ye doors of the ye Towne House at early candle-light, wh is sett down in ye Olde Almanack at 7 o'clock in ye twilighte.

Issued from ye Printing House of S. S. Foss, Patriot Building, Woonsocket, R. I.

A special centennial dinner was held at the town hall to celebrate our country's 100 years of independence.

ENTERTAINMENT.

Ye followinge is as complete a recorde of what will be done, as ye Committee is able to give at ye present tyme.

N. B. At ye announcemente by Nabor Eaton, all conversatione will stop, and ye companie will heare ye Fiddlers tune their Fiddles, and ye Singers get their pitche.

Ye Worldleye Amusements

will begin withe some sacrede tunes, and some worldleye songs on ye wind and ye stringed instruments, under ye Greate Veteran Fiddler Burr, whose fronte name is Dave, with some more pastimes, at wh ye companie may prudentlye smile.

FIRSTE.

PLEYEL'S HYMN.—By all ye men and women singers, and ye fiddlers.

ODE ON SCIENCE.—By all ye wind and ye stringed instruments.

NEXTE.

PUPPET SHOWS.—By a goodlye companie of ye old and young men and maidens.

MUSICK.

GUILDROY. FISHER'S HORNPIPE. LIME ROCK. } By request of ye many worldleye minded people.

NEXTE.

PUPPET SHOWS.

MUSICK.

By ye Pipers and ye Fiddlers.

N. B. Precision Rocket will have Rooms filled withe Relics of ye olden tyme, in wh Greate-Grande Mother Sherbet will preside at ye spinning wheel, and Nabor Holbrooke, whose fronte name is Amos, will hatchel ye flax.

Dorothy Whitney, ye Tithing Woman, will collect ye money at ye doore.

Jedediah Rocket, Wealthy Ann Baker, Charity Bates, Bashaby Allen, withe a greate number of Nabors and girls, will have Companie at ye Olde Tyme Supper Table, at 8 and 1-2 o'clock of ye twilighte.

N. B. Nabor Varmiboge Rocket will be there to see that nobodye yeilds to more levitye than is becominge, and to see that no one takes more Baked Beans than is consistente withe these fashionable tymes.

Ye following is a description of ye Supper.

Baked Beans,	Bean Porridge, hot,	Biled Pot Garden Sass,	Biled Indian Puddings,	Biled Doughnouts,
Punkin Pie,	Cornede Beefe,	Lection Cake,	Ginger Breade,	Apple Pie,
Mince Pie,	Custarde Pie,	Oranges,	Loafe Cake,	Pickles.

N. B. Ye Women Folks at Nabor Saxton Whiting's will bile Doughnouts for a goodleye Companie.

N. B. It is hoped ye large men will consume 50 penneyes worthe. If ye conscience and pocket-bookes are at all burdened, ye can drop ye balance into ye little boxes at ye doore.

If ye tyme is not too late, some more pieces will be said.

Ye entertainment will be stopped by singinge of ye newe tune wh is called 'Amerika,' in wh ye whole assemblye are asked to join ye goodlye Companie of Singers.

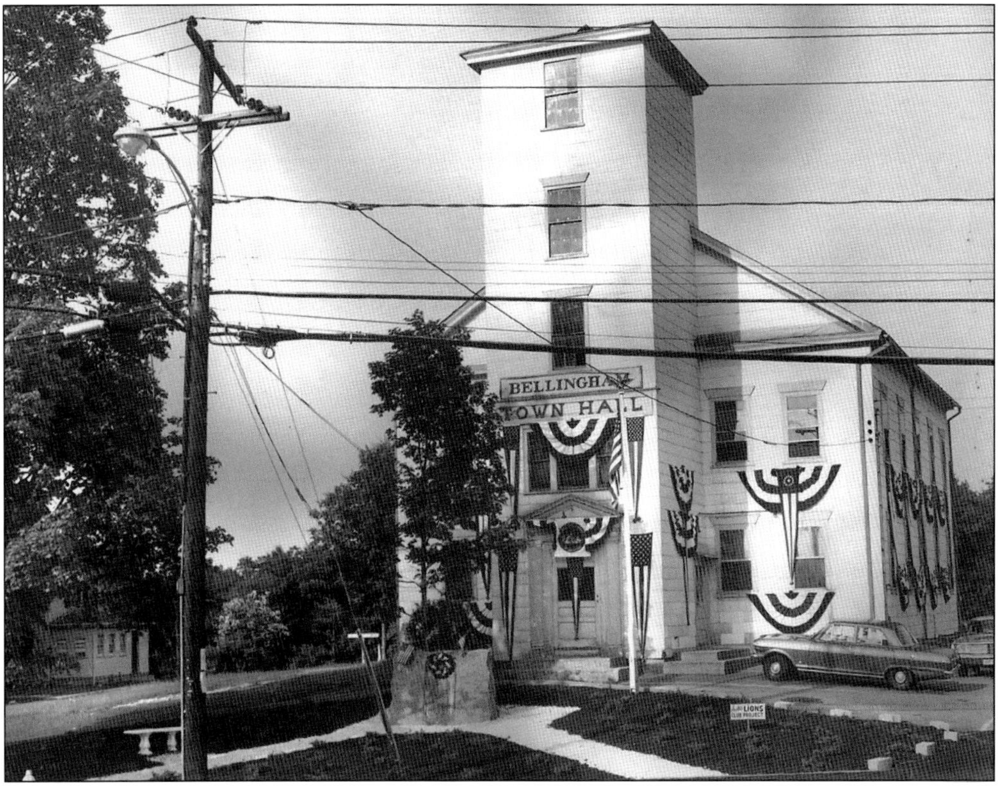

The 1969 bicentennial celebration was the biggest event to ever take place in town. The celebration lasted throughout the year. This World War I memorial beautification project was one of the many Lion's Club contributions to that occasion.

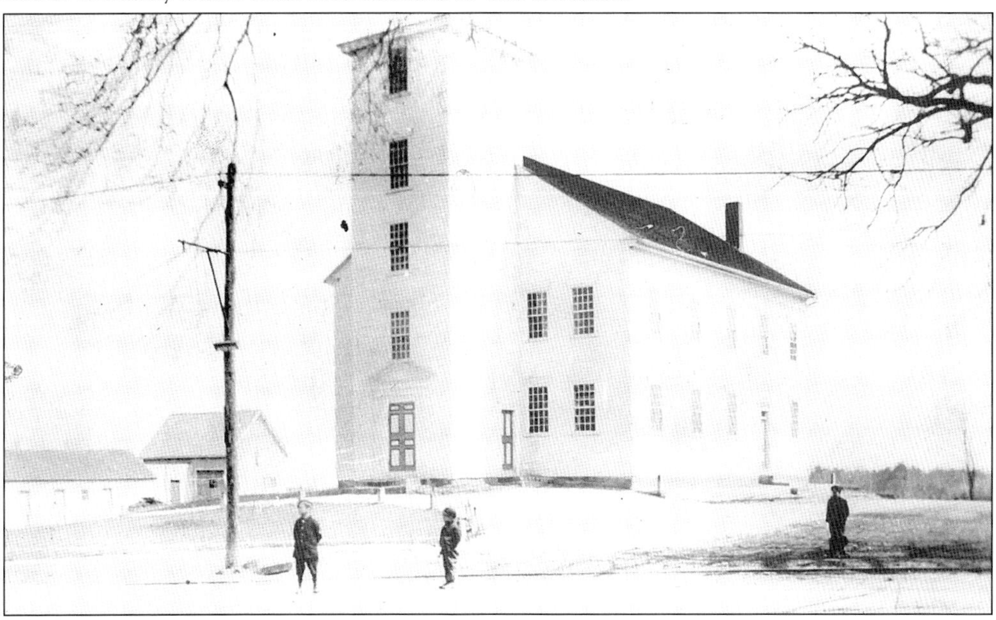

This 1898 photograph, which was taken before the building's renovations (1910), shows a very typical simple Colonial New England–style building.

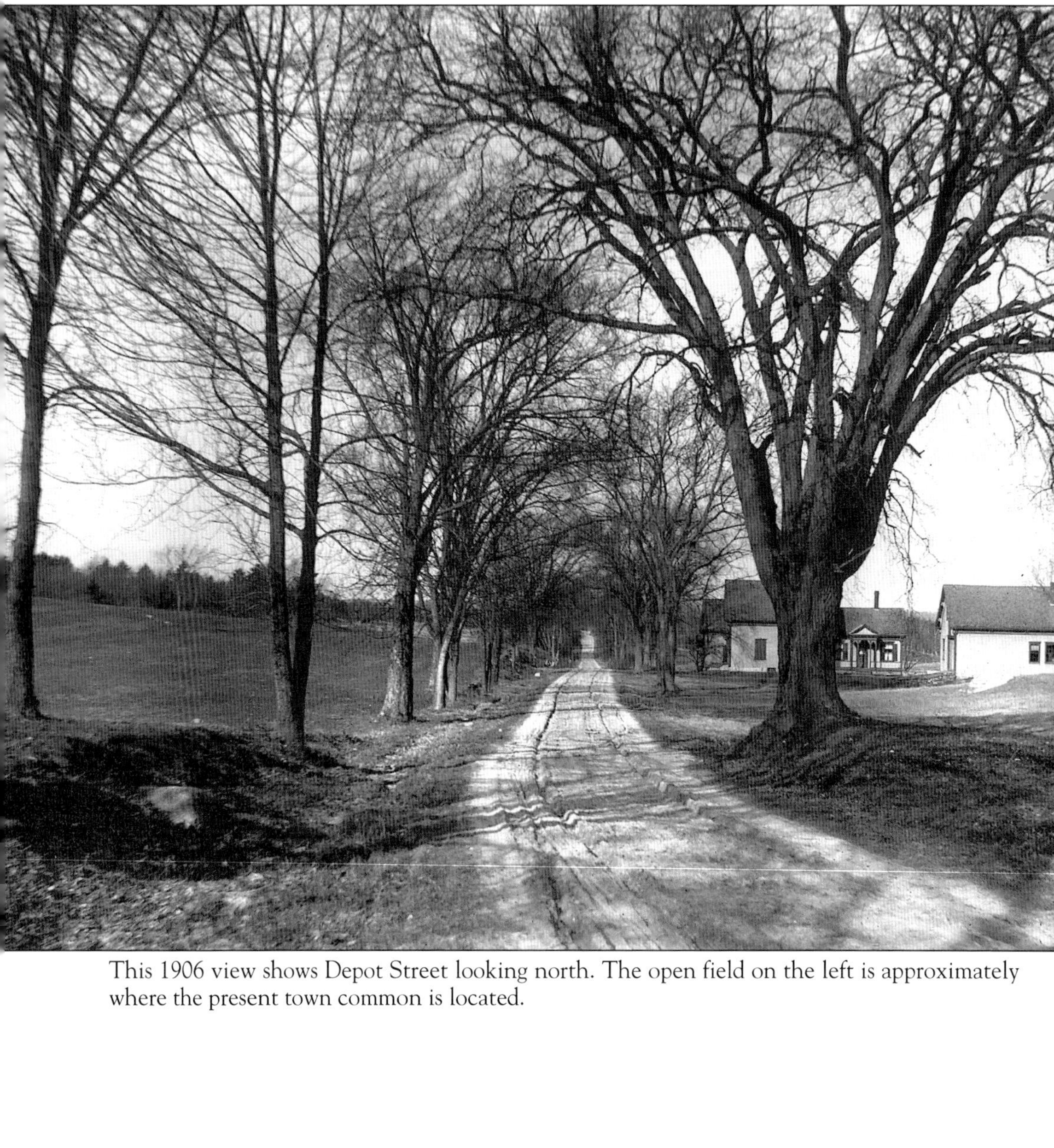

This 1906 view shows Depot Street looking north. The open field on the left is approximately where the present town common is located.

Two

CHURCHES

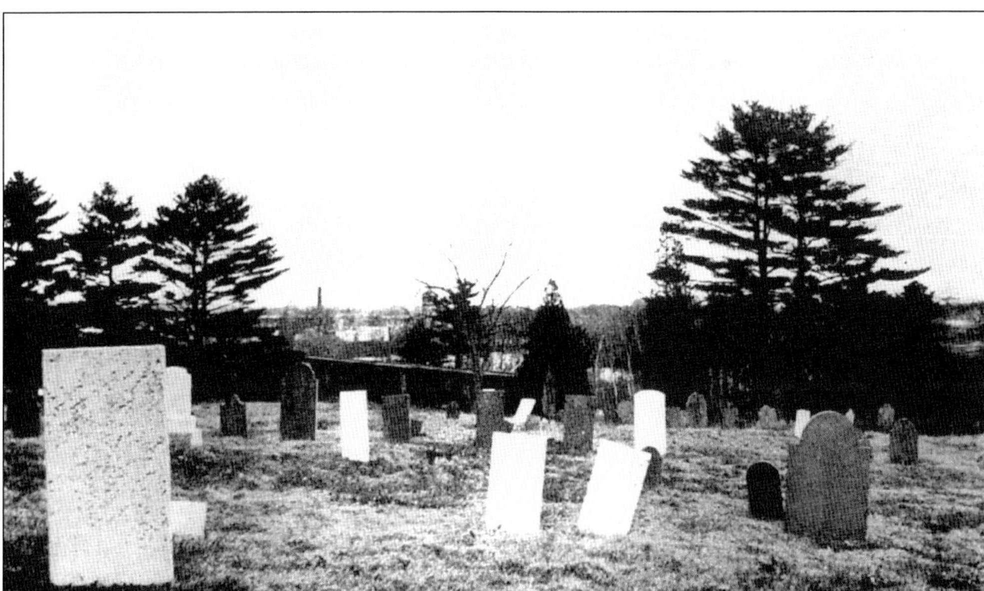

The North Bellingham Cemetery located on Hartford Avenue is actually older than the town itself. The first burial to take place here was in 1718. In 1804, a vault was built for winter burials. This cemetery and the adjacent Oak Hill Cemetery are still in use.

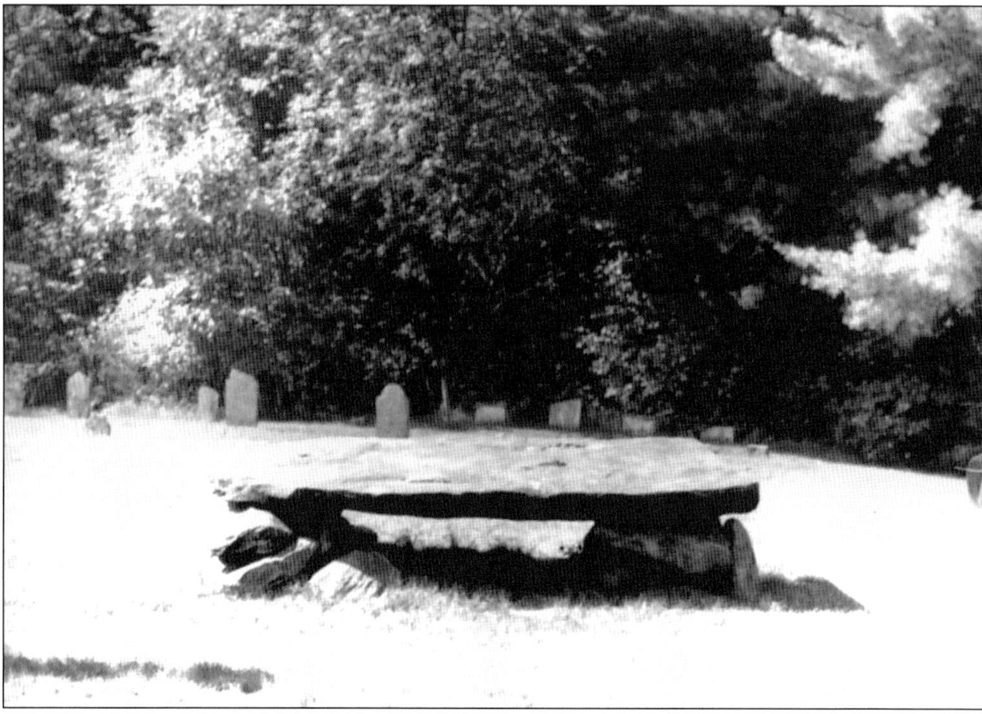

The Scott Cemetery on Center Street was laid out in 1717. The land belonged to the Scott family. Legend has it that Native Americans are buried here. Pictured is a rare mounting stone. This stone was used to make it easier to get up on the back of a horse.

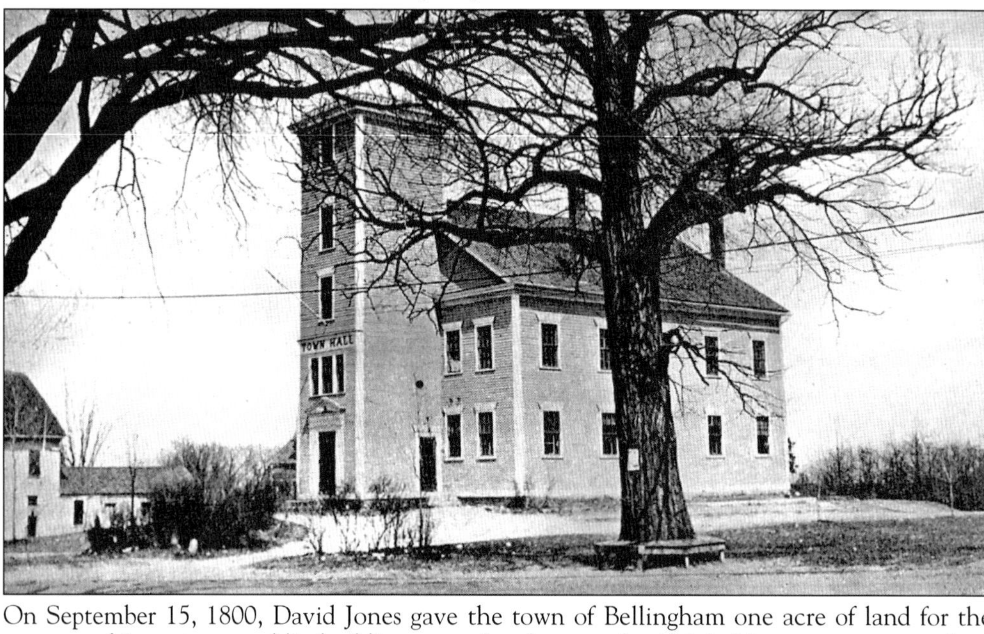

On September 15, 1800, David Jones gave the town of Bellingham one acre of land for the purpose of "erecting a public building upon for the use of said inhabitants to transact their public concerns in, at all times . . . and also for the accommodation of said Religious Society for a House of Public Worship, forever or so long as said inhabitants shall continue to keep a convenient house upon said land."

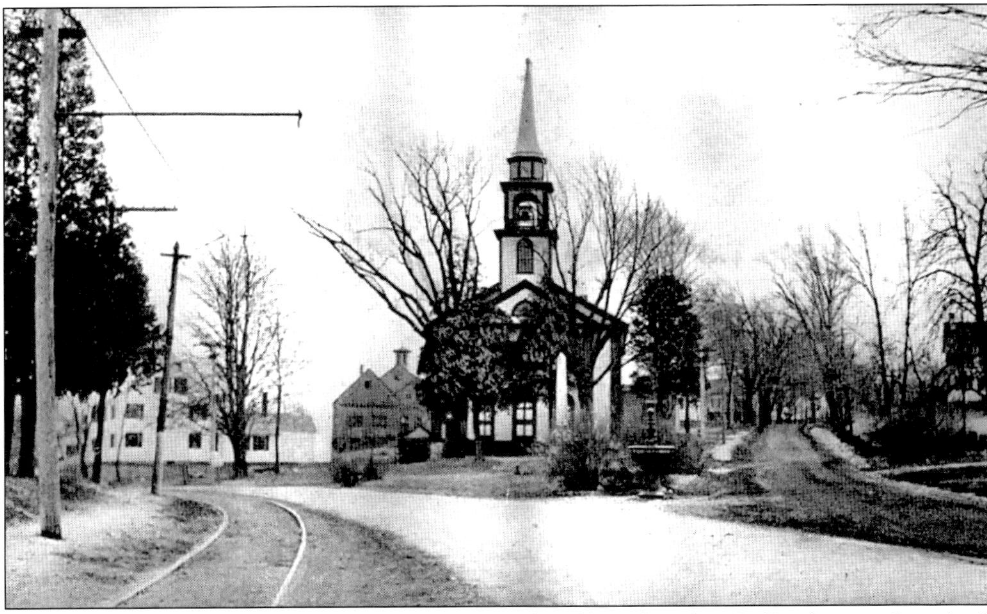

The First Baptist Church at Bellingham Center is the oldest church in Bellingham and was built in 1826 at a cost of $2,600.

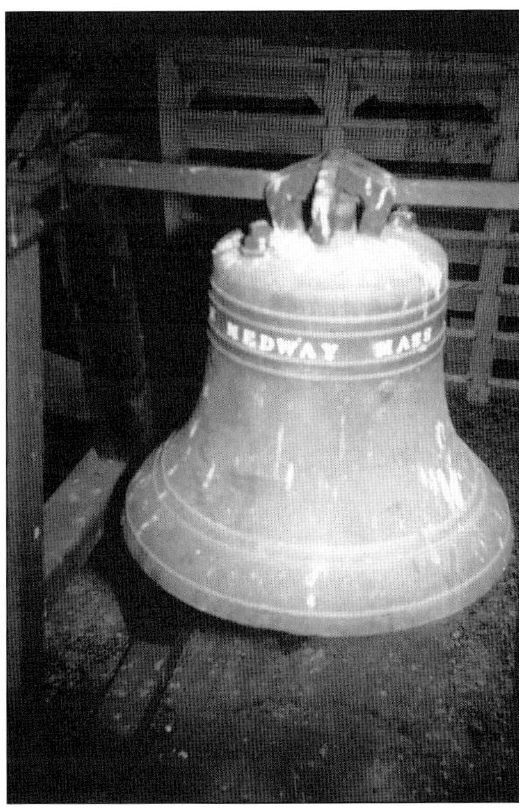

A bell was purchased for the steeple of the First Baptist Church at Bellingham Center in 1833. An inscription on the bell reads, "cast by G. H. Holbrook, East Medway, Massachusetts, 1833." The church bells were rung on Sundays and also to alarm the community in the event of an emergency.

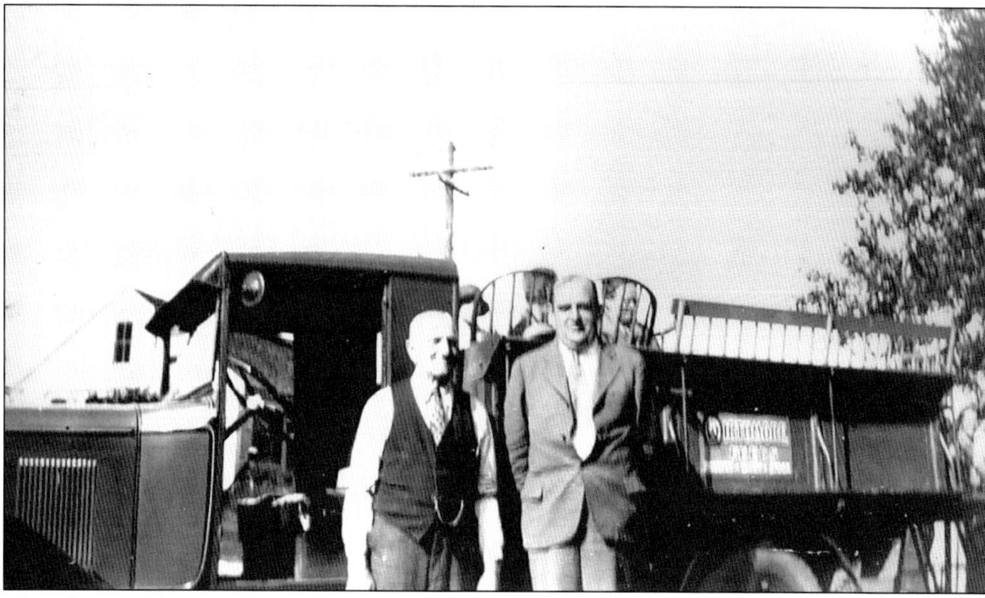

This photograph was taken in 1932 at the Ladies Aid Picnic. L.F. Thayer (left) is pictured with the Reverend Clarence Chamberlain at the First Baptist Church.

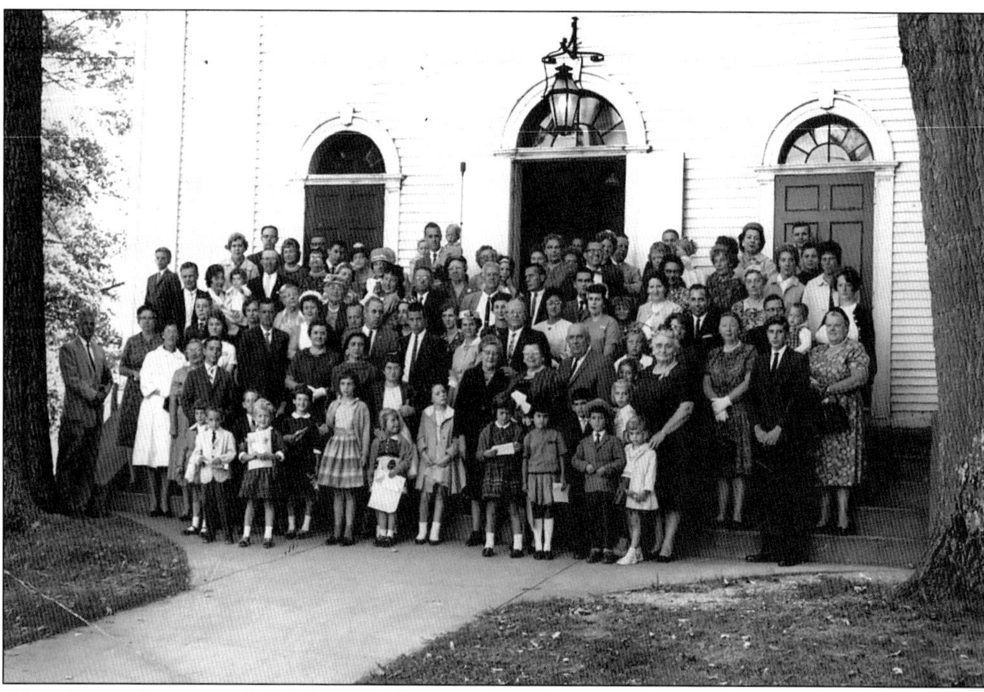

Church parishioners of the Baptist church located at Bellingham Center are seen here on September 16, 1962.

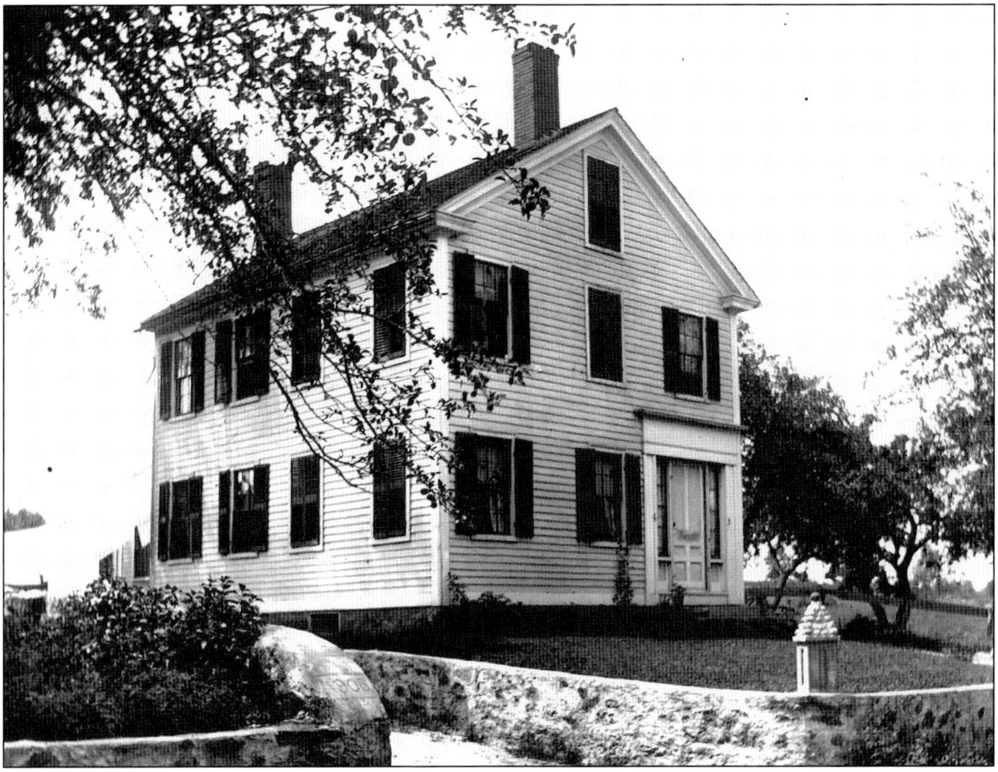

The Baptist pastor Joseph T. Massey was the first to reside at the Old Parsonage House located on Mendon Street from 1834 to 1840. The First Baptist Church sold the home and property in 1946.

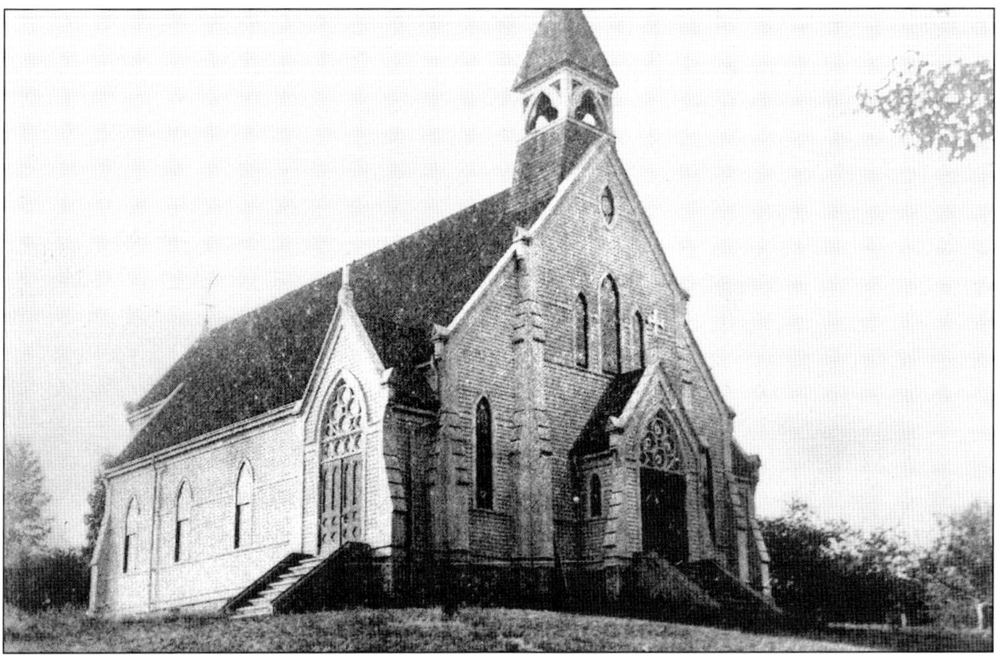

St. Brendan's Church was dedicated on September 8, 1895. This church seats 400 people. It is the first and oldest Catholic church in Bellingham.

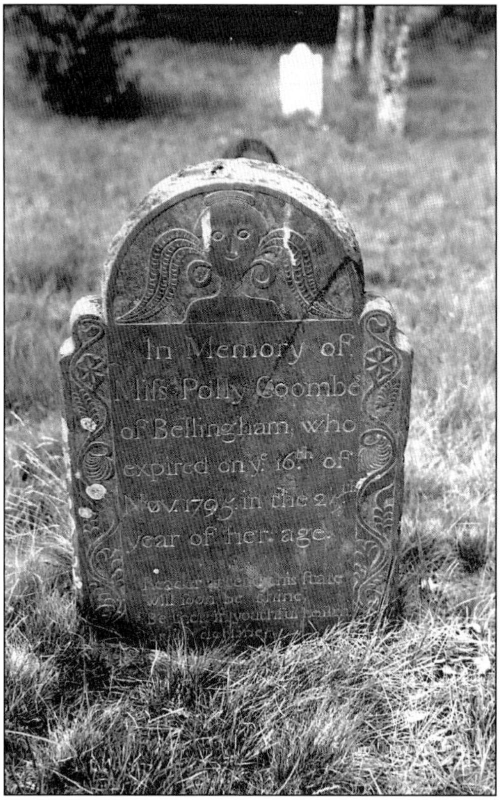

The famous Polly Coombs gravestone is in the North Bellingham Cemetery. This gravestone rubbing has been featured on television and has been written about in books because of the unusual markings on the top of the stone. The stone reads, "in the memory of Miss Polly Coombs of Bellingham who expired on ye 16th of November 1795 in the 25th year of her age."

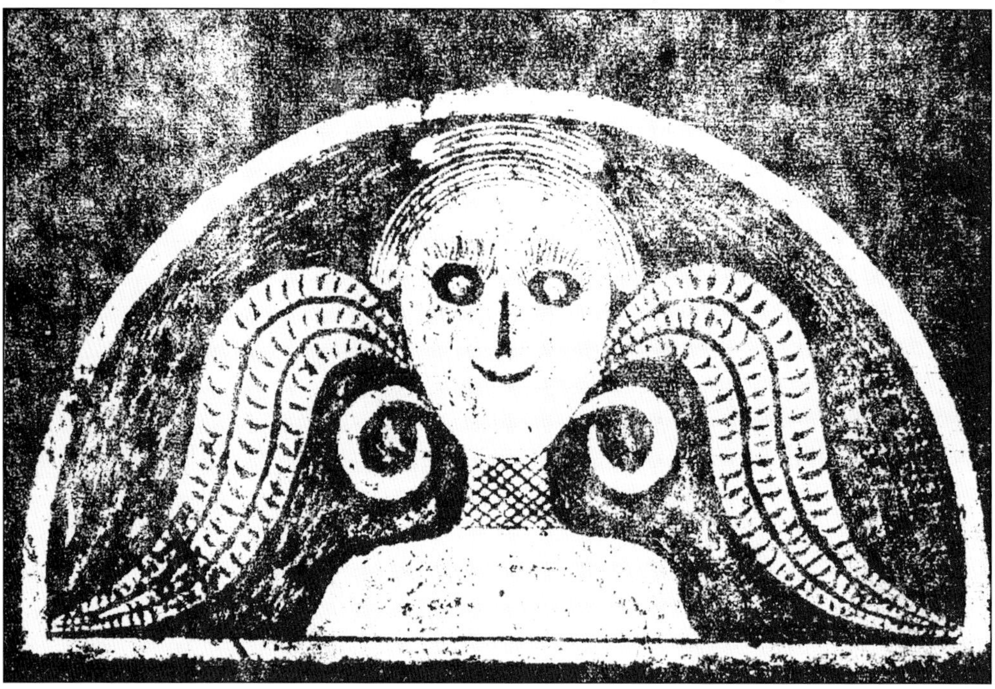

Attendance Week at Baptist Church

Attendance Sunday, April 27th

Sunday Morning at 10 30. Subject: "The Joy of Giving."

Sunday Evening at 7 30. Speaker, Dr. W. E. Witter.

Wednesday Evening, Apr. 30th. A "Get-to-gether and Talk-it-over" sociable social.

Games, Entertainment, Three minute addresses.

Ice Cream and Cake.

YOU are cordially urged to attend all of these "Attendance Week" events.

JOHN S. LOVEJOY,
CHAS. FEARING,
ALONZO GREENWOOD,
RICHIE D. SHERMAN,
A. MAUD GRANT,
Finance Committee.

This *c.* 1913 postcard was sent out to the church parishioners.

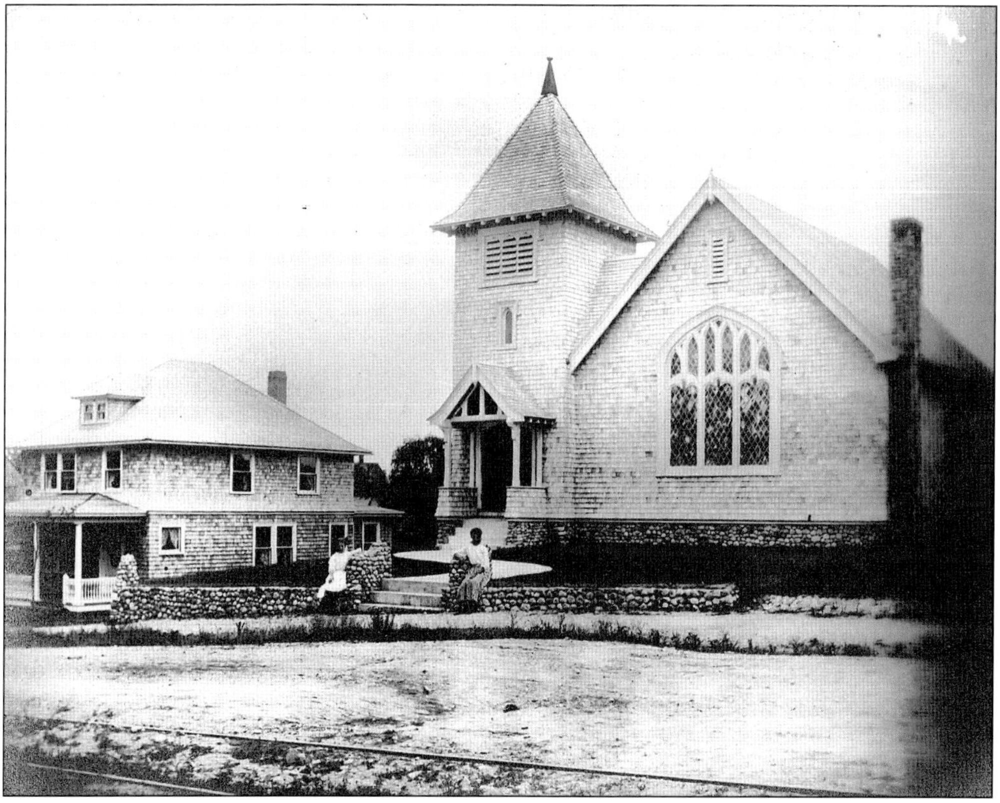

The North Baptist Church was opened and dedicated on March 12, 1908. The total cost for the building was $4,500. The church had 27 members in 1917. That same year a Holbrook bell was donated to the church. This church is now known as the Bellingham Bible Baptist Church.

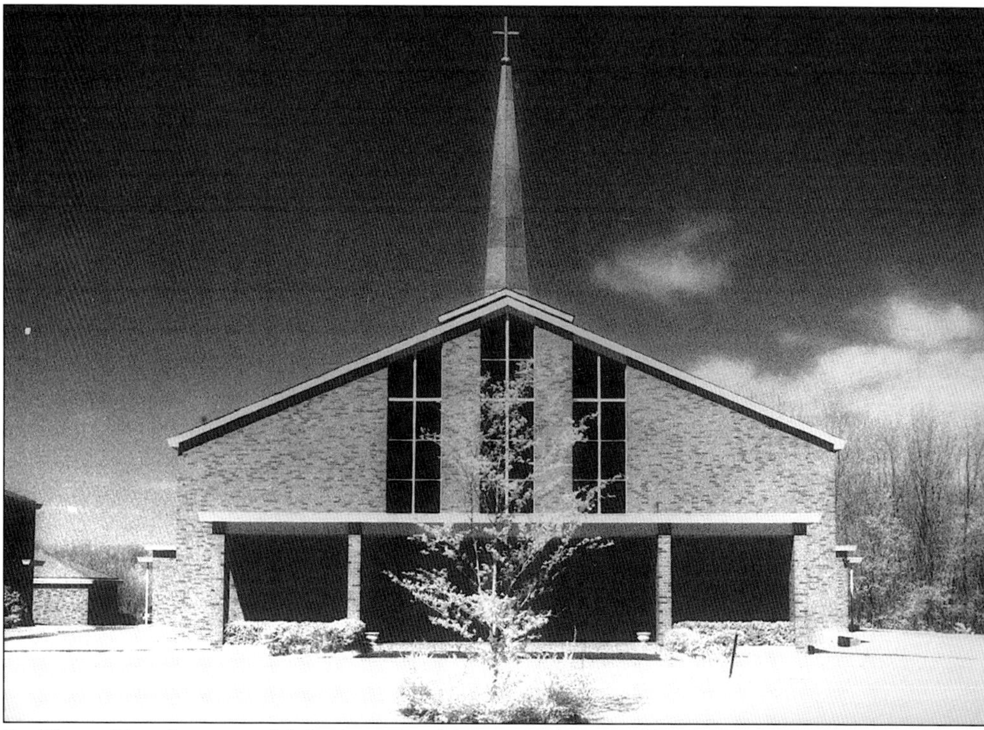

St. Blaise Church was established on April 3, 1962. This is Bellingham's third Catholic church. The first pastor at St. Blaise was the Reverend Father Joseph P. Mahoney.

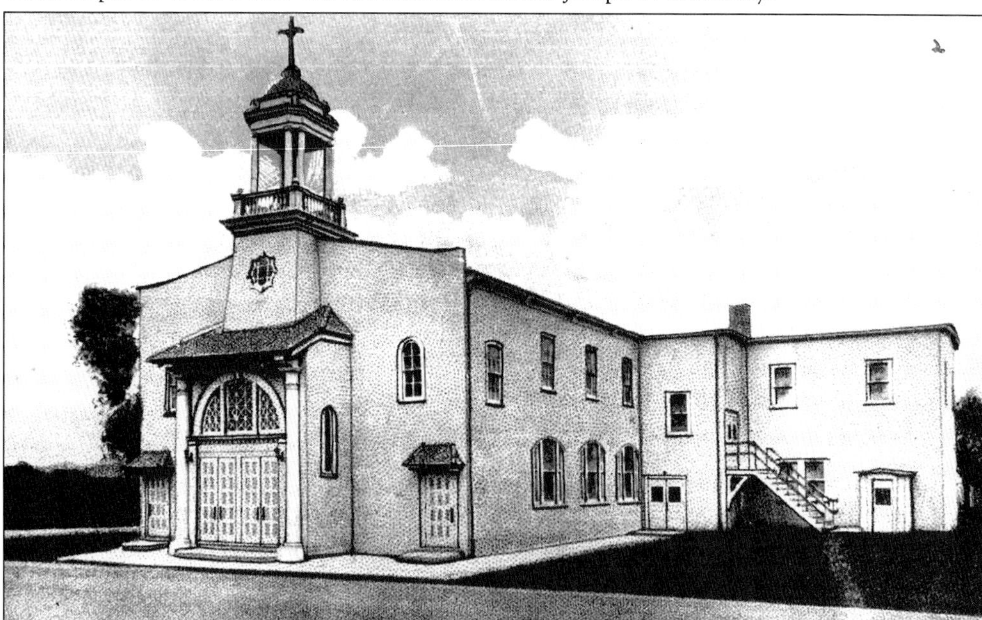

The Assumption Church parish, located on Pulaski Boulevard, was established in 1927. The church seated 320 people and was opened on September 17, 1927. A bell for the belfry was installed on May 28, 1928. In 1965, the church moved to the basement of the Assumption School on Moody Street.

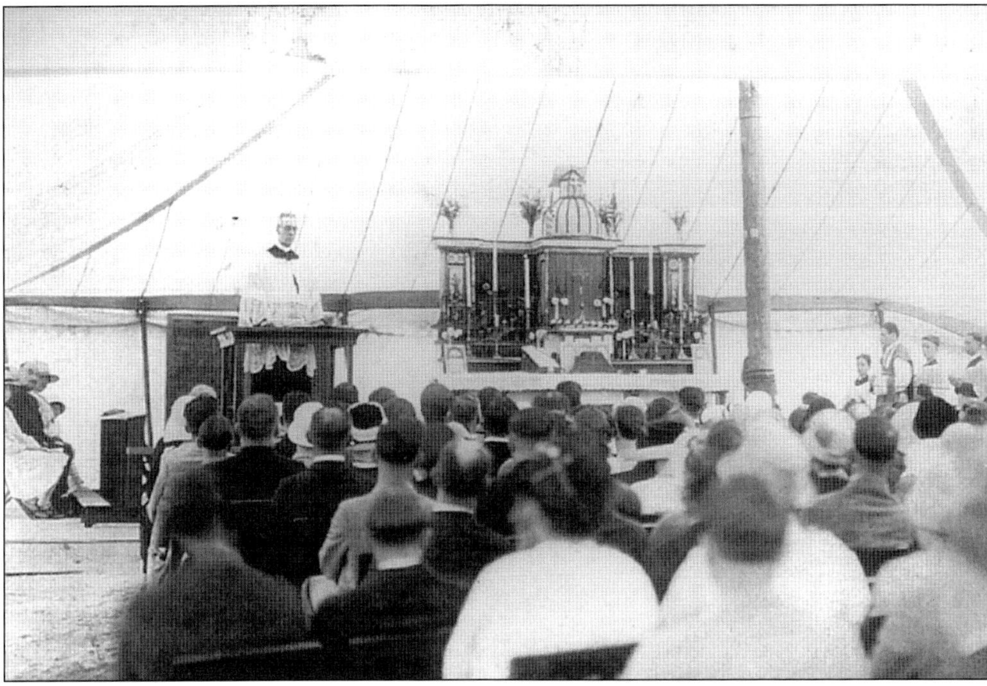

The first Mass for the Assumption Church parish was celebrated on July 31, 1927, under a tent in the parking lot.

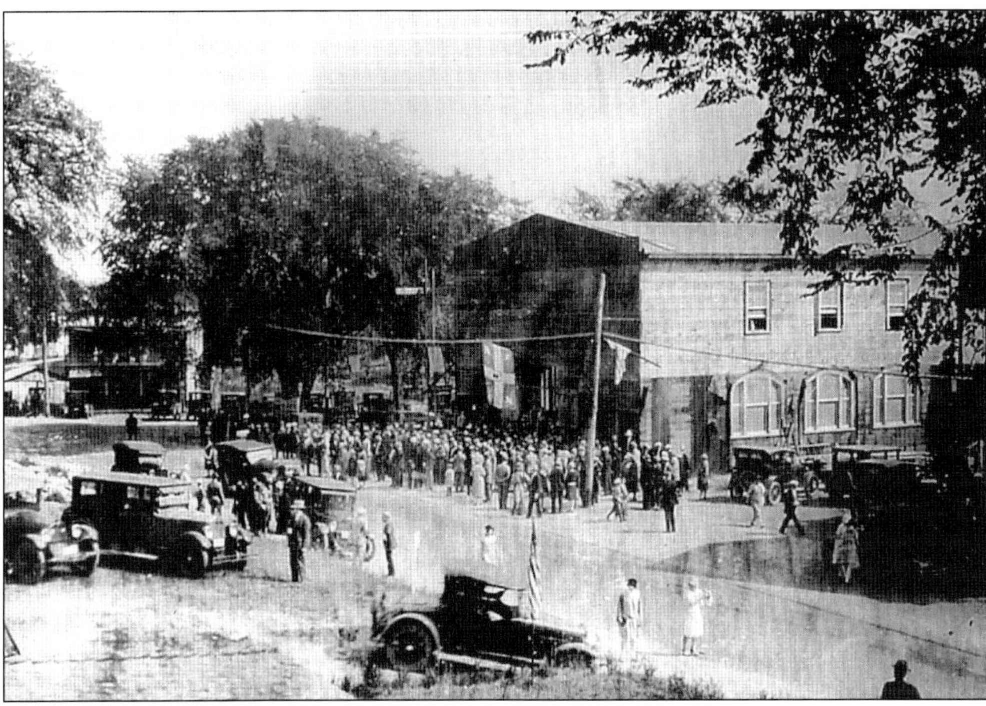

First Mass in the unfinished church was held on September 17, 1927.

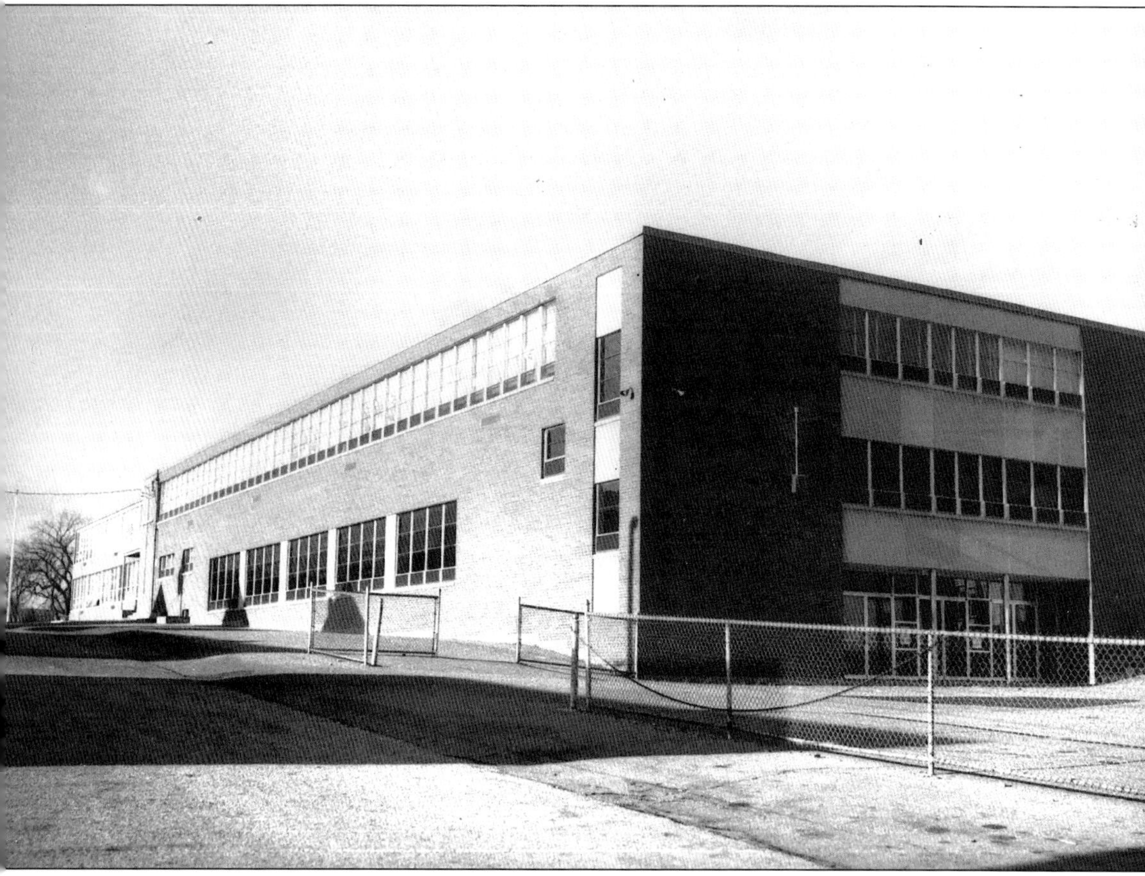

The lower level of this building serves as the Assumption Church. The upper level once housed the parochial Catholic school. This photograph was taken in 1969.

Three

BUSINESSES AND FARMS

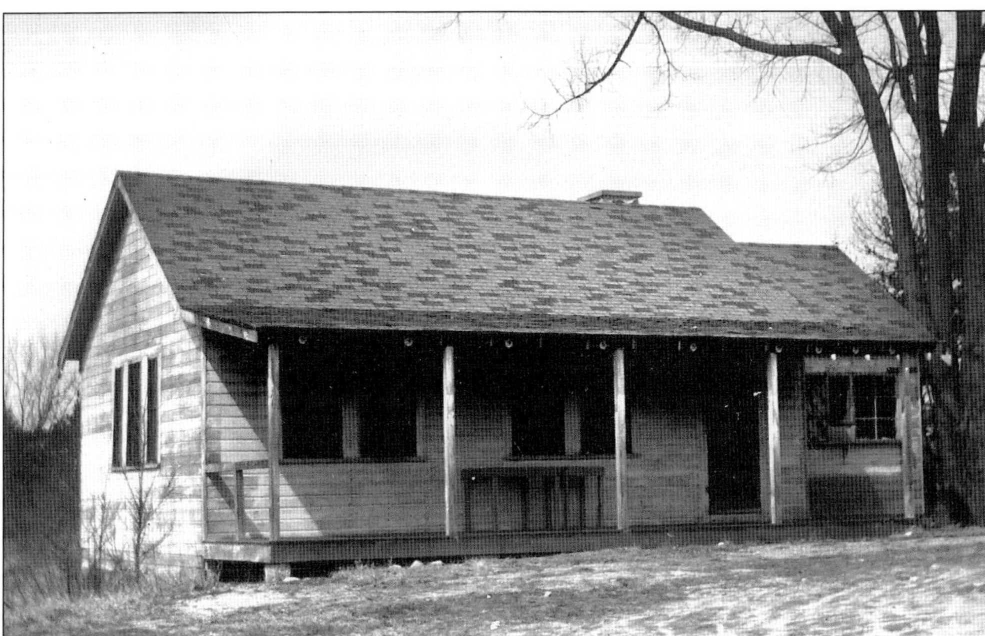

Aw'Comon In, located at 98 Hartford Avenue, was a popular local gathering spot during the 1930s and 1940s for whist parties on Friday nights, home cooked food, and dancing. It is now a private residence.

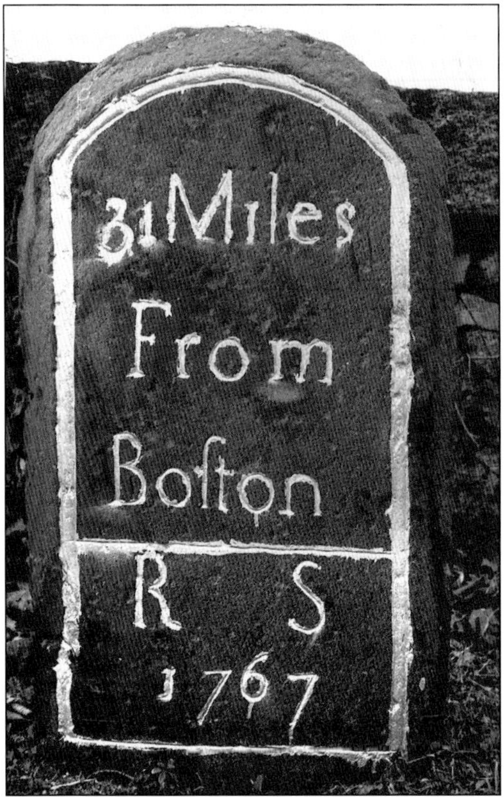

This Middle Post Road milemarker stands in front of the North School on Hartford Avenue. In 1753, Benjamin Franklin placed the original stone marker near here. A slate stone, pictured here, replaced the original stone. Note that R.S. stood for Royal Service, as the postal operation at that time was under the direction of the king of England.

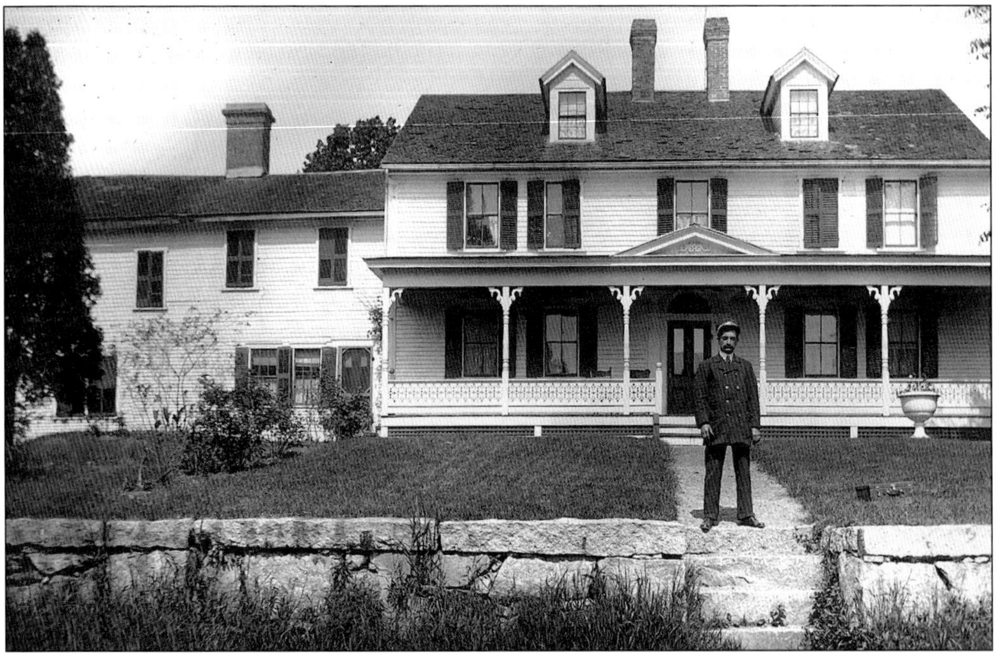

The Pelatiah Smith Tavern was built in 1702. The tavern burned in the early 1800s and was rebuilt. This building is still known as the Smith Tavern and is located adjacent to St. Brendan's Church. The 1767 milemarker originally stood in front of the stone wall.

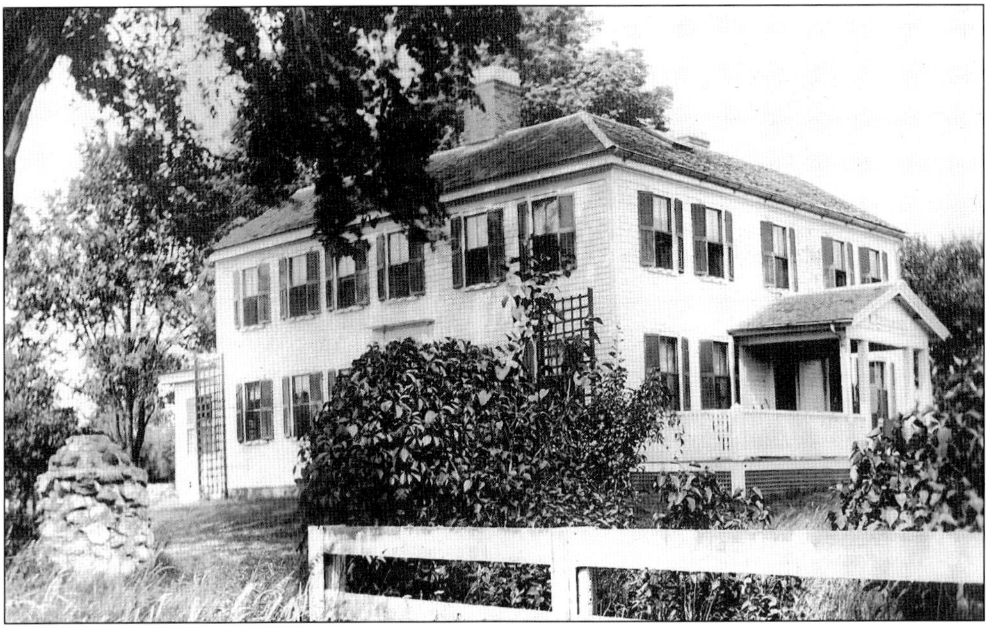

The house pictured here was known as Pinewood Farm and was located on North Main Street, where the circle C.G. Ranch is now. It was built in 1893. The farm was mostly used by members of the Grace Episcopal Church of Providence for summer outings and vacations. It had a windmill on the property used to pump water. This beautiful home was destroyed by fire in 1921.

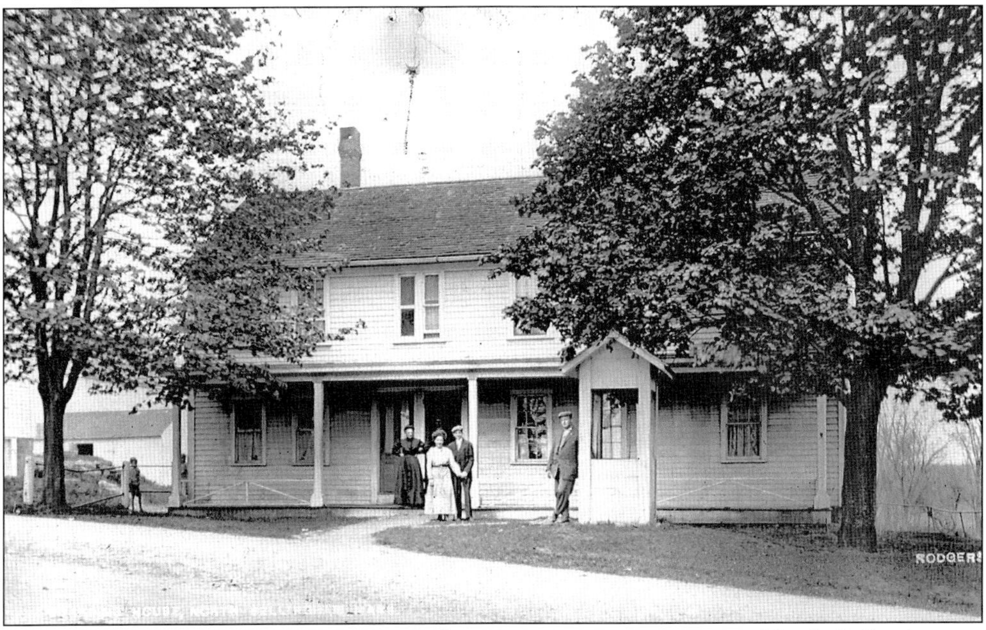

Fifteen veterans of World War I organized an American Legion post in North Bellingham in 1919. They held weekly meetings at the old depot on Maple Street. The post decided to get their own meeting place and selected a vacant room upstairs in the old boardinghouse at 26 Maple Street. Francis Diggins was the first fort commander in 1934. The post was reorganized under the name of Arnold-Spencer Post No. 218 American Legion. Arnold and Spencer were two soldiers from Bellingham who died in World War I. Alice Beausoleil (Lussier) was the first president.

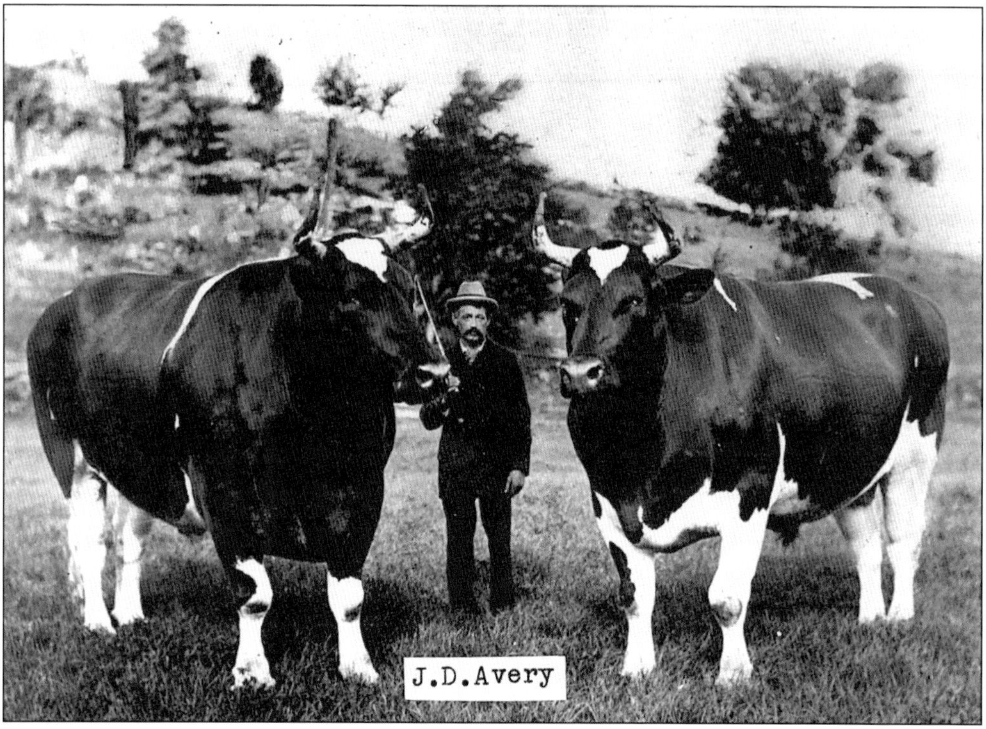

Joseph Ray of Bellingham bred these thoroughbred Holsteins that were almost full brothers by blood. Walter E. Cook purchased the animals and worked them at farming and lumbering. They were campaigned at the Fairs of 1893 and 1894 as draft oxen and never met their equal. These oxen could draw 11,061 pounds on a drag and eight feet at one pull in the dirt and on dead level—a feat never accomplished by any other team.

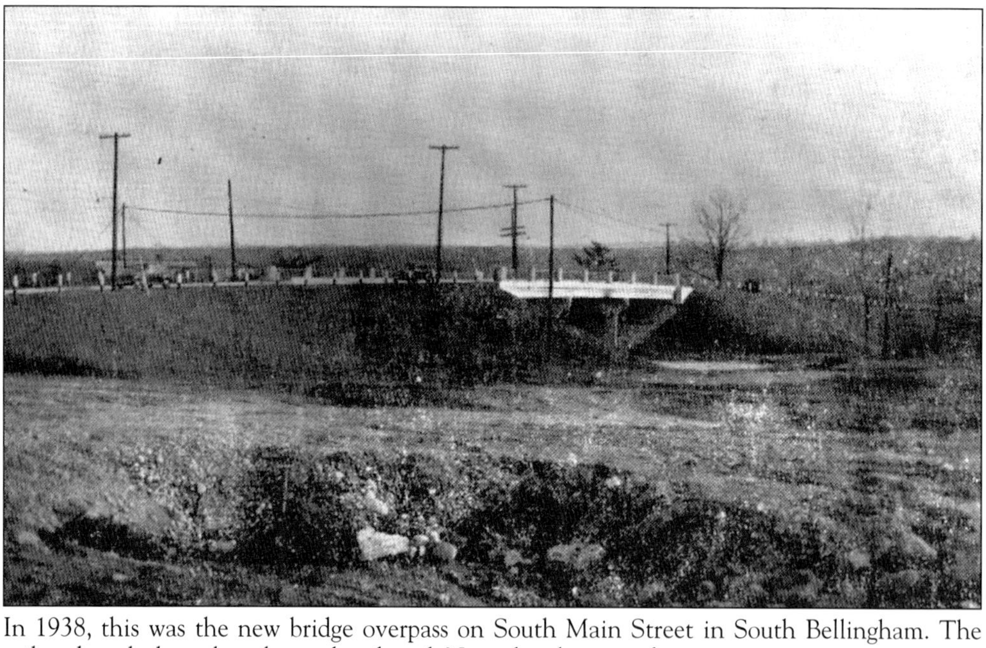

In 1938, this was the new bridge overpass on South Main Street in South Bellingham. The railroad tracks have long been abandoned. Note the absence of trees.

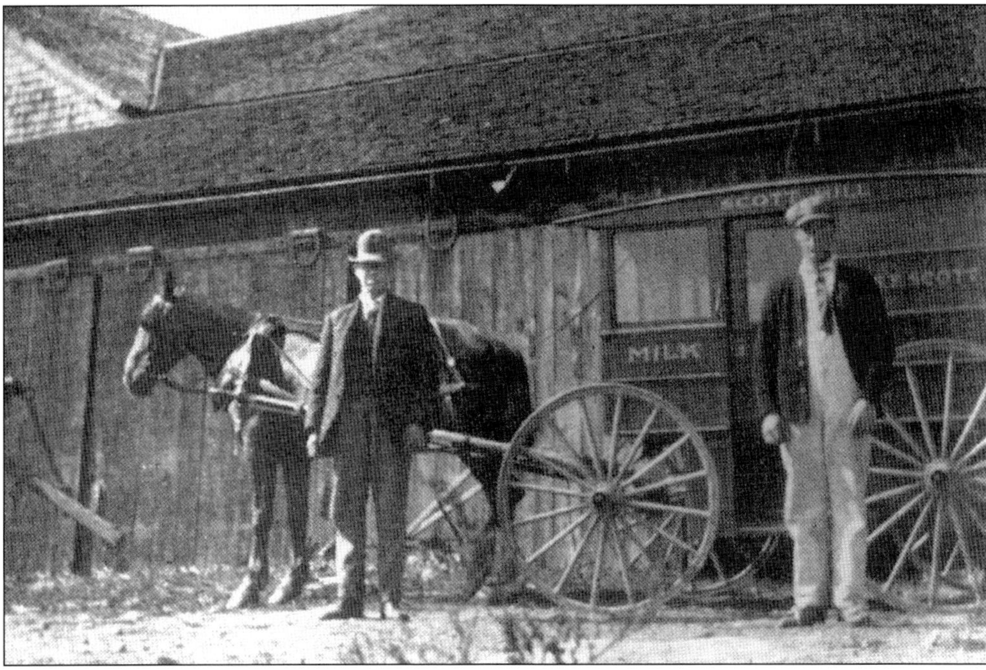

Stephen and Edgar Scott stand in front of their dairy barn with their milk delivery wagon. Their dairy farm was located on Scott Street. Scott Hill Road was named after this prominent family.

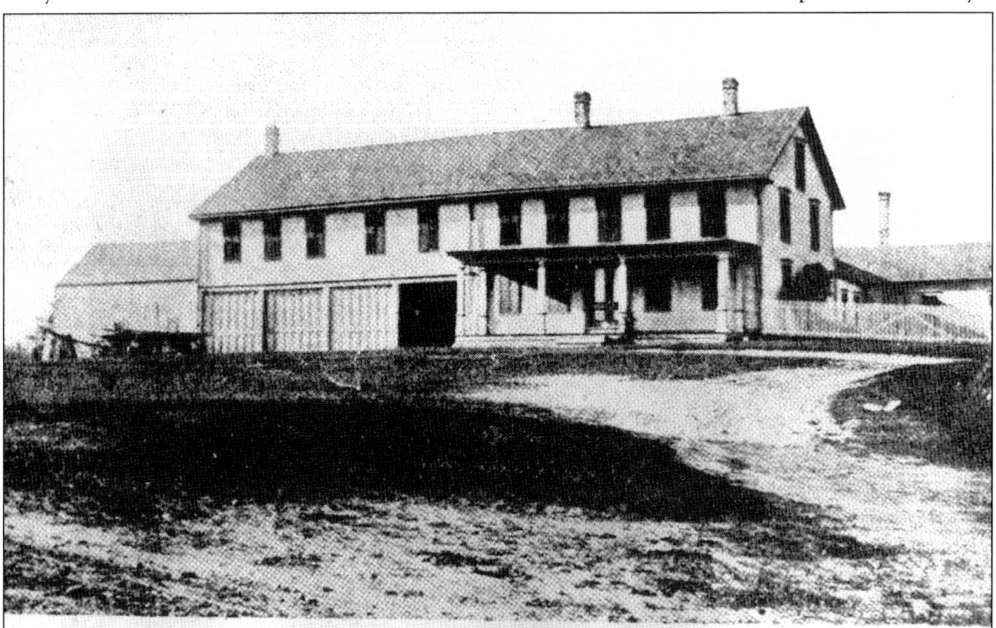

CROOK'S TAVERN, kept by Jeremiah Crooks 1834 - 1860.

Located on this spot in 1750 was the Universalist church. Between 1800 and 1834, Wright Curtis ran the town's first tavern here. Jeremiah Crooks bought this property in 1834 and continued to have the tavern here until 1860. Up until 1900, the tavern served as a stagecoach station for the Providence to Worcester stage. This fine historical building was torn down in 1952. It stood close to Crooks Corner.

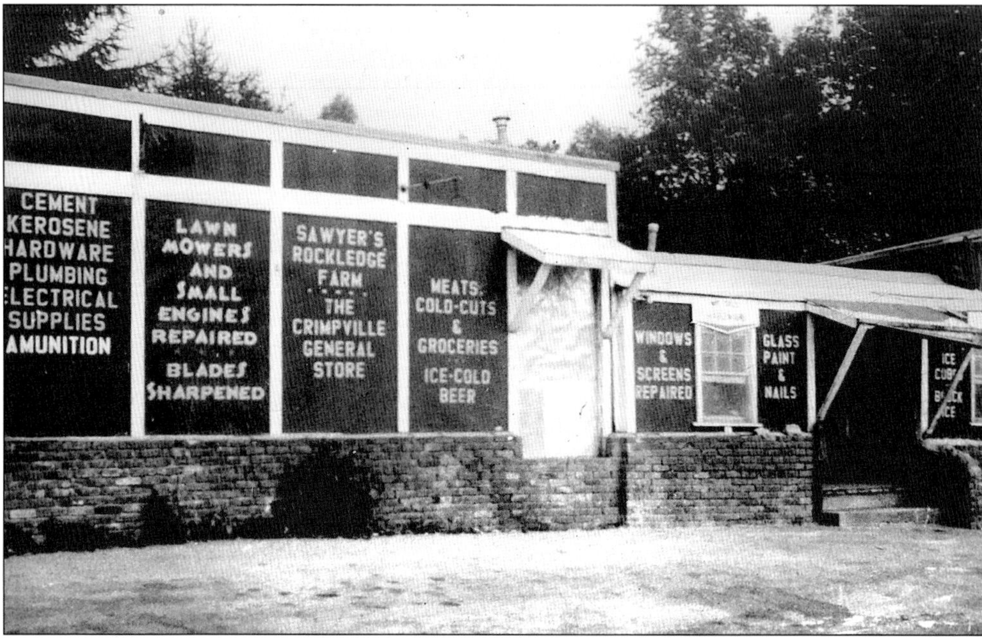

Sawyer's Rockledge Farm was located at the corner of High and North Main Streets. Ed Sawyer—founder of the historical newsletter *Crimpville Comments* and the moving force in the formation of the Bellingham Historic Commission—lived in this combination store and house. Around the wood-burning stove below, Ed Sawyer would tell his stories of historic Bellingham.

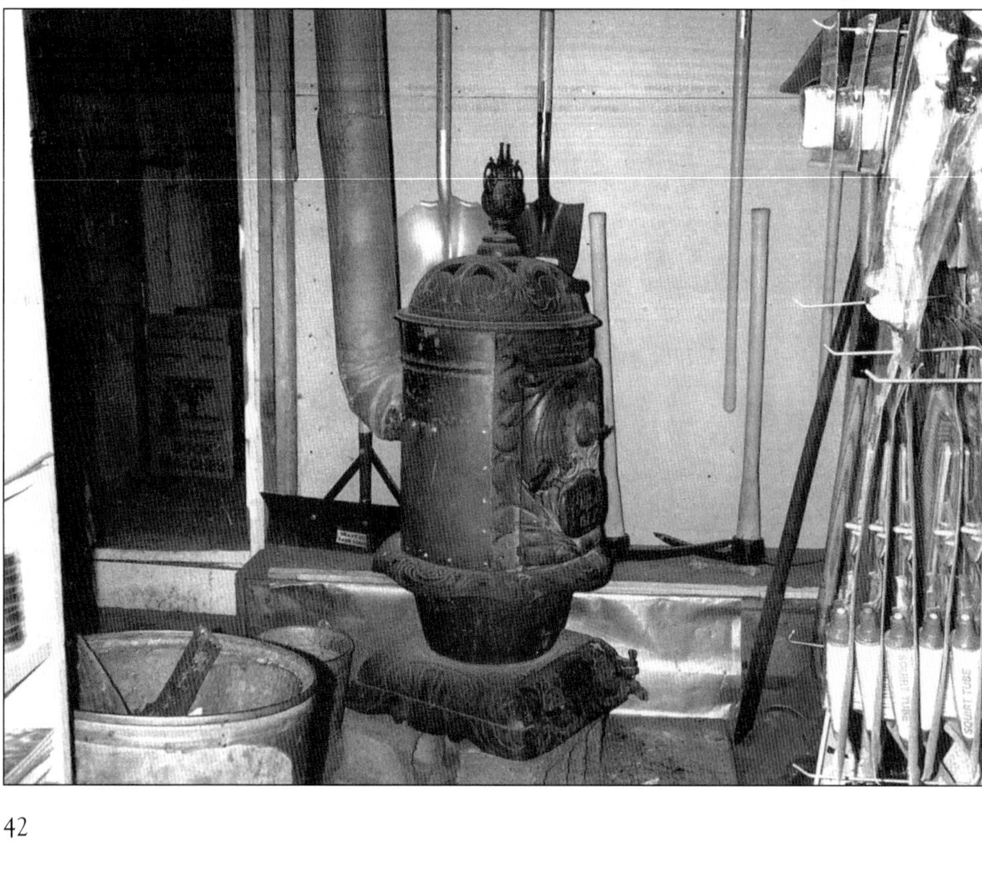

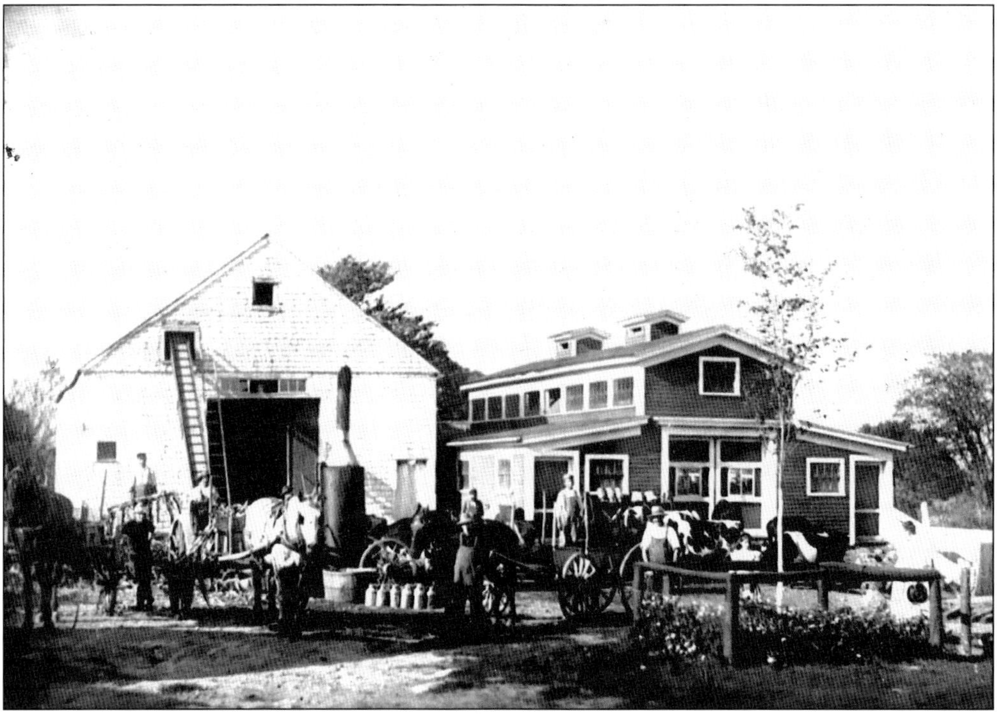

A 1901 photograph of the town farm shows an old barn on the left and a new cow barn on the right. The inmates or residents helped by working here. The farm produced milk, garden crops, cordwood, and lumber. No one was allowed to sit around idle unless they were sick or too feeble to work. This place was also known as the poor farm. The home was known as the almshouse.

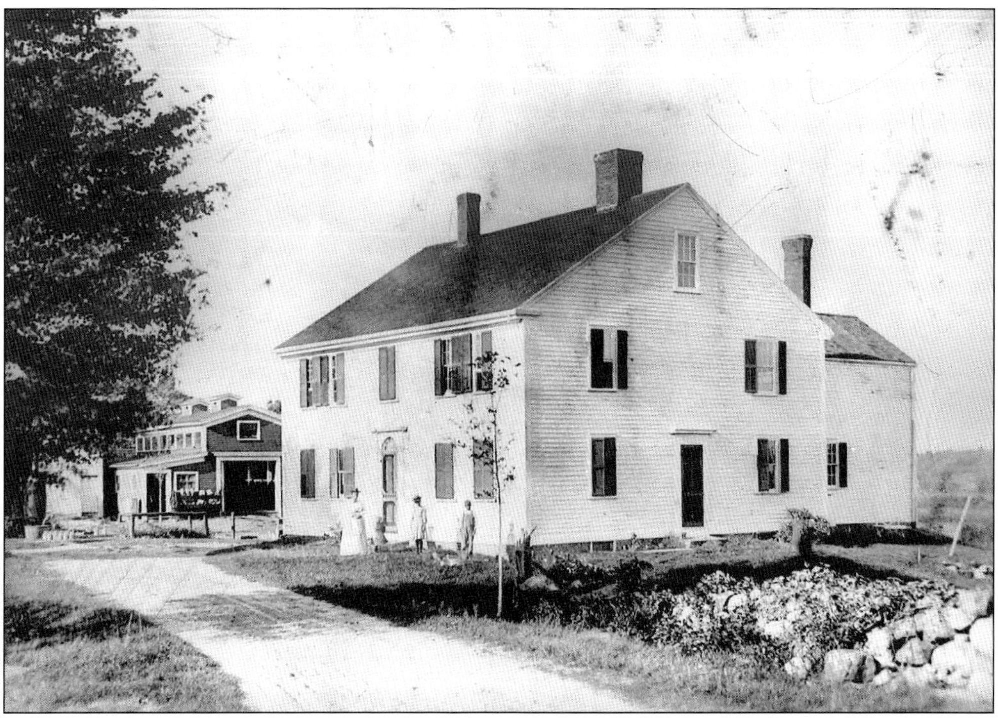

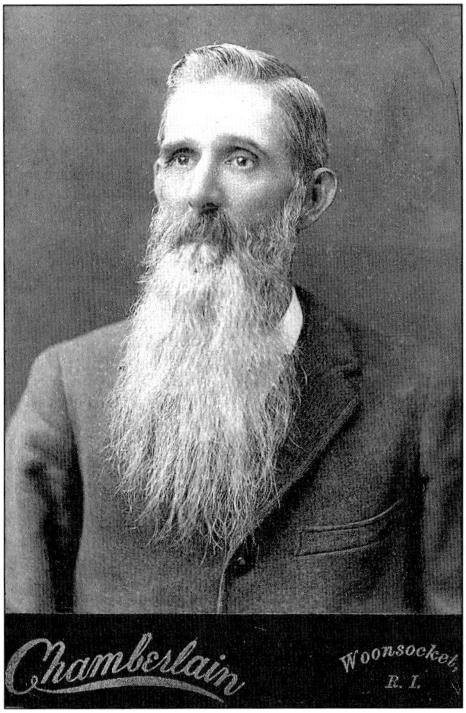

Senaca Burr lived at this farm in South Bellingham. In 1872, he was representative to the General Court.

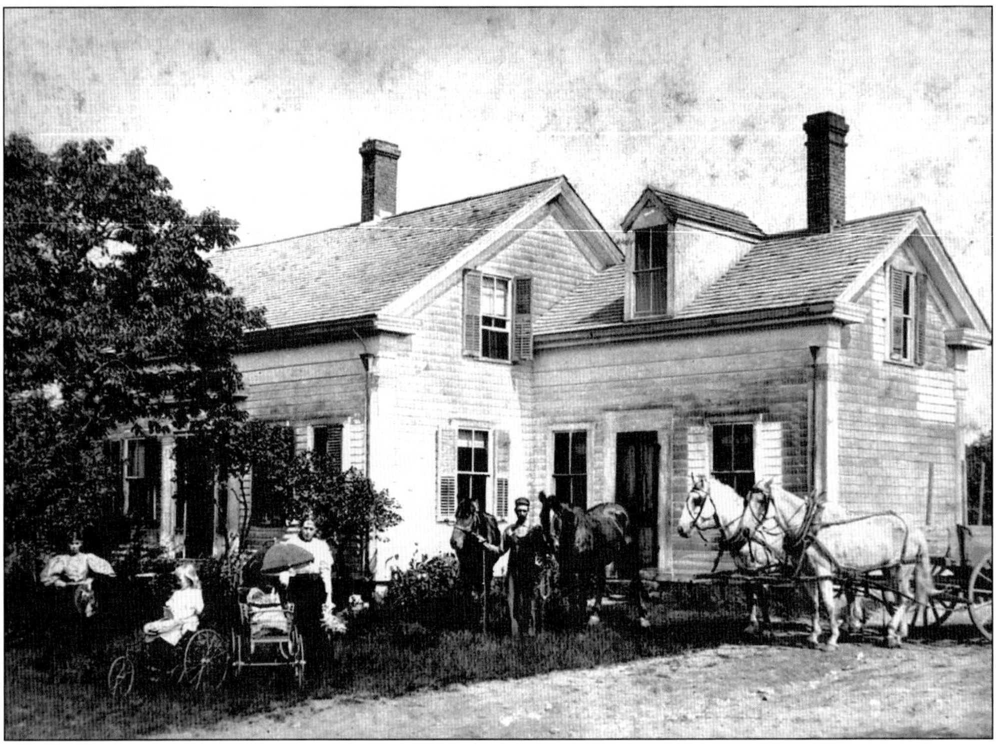

Burr Farm on Railroad Street in South Bellingham is shown here. Willie A. Burr is near the horses. Alice Chilson Burr is with the baby carriage, in which sits a very young Hazel Burr. Vestella L. Burr is on the tricycle. Katie, a helper girl from Nova Scotia, is also pictured.

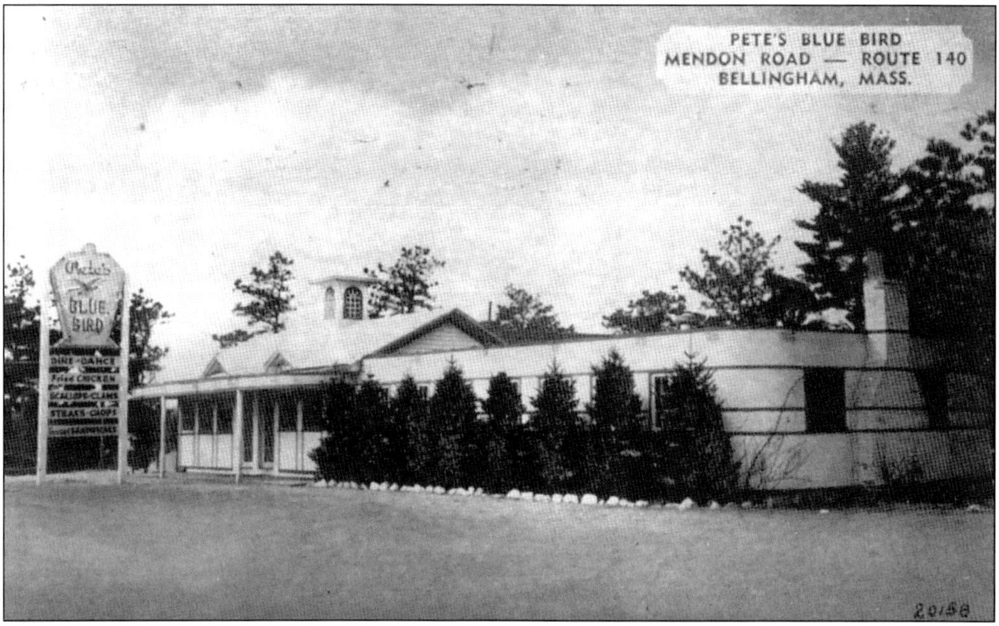

Pete's Bluebird Restaurant located at 93 Mendon Street was first opened in 1940 by Pete and Georgia Coniaris. The reverse of this postcard reads, "Road to Cape Cod, Camp Devens, Camp Edwards, where fine food is served. Dine and dance. Special dinners served in our beautiful blue room. Full accommodations for all occasions. Stop and rest on our beautiful pine tree grounds. Tourist's cabins rented."

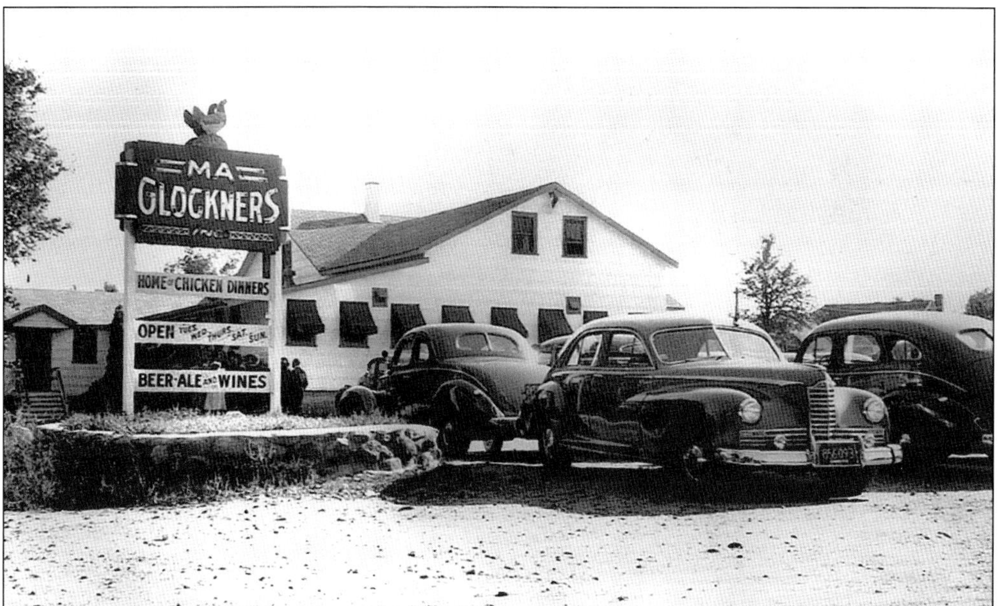

Ma Glockners has been a major attraction since 1937. People came from great distances to eat their unique, "berched-style" chicken. During the days of the Great Depression, it was difficult for the Glockners to get chickens to market, where there were few buyers. So the Glockners decided to open a small 24-seat restaurant, selling only chicken dinners. The business caught on and has been a success ever since.

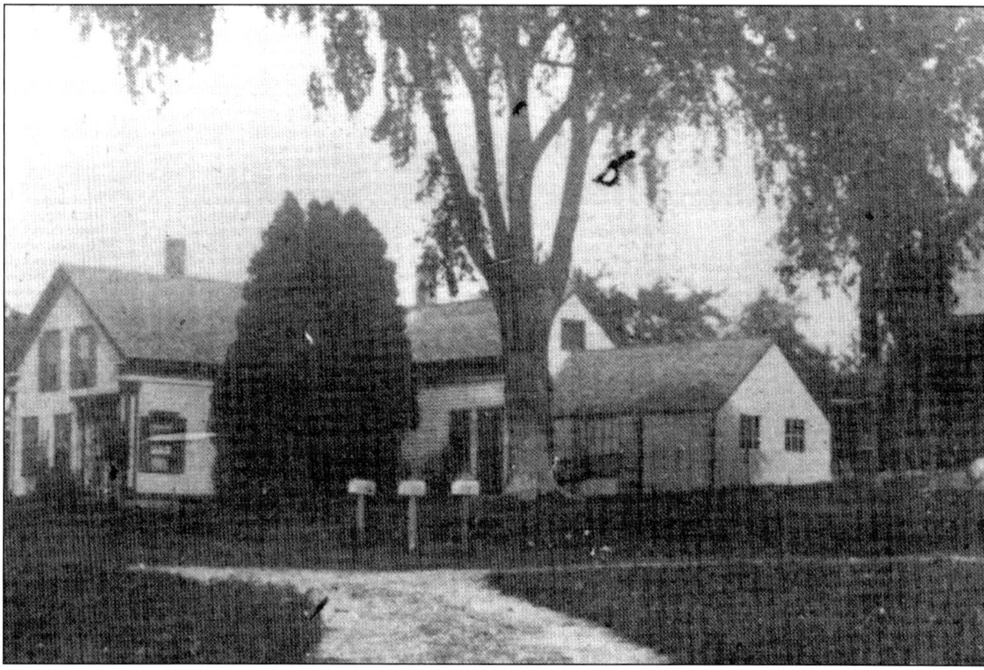

At one time, on the west corner of Hartford Avenue and North Main Streets stood a stable where, in the 1700s, the Boston to New York stage would stop to change horses. Tired and hungry passengers would cross the road to this home. Here, their needs were taken care of. They got a good night sleep and were refreshed for the next day's stage ride. The former Forbes home is now the Ozimek Insurance Company.

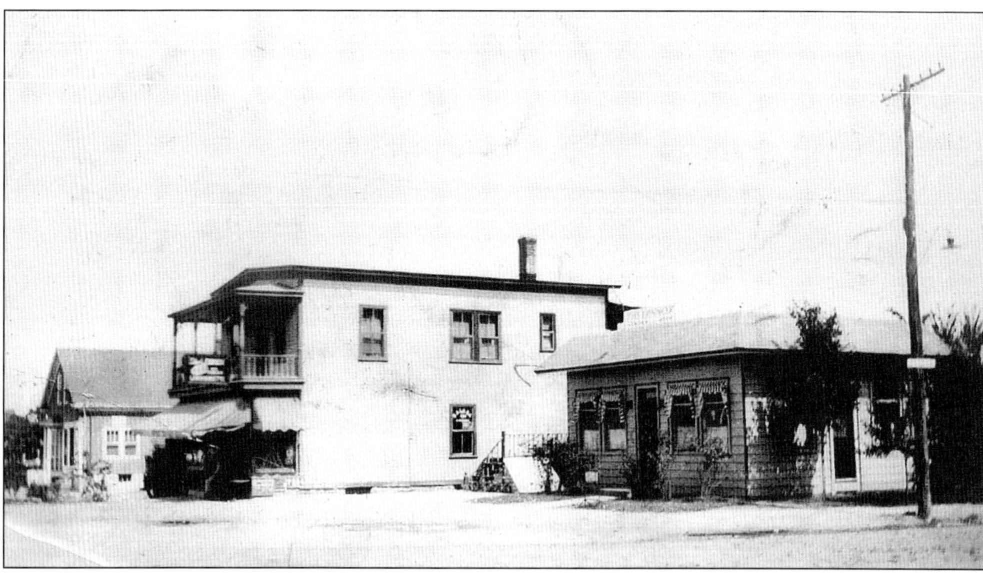

The Lennox Grill was once located at Crooks Corner. The old log lounge was added later. During the 1940s and 1950s, students from the South School who had money were allowed to come here for fish and chips. The Lennox was in business from the late 1930s to the early 1970s. The Dean Bank and Crooks Corner Pavilion are currently at that site.

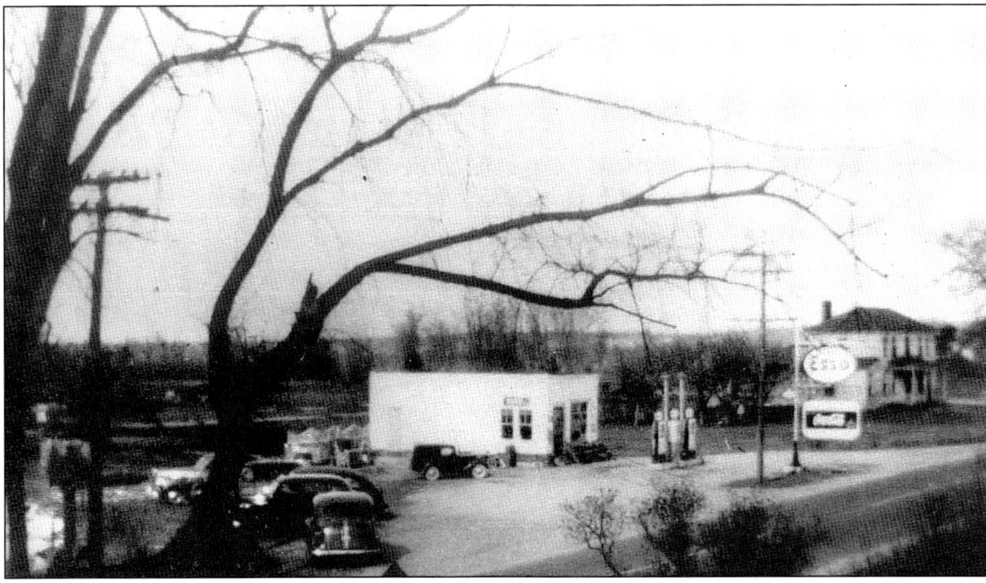

The area of town where Maple Street crosses Mechanic Street is called the Four Corners. Mechanic Street, or Route 140 since 1930, was called the Cape Road. At this northwest corner in 1946, Donald J. Moore bought a gas station called Littlefields. He soon established a Hudson car dealership. Today, Moore's Bellingham Auto Sales is well known throughout New England and the East Coast for its classic automobiles.

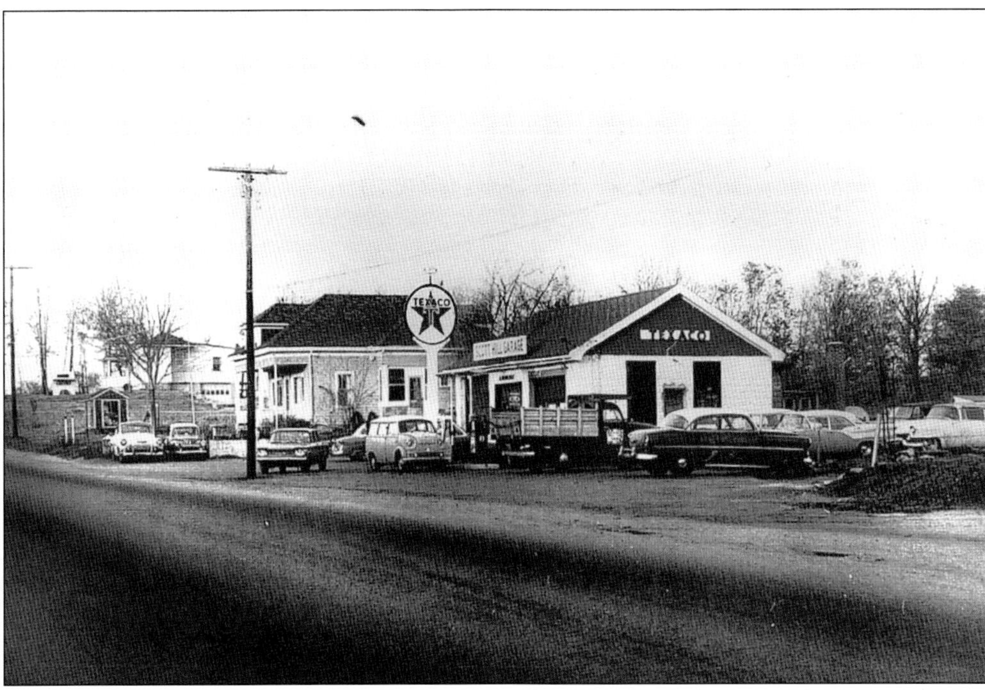

Alfred Puoliot rebuilt an automobile repair garage here in 1931. The original garage at this site was built in 1925 but burned in 1930. The property was sold in 1963. The site at 825 South Main Street is now the home of Charlie's Tire and Service Center.

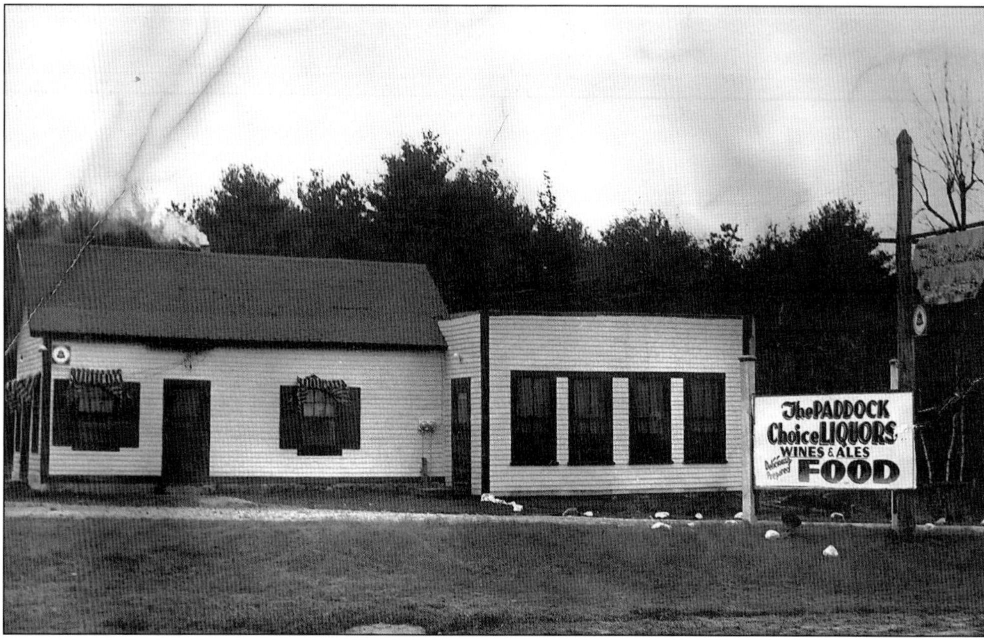

The Paddock located on Mendon Street by the town line remained one of Bellingham's popular nightspots from the 1930s through the 1970s. Under a new owner, it was G.W.'s, and currently, it is the Fifty's Lounge.

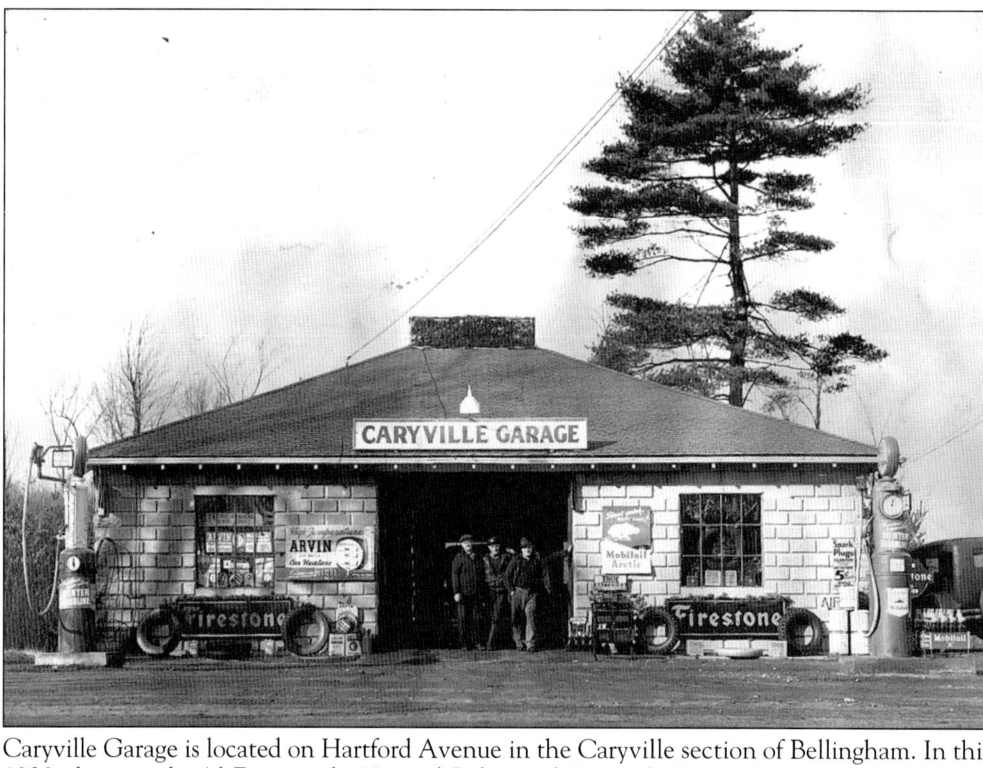

Caryville Garage is located on Hartford Avenue in the Caryville section of Bellingham. In this 1930 photograph, Al Fitzpatrick, Howard Bebe, and Howard "Rusty" Rogers are seen in the garage doorway.

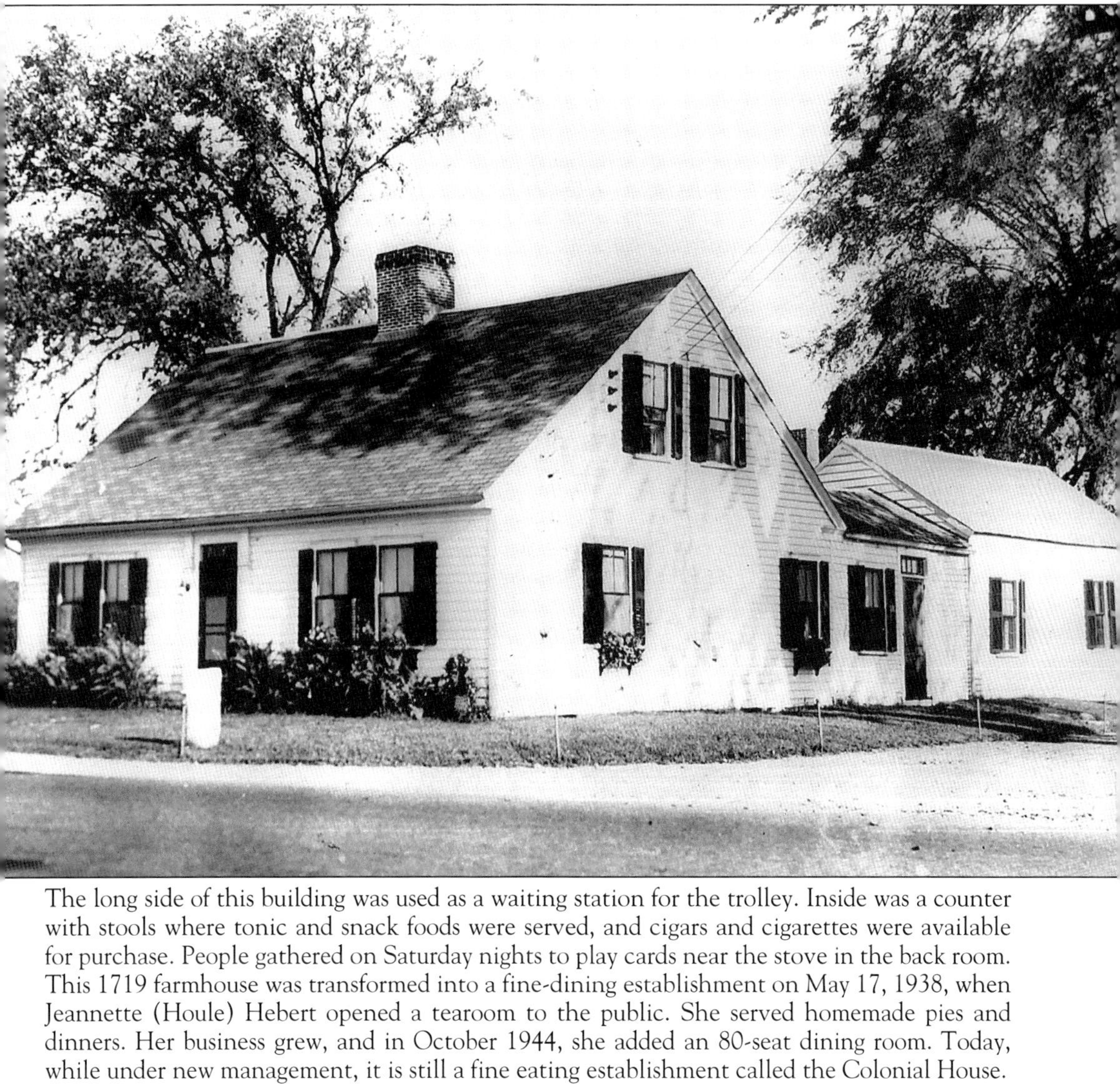

The long side of this building was used as a waiting station for the trolley. Inside was a counter with stools where tonic and snack foods were served, and cigars and cigarettes were available for purchase. People gathered on Saturday nights to play cards near the stove in the back room. This 1719 farmhouse was transformed into a fine-dining establishment on May 17, 1938, when Jeannette (Houle) Hebert opened a tearoom to the public. She served homemade pies and dinners. Her business grew, and in October 1944, she added an 80-seat dining room. Today, while under new management, it is still a fine eating establishment called the Colonial House.

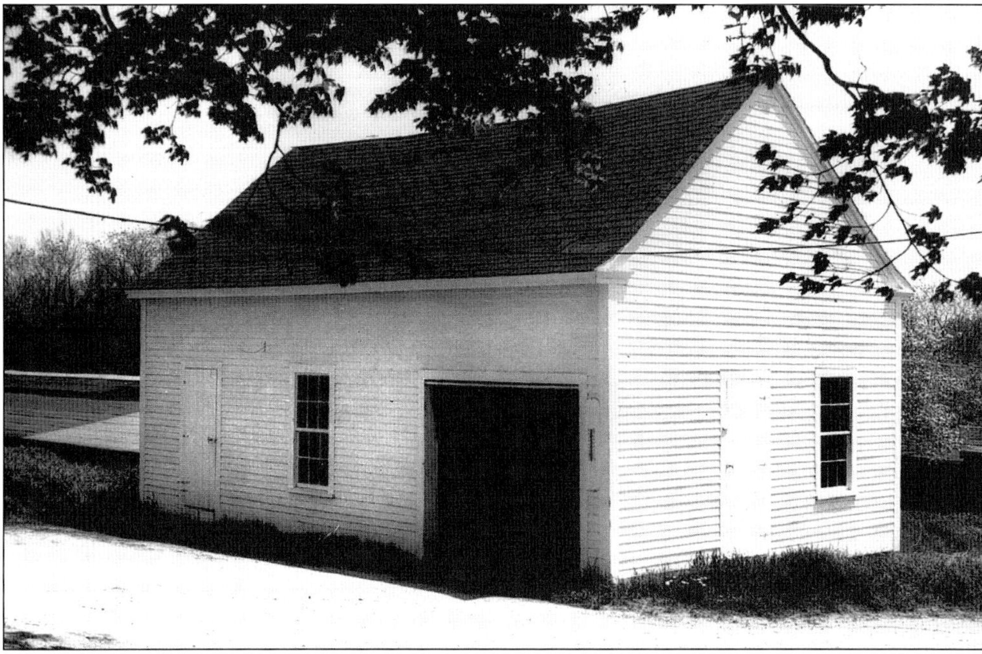

A small white shed upon the Whiting property on Scott Street once housed the Barber glue factory. In the late 1800s, freight cars carrying barrels of animal hoofs were unloaded at Rand's railroad crossing in South Bellingham. The hoofs were taken by horse and wagon to this factory to be boiled down into glue.

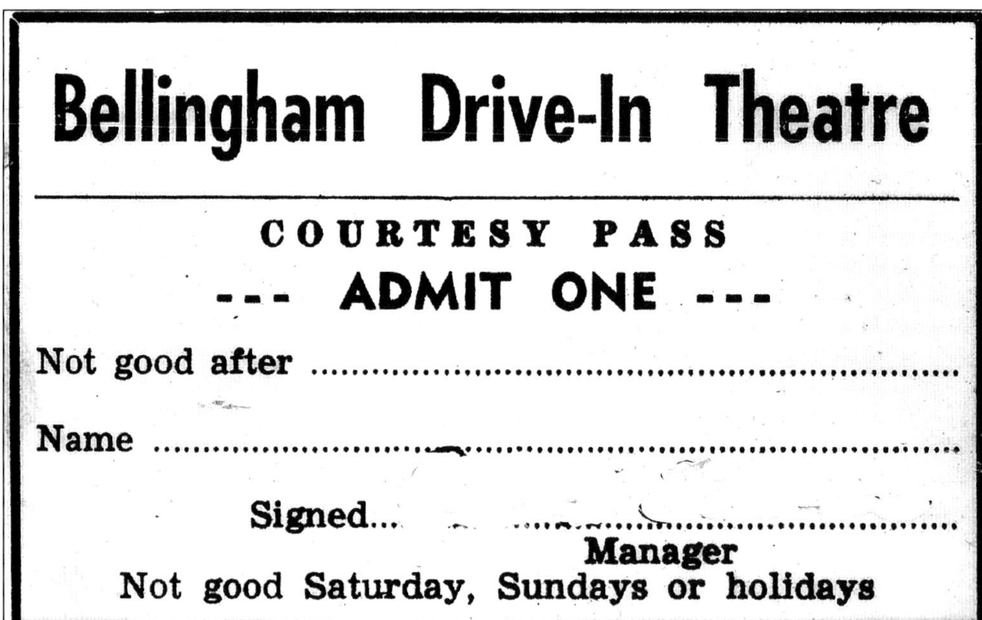

Bellingham Drive-In Theatre

COURTESY PASS

--- ADMIT ONE ---

Not good after ....

Name ....

Signed..

Manager

Not good Saturday, Sundays or holidays

The earliest reference to the Bellingham Drive-In Theatre on Pulaski Boulevard is included in accounts of the 1938 Hurricane, when the wooden screen was blown over. This popular family theater existed until 1985.

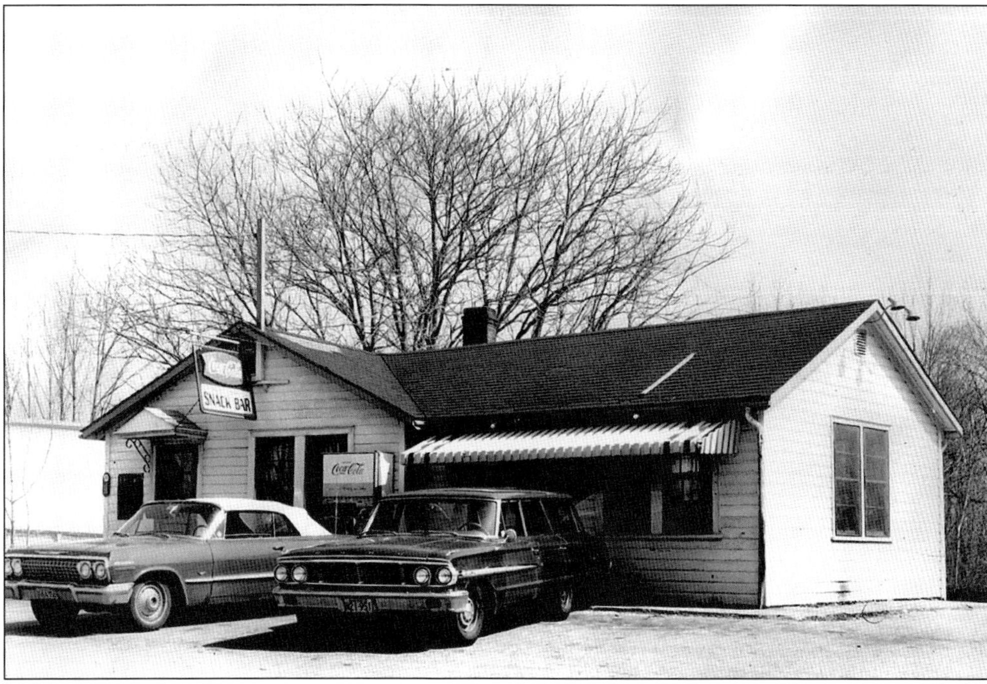

This restaurant at Bellingham Center on Mechanic Street had a variety of names. It started out as (Mae) Vater's snack bar. Then it was Ma's (Rogozyn) restaurant. Later, it became Marie's. The business, now called Joanne's, is still open and under new management.

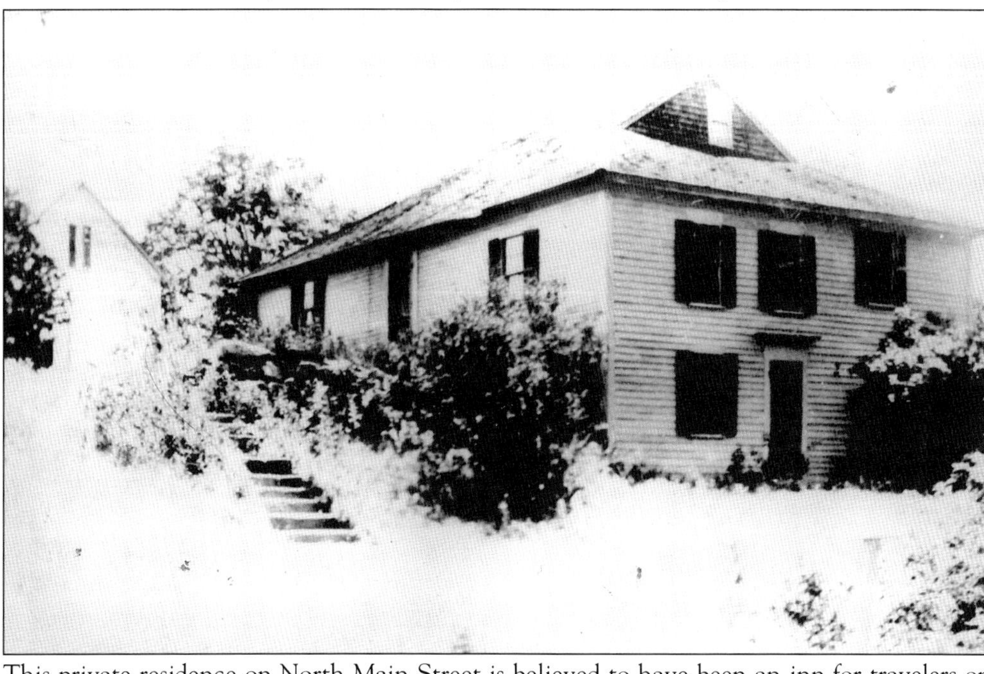

This private residence on North Main Street is believed to have been an inn for travelers on the stage line between Taunton and Worcester. Legend has it that on May 20, 1782, Deborah Samson (also Sampson), disguised in men's clothing, enlisted in the Continental Army here as Robert Shurtlieff.

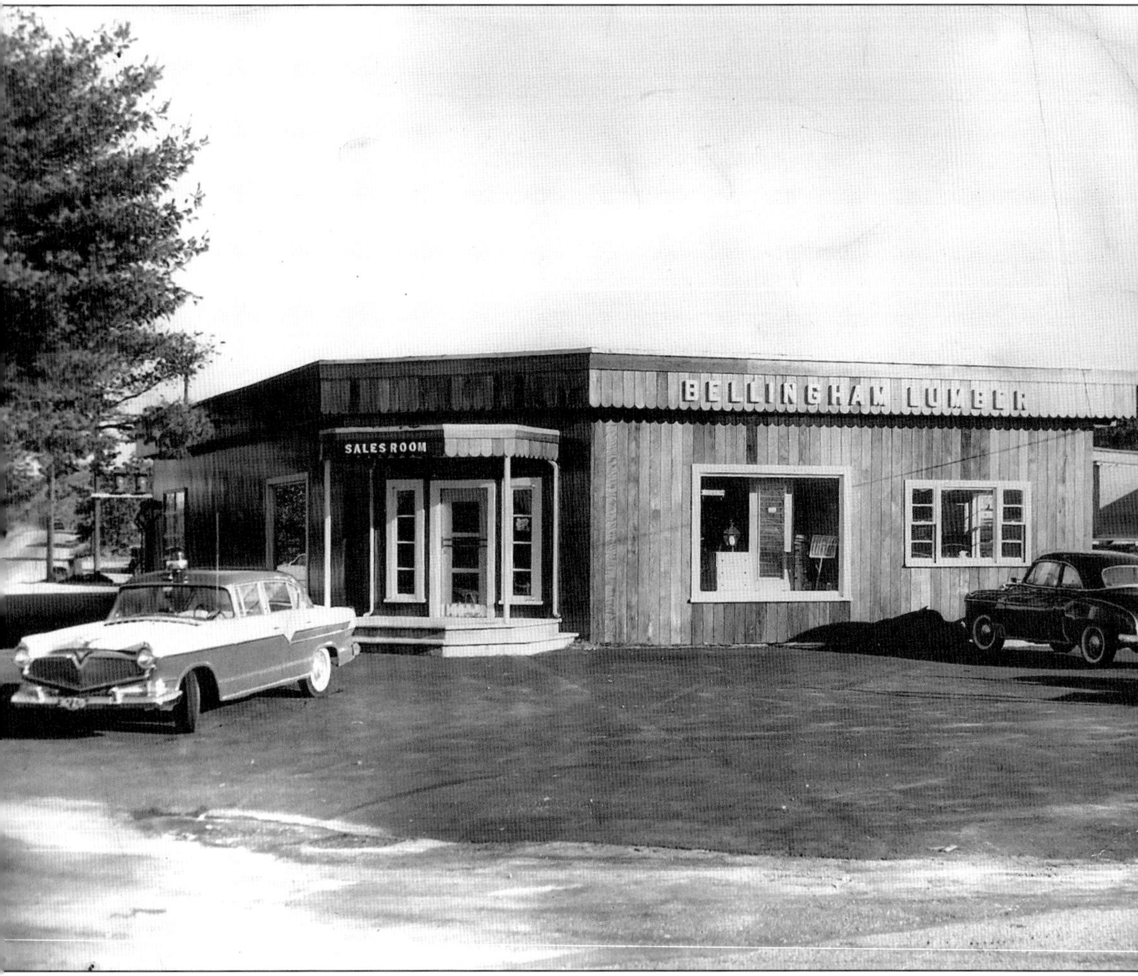

Eldridge Avery Rhodes founded a lumber company in 1900. It was first called the E.A. Rhodes Company and later the Bellingham Lumber Company. In this photograph is Bellingham's first police cruiser, a 1956 Hudson Hornet.

Four

Silver Lake, Trolleys, and Railroad Depots

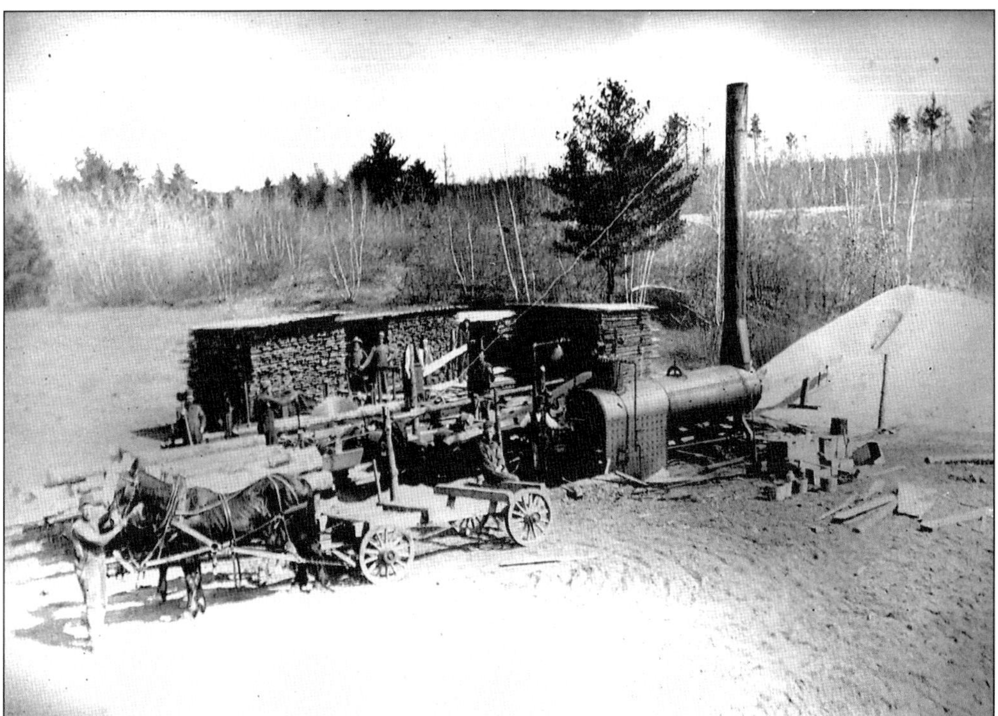

Elmer Nourse is sitting on the back of a wagon at Steam Saw Mill, Hoag Lake, in 1912. In 1922, the Hoag Lake was renamed Silver Lake.

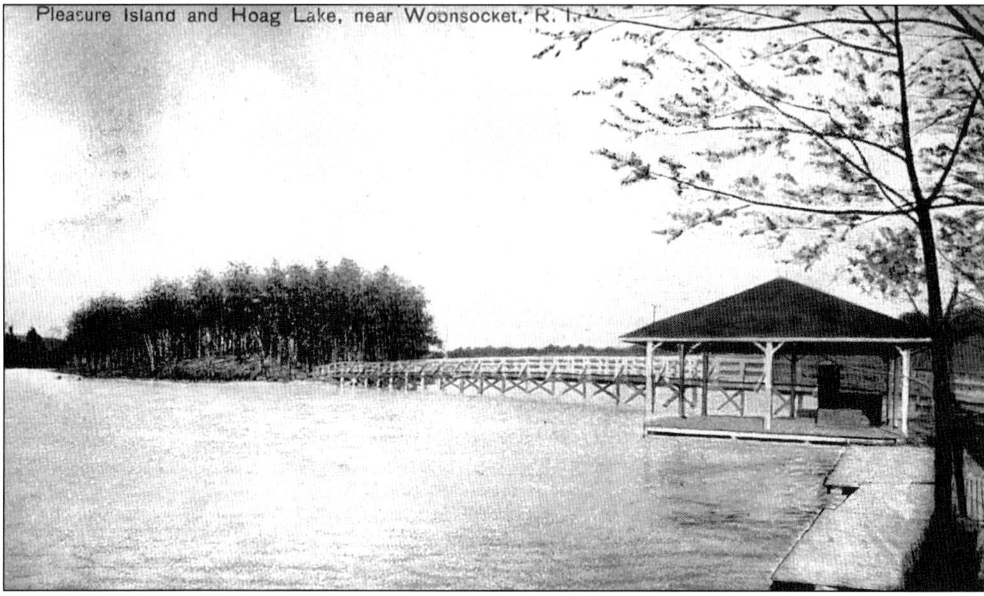

This area was a swamp until 1828, when William Chilson dammed up the stream so he could harness the water to power his cotton-manufacturing mill. In 1899, the Milford, Attleboro and Woonsocket Street Railway Company purchased the lake and ran an amusement park until 1922, when it came under new management. Throughout the years, the lake has had a number of owners and remained without the success of bygone days. The town now owns the lake and keeps the beach open for recreational use.

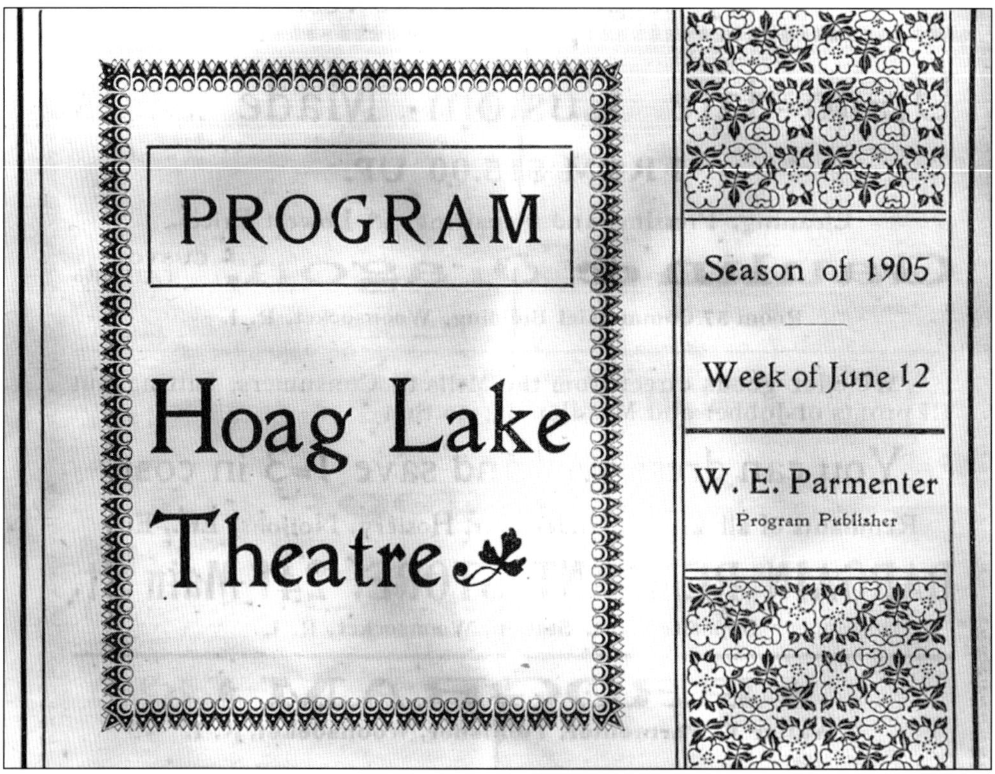
PROGRAM

Hoag Lake Theatre

Season of 1905

Week of June 12

W. E. Parmenter
Program Publisher

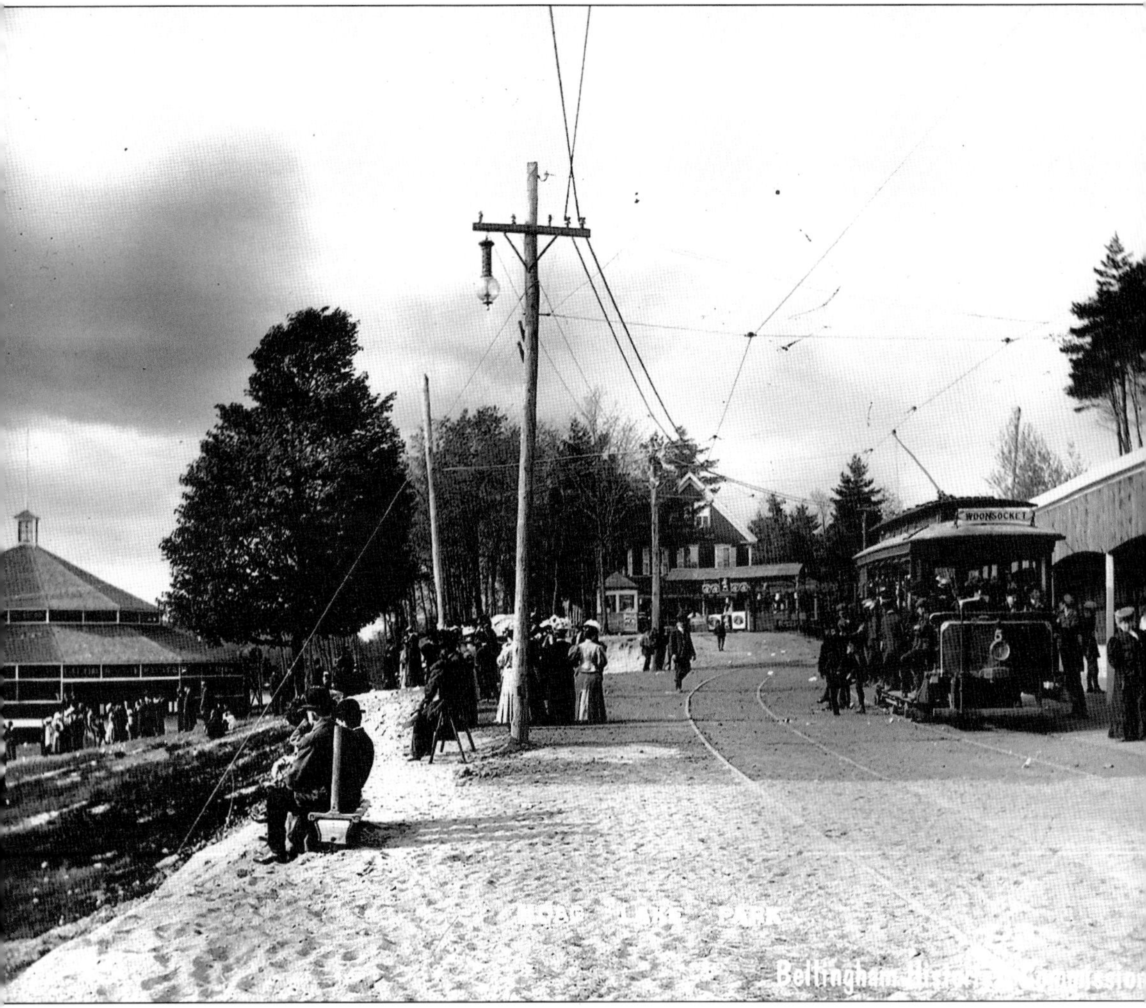

This photograph taken in 1910 shows Hoag Lake, now Silver Lake, located on Cross Street. The Milford, Attleboro and Woonsocket Street Railway Company developed and opened this popular summer amusement park in 1899. It cost 5¢ to ride the trolley to Silver Lake. Once at the amusement park, one could enjoy swimming, band concerts, and vaudeville acts. There were boat rentals, live animal acts, carousel rides, and evening dances at the Island Dance Hall. The decline in the trolley system led to fewer people visiting this resort area. In 1922, the park was closed. There were many attempts to revive this once beautiful resort area, but the lake has never recaptured its popularity.

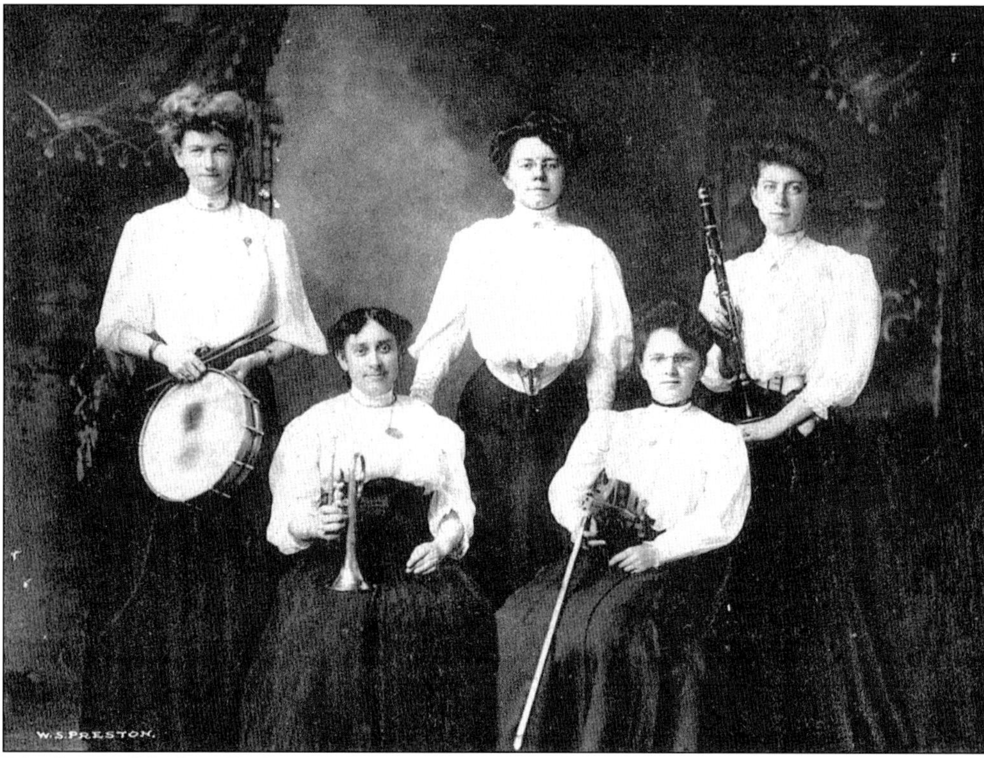

The Imperial Ladies Orchestra is pictured at Hoag Lake in the early 1900s. Members include Bertine Converse Marsh, Etta Highland, Sadie Bissell, Hattie Litchfield, and Lizzie Otto.

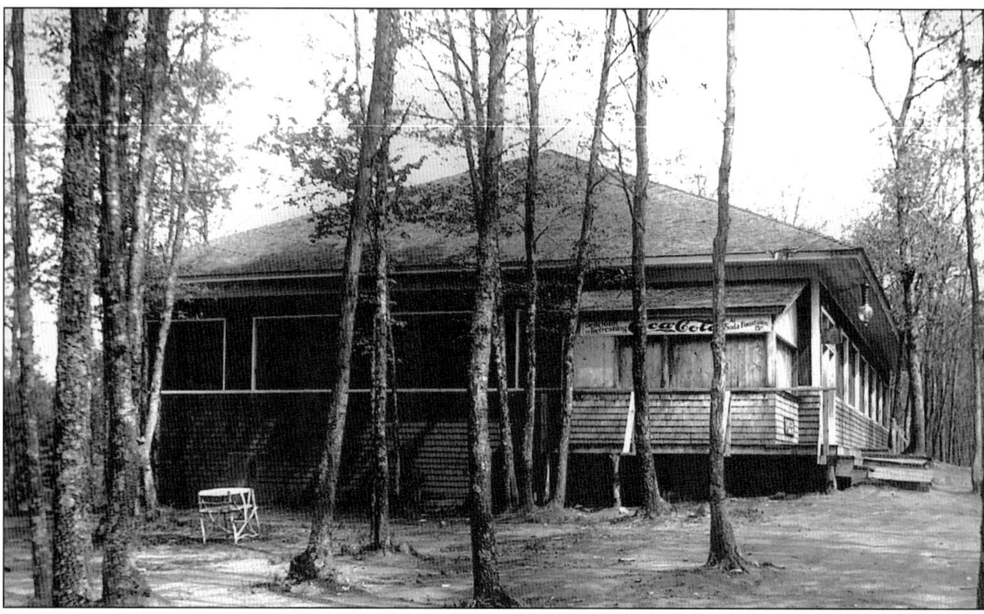

This dance hall at Hoag Lake Park was located on Pleasure Island. A special wooden bridge was built for a cost of $1,000 to connect the island to the mainland. With the decline of the lake resort, the island bridge was not maintained, and by the mid-1930s, it became unsafe and was dismantled. The dance hall burned in 1968.

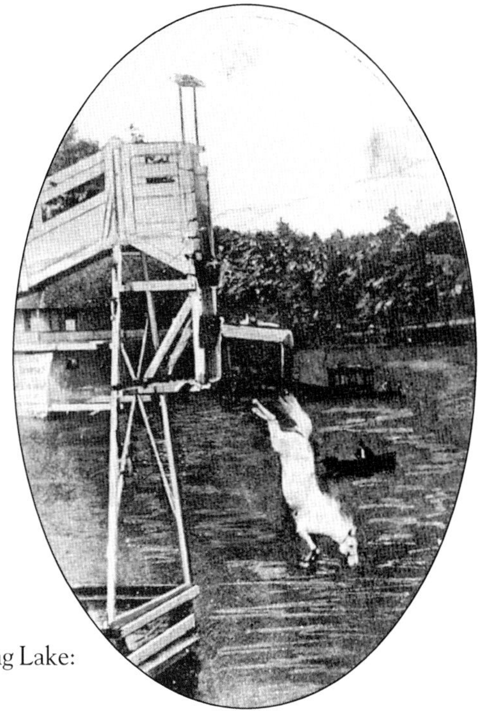

In 1902 and 1903, a major attraction came to Hoag Lake: the diving horses King and Queen.

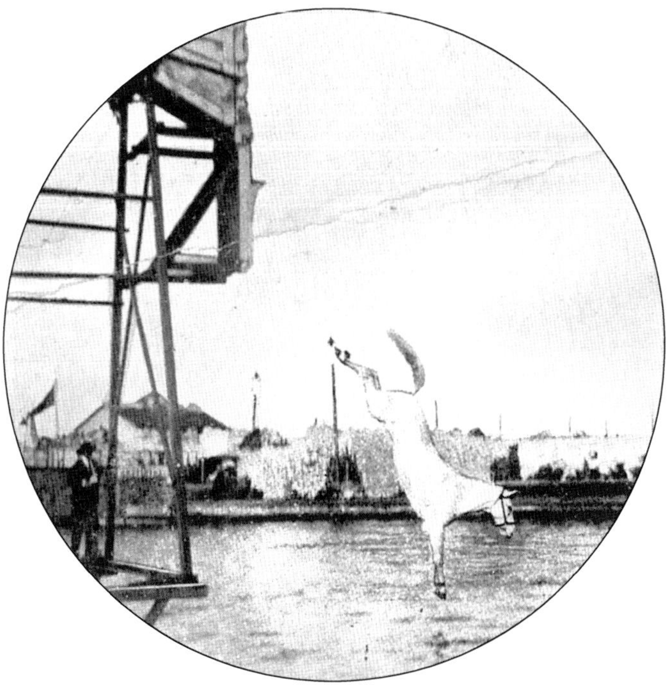

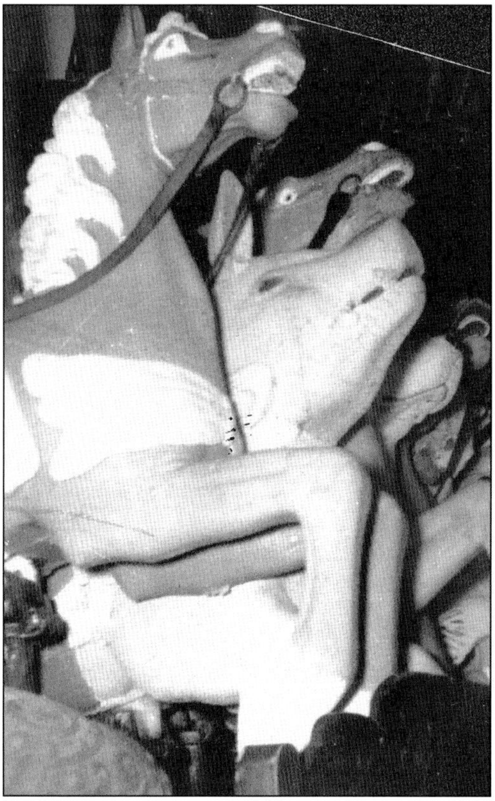

This is only one of two photographs known to exist of the Hoag Lake carousel figures. Chet Hood gave the following details about the carousel: "The merry-go-round was not very big; it measured only about 40 feet across. There were only 2 animals in each row. The combination of animals was 20 horses, 2 chickens, 1 dog, 1 pig, and 1 chariot." The music was provided by a calliope, or steam organ. In 1962, the carousel was dismantled and sold.

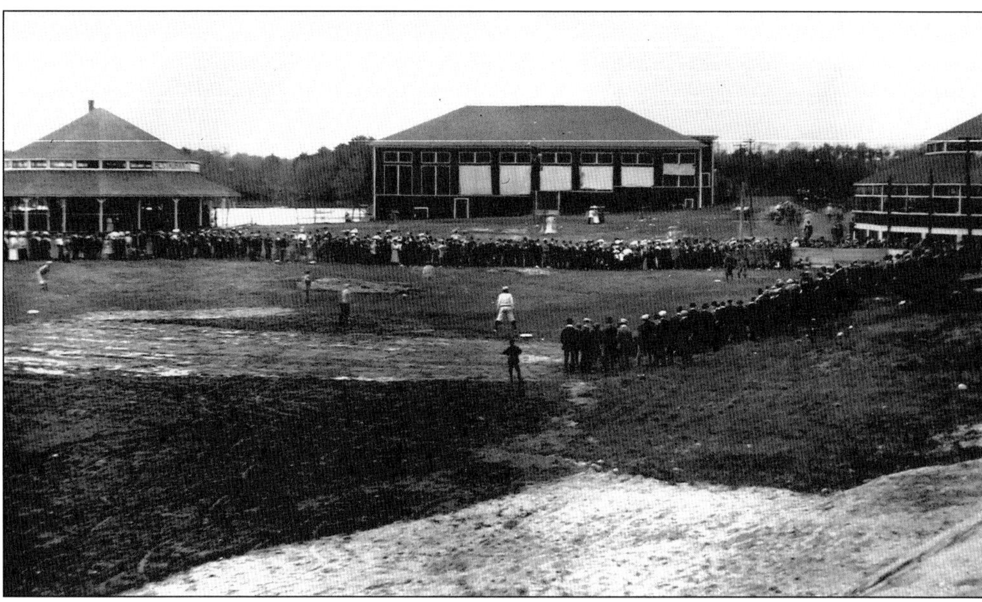

In this 1906 photograph, the crowd is enjoying an afternoon baseball game. On the left is the Hoag Restaurant; on the right is the carousel. In the center of the photograph is the great Hoag Theater. On May 18, 1900, work progressed on the construction of a 1,200-seat summer theater. The theater was 130 feet long by 66 feet wide and was completed and opened on June 26, 1900. The building burned in 1922.

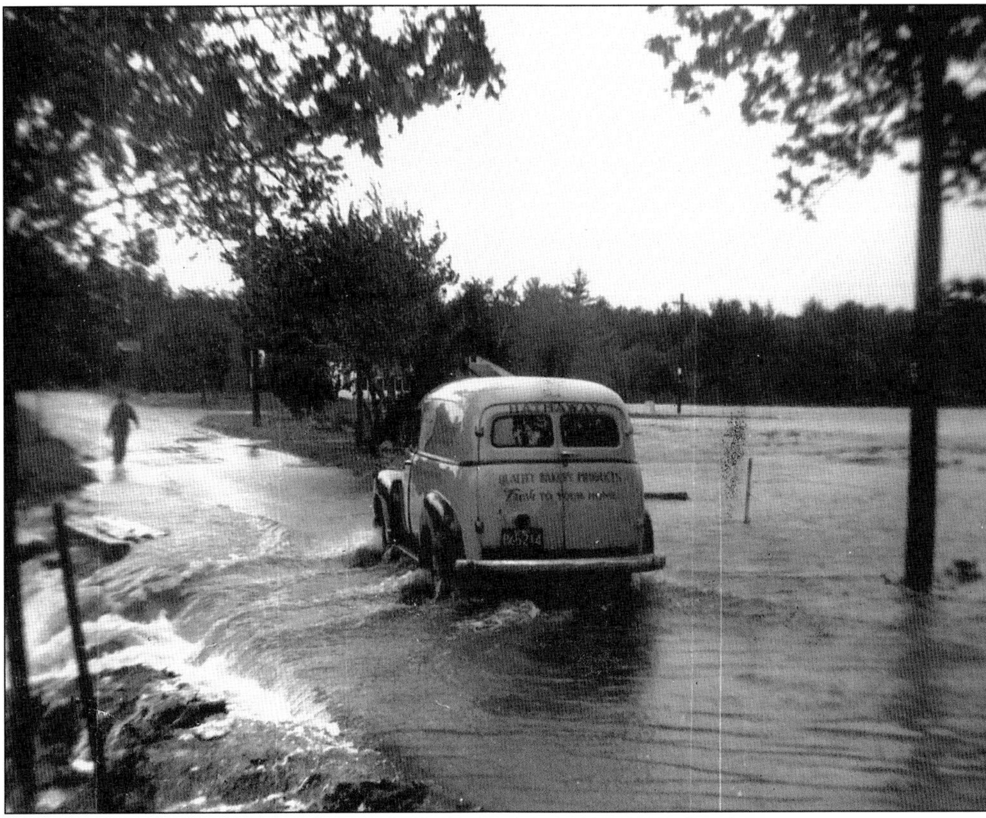

A truck crosses the swollen lake at Cross Street during the 1955 flood.

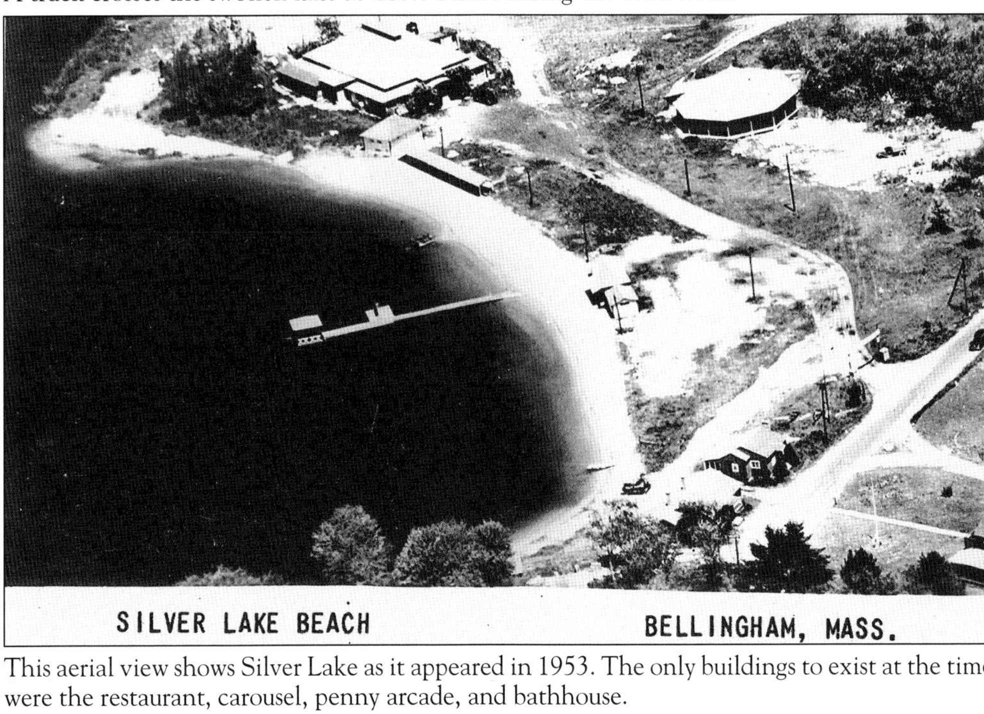

This aerial view shows Silver Lake as it appeared in 1953. The only buildings to exist at the time were the restaurant, carousel, penny arcade, and bathhouse.

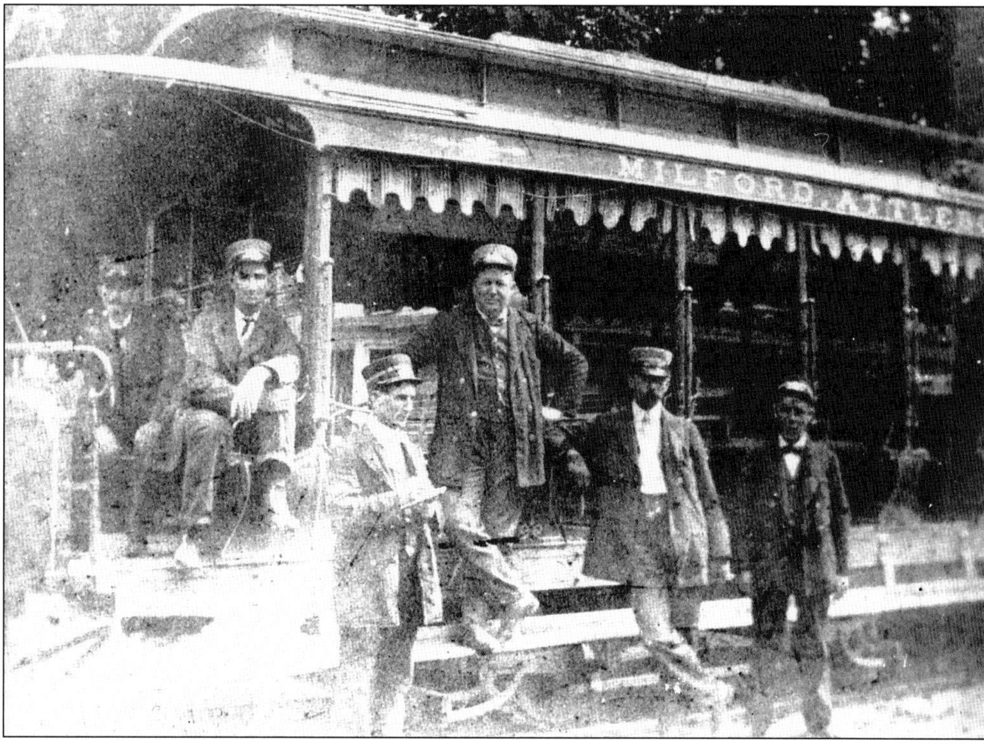

Trolley men of the Milford, Attleboro and Woonsocket Street Railway Company are pictured in this 1910 photograph. Sitting second from the left is Rodney Tyler, and standing, from left to right, are Mike Cullen, unidentified, Gordon Ross, and unidentified.

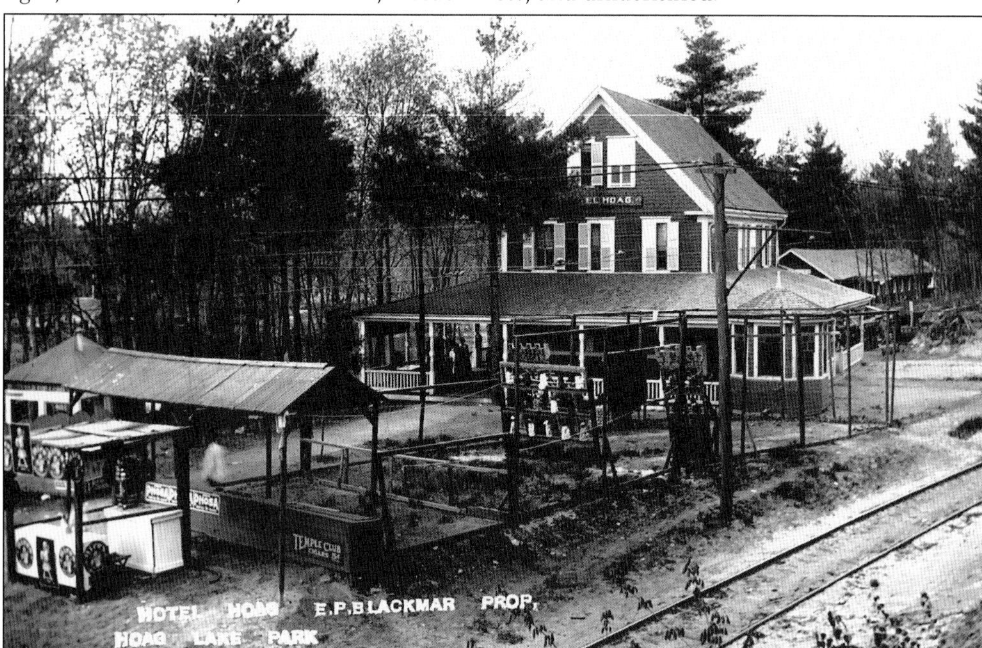

In 1922, the once popular Blackmar Hotel was sold off from the main park and became a private residence.

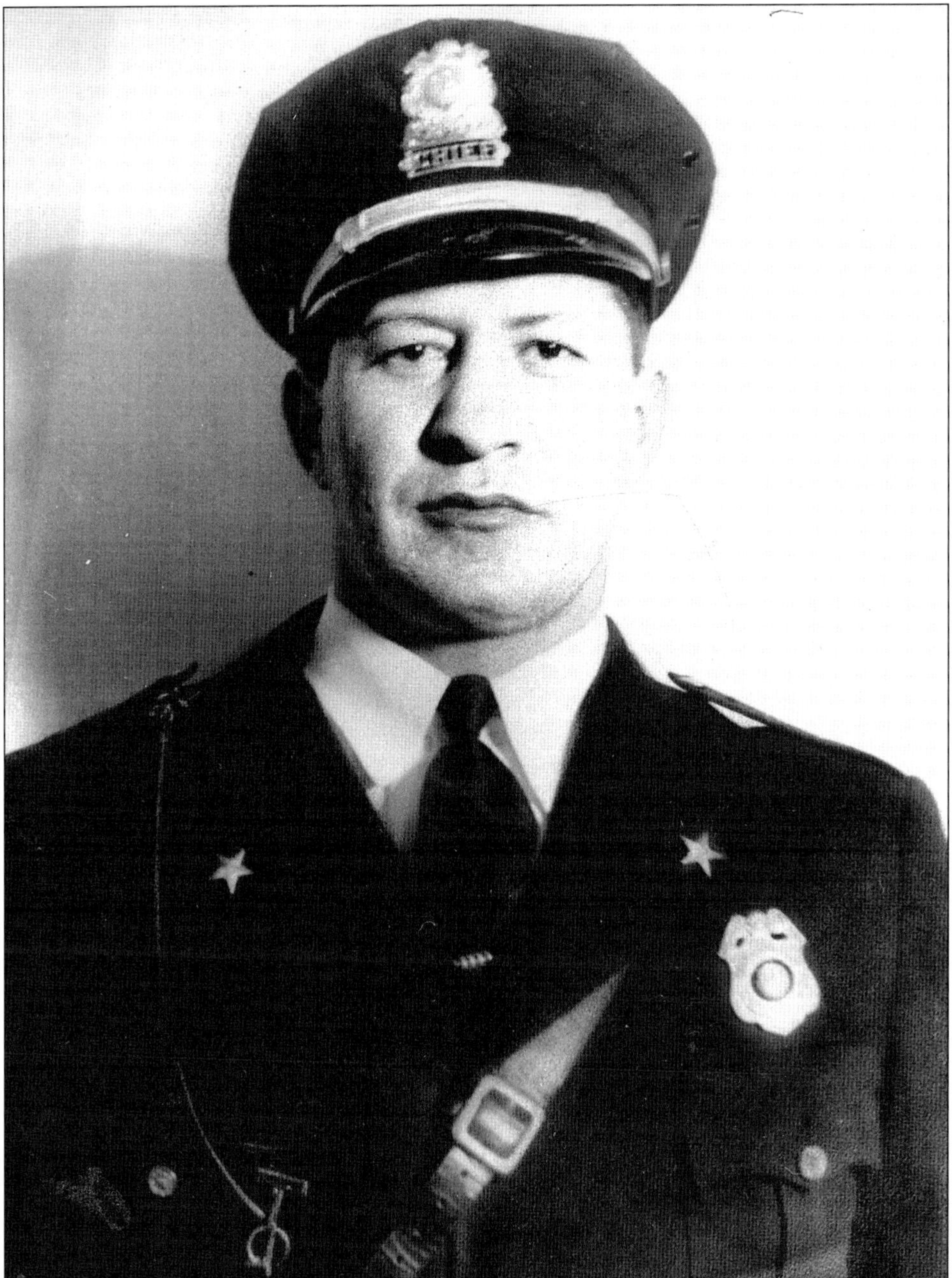

Euclide Fleuette was born in Canada on June 19, 1908, and died on December 19, 1967. He became a policeman in Bellingham in 1933 and chief in 1937. He was the police chief for 30 years. The police department had an office in the town hall but basically operated as a one-man police force. For years, Fleuette operated from his home on Cross Street at Silver Lake. He was on call 24 hours a day, 7 days a week. Chief Fleuette, who was a Golden Gloves boxing champion and in excellent physical condition, swam across Silver Lake everyday in all kinds of weather until the ice over the lake became too thick to swim through. He was a highly respected member of the community.

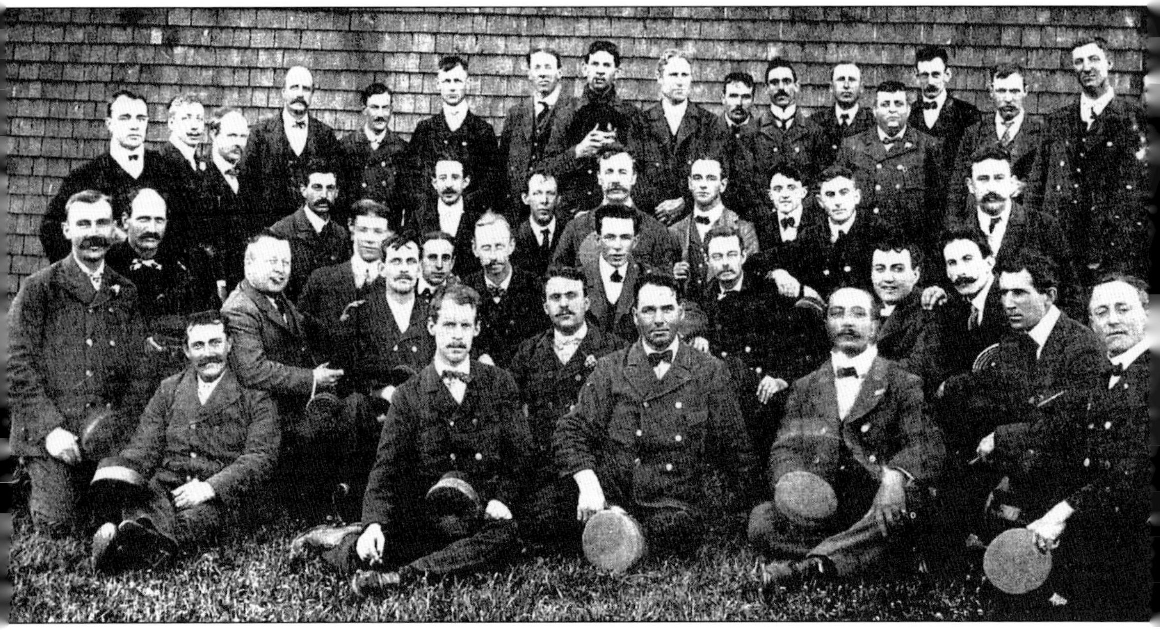

Part of the crew of the Milford, Attleboro and Woonsocket Street Railway Company enjoyed a clambake at Hoag Lake. Seen here are, from left to right, the following: (front row) Gordon Ross, ? Senacal, Henry Simmler, Fred Horton, Joe Dupre, Willard Ross, Bert Connors, Jesse Wright, Win Nye, Martin Morrisey, Charles Aldrich, Dan Coutler, Mark Knowlton, Donald Ross, Patrick Clancy, Virgil Grignon, Gus Boucher, Daniel McKenna, Thomas Powers, Thomas Fogarty, Joe Desrosiers, Lloyd Cook, Tony Carpenter, William Fox, Michael Cullen, and Archie Fontaine; (back row) unidentified, ? Brown, John Cook, Ernest Potter, Fred Rhodes, Herbert Cass, Percy Burr, Daniel Gilmore, Nick Chilson, Fred Bacon, Jerry Cross, ? Martin, Amos Leclair, Frank Gassett, George Cook, James Trent, and William Gorton. This photograph was taken sometime in the second decade of the 20th century and donated by Mrs. Wesley Bibbins of Franklin, who is the daughter of Gordon Ross. He was the first and last motorman on the line (1898–1924), and he started at 16¢ an hour and retired at 81¢ an hour.

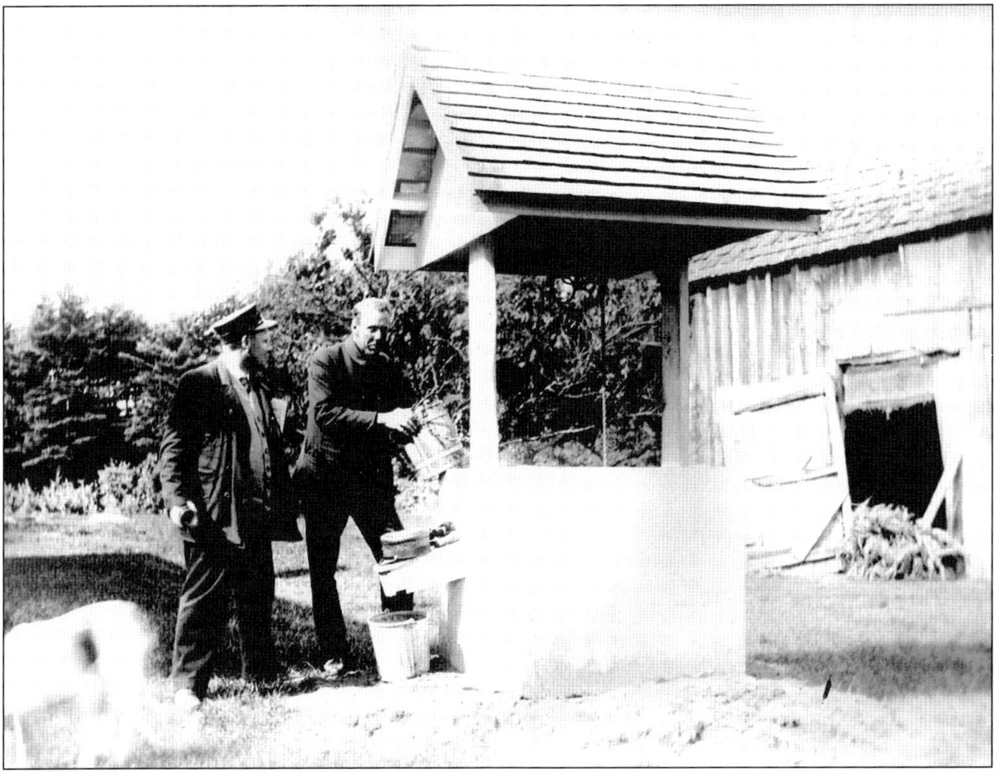

Trolley men Jenks and Percy Burr pause during work duties to get water from a local well. The property is believed to be the Burr Farm on Railroad Street.

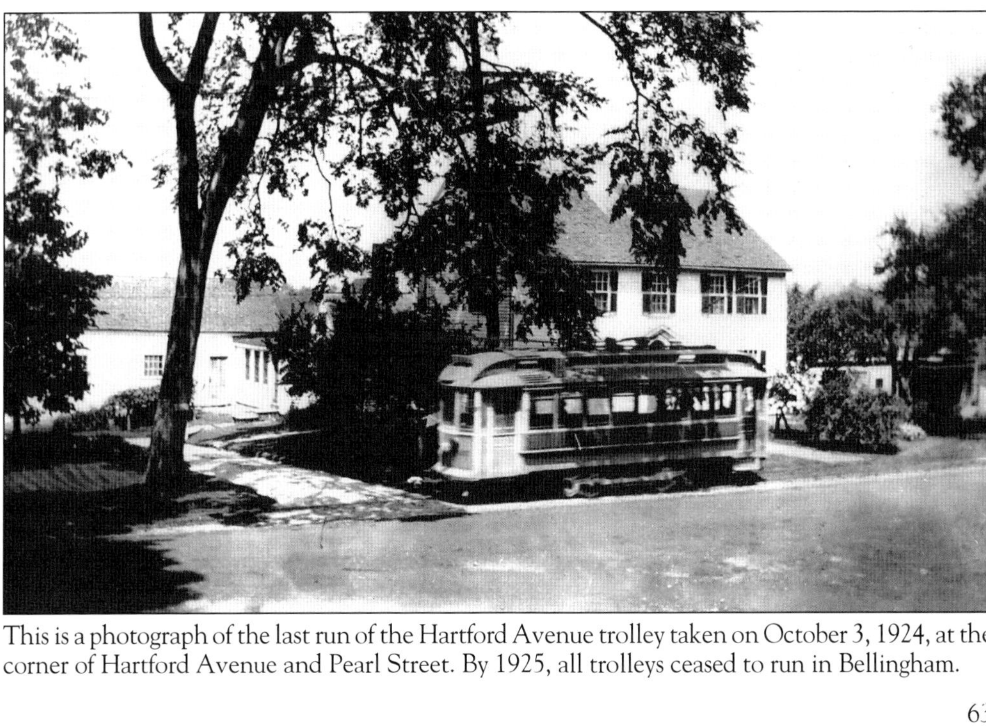

This is a photograph of the last run of the Hartford Avenue trolley taken on October 3, 1924, at the corner of Hartford Avenue and Pearl Street. By 1925, all trolleys ceased to run in Bellingham.

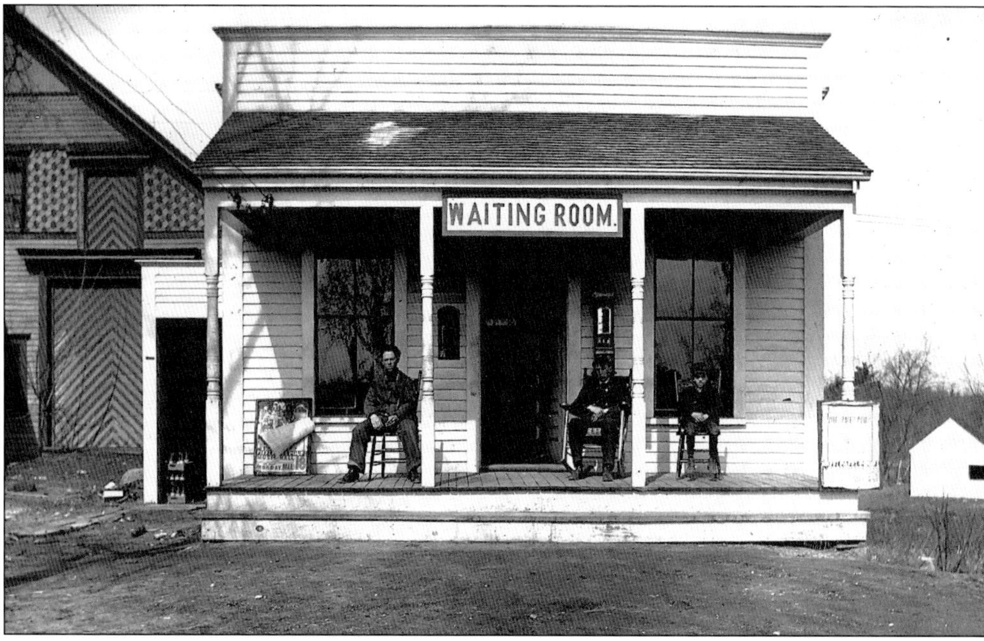

Waiting room stations were established along the route of the Milford, Attleboro and Woonsocket Street Railway Company. It was a place for passengers to wait, get something to eat, and maybe catch up on the local news. This particular waiting room was located at the corner of Hartford Avenue and Stone Street.

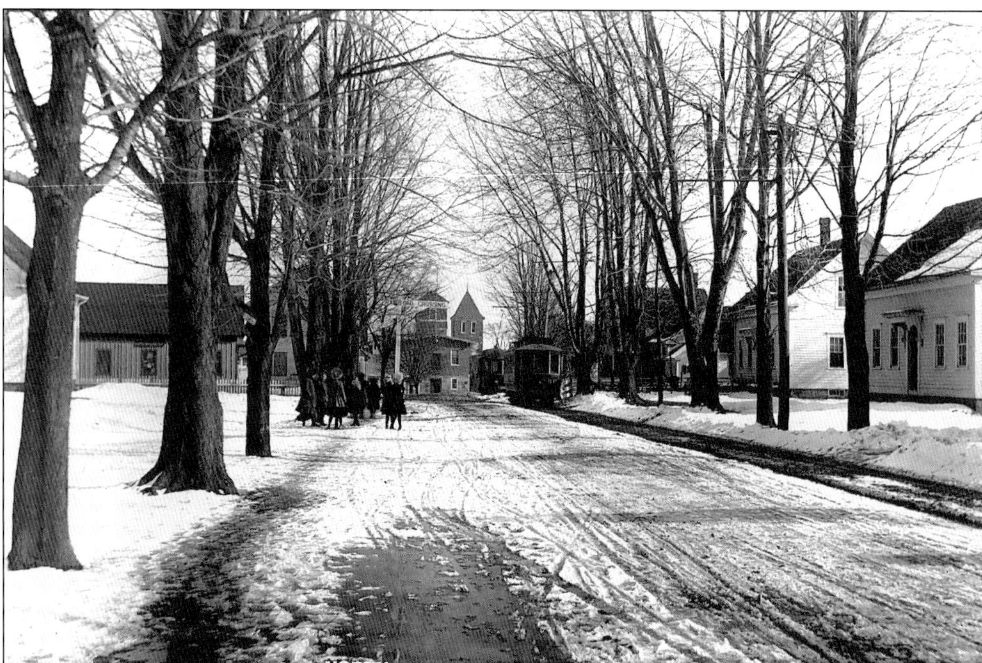

This photograph shows a distant view of the Maple Street railroad crossing. Note the two trolleys. The trolley tracks could not cross over railroad tracks, so passengers had to get off the trolley, walk across the tracks, and re-board another trolley on the other side of the tracks.

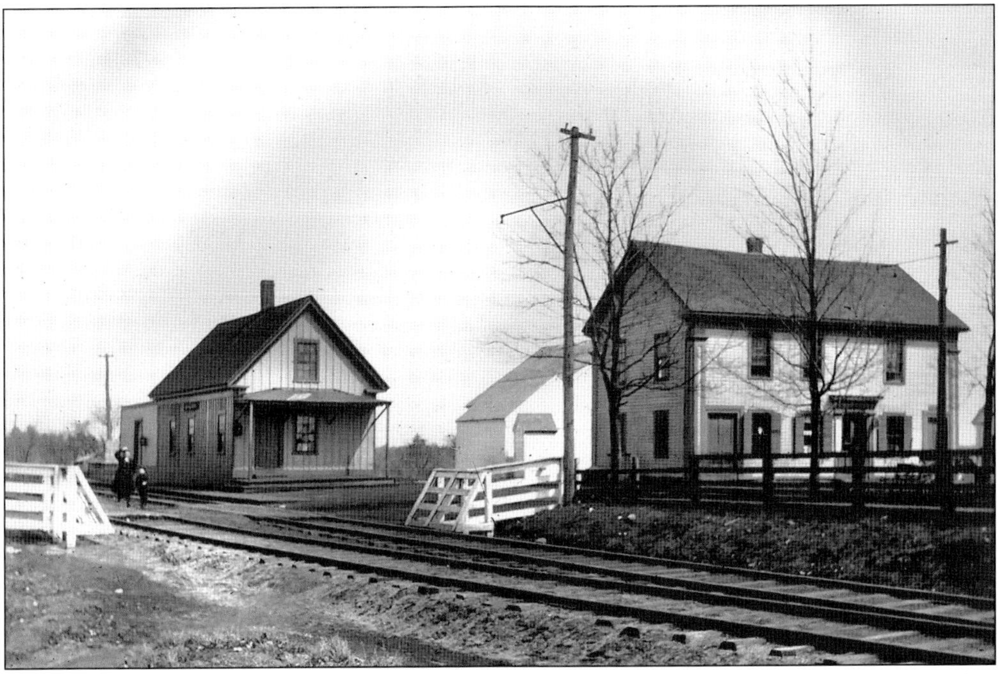

This is the Maple Street railroad crossing in 1904. The North Bellingham depot is on the left and the post office block is on the right. At one time, this building housed a post office, a grocery store, and a church.

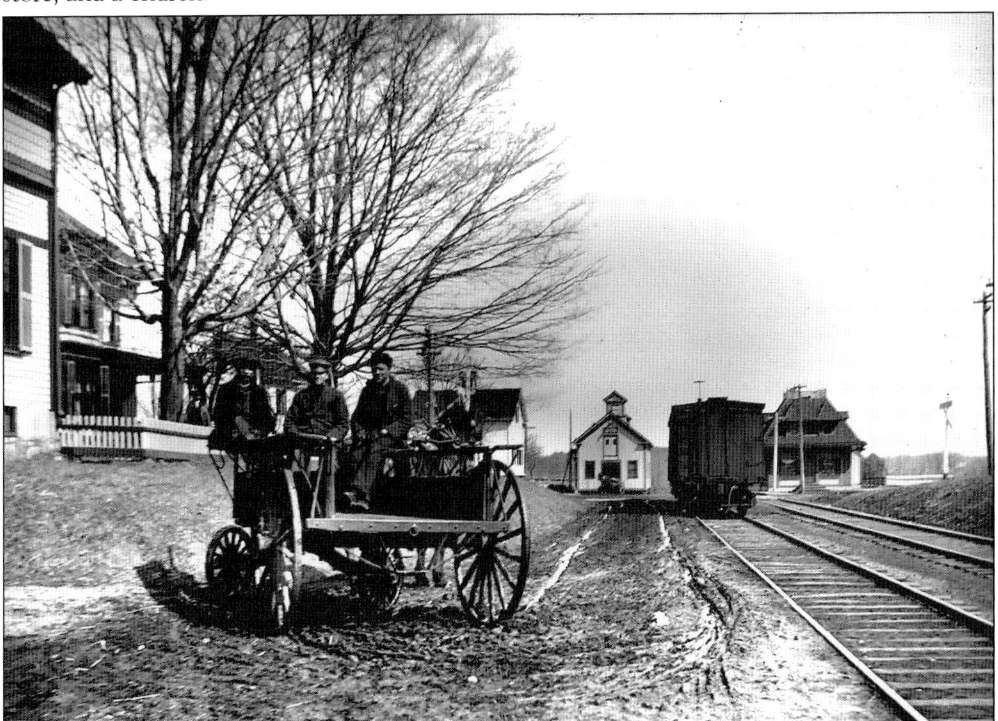

Railway workmen take a break in this 1904 view near the E.B. Stowe store and railway depot on Pearl Street.

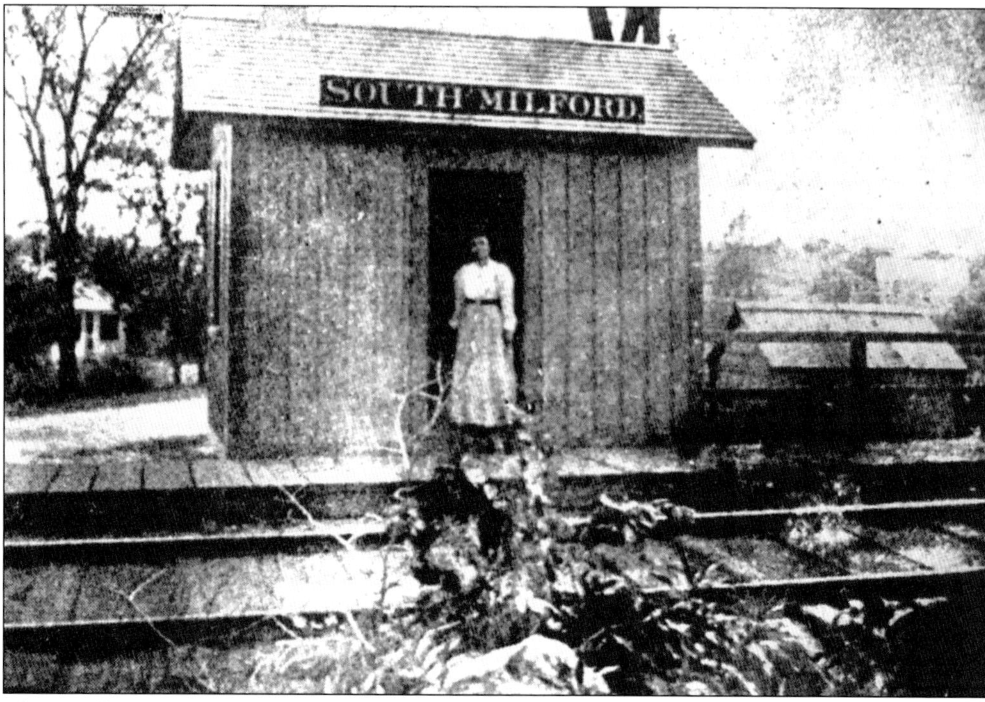

This small one-room depot was built in 1868. It was located on Hartford Avenue in the South Milford section of Bellingham. These railroad tracks from Franklin to Milford are the only rail tracks still existing in Bellingham. The depot was only used for passengers or milk and mail runs. Clara L. Thayer was the stationmaster.

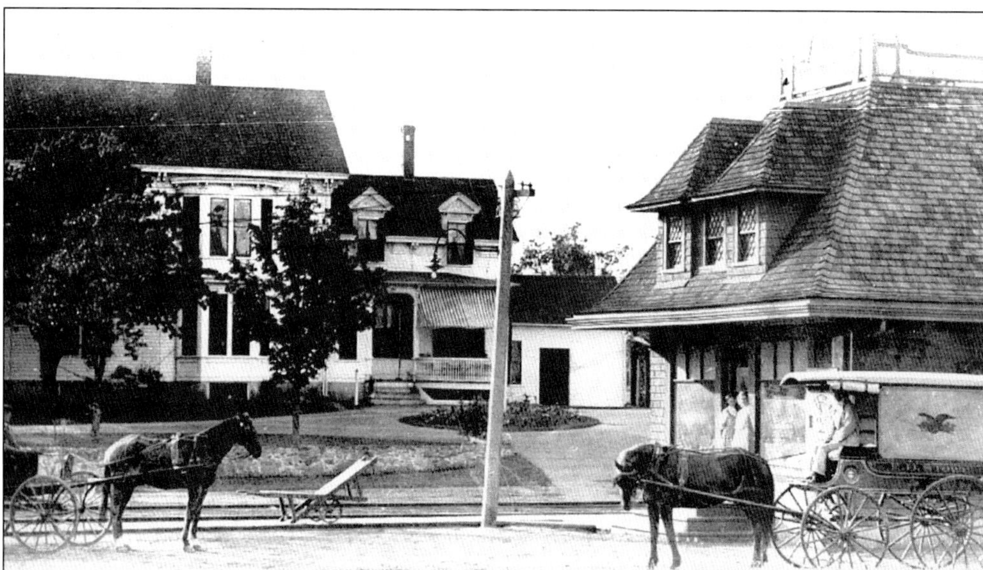

This is a great 1903 photograph of the E.B. Stowe residence, store, and railroad depot. In 1866, a post office was established at the railroad depot on Pearl Street. E.B. Stowe was appointed postmaster with his wife, Edith M. Stowe, as his assistant. Stowe also served as a station agent and kept a store off Pearl Street. This house was built in 1877. In its heyday, c. 1910, seven trains stopped at this station daily. The railroad line was abandoned in 1929.

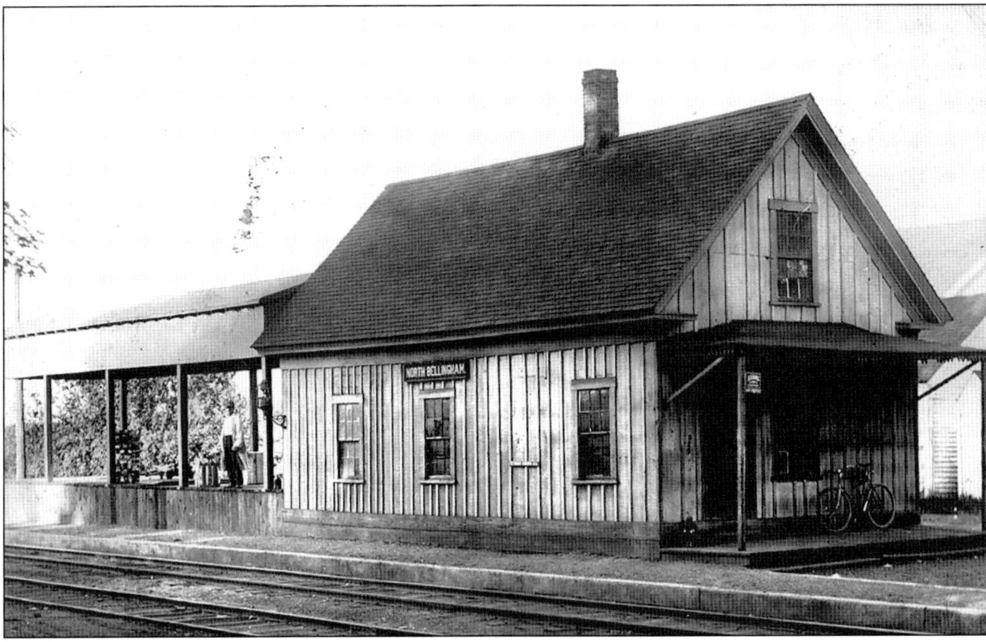

The Charles River Railroad opened in 1852. This line ran through the north section of Bellingham. Shown here is the North Bellingham Railroad Depot, once located on Maple Street.

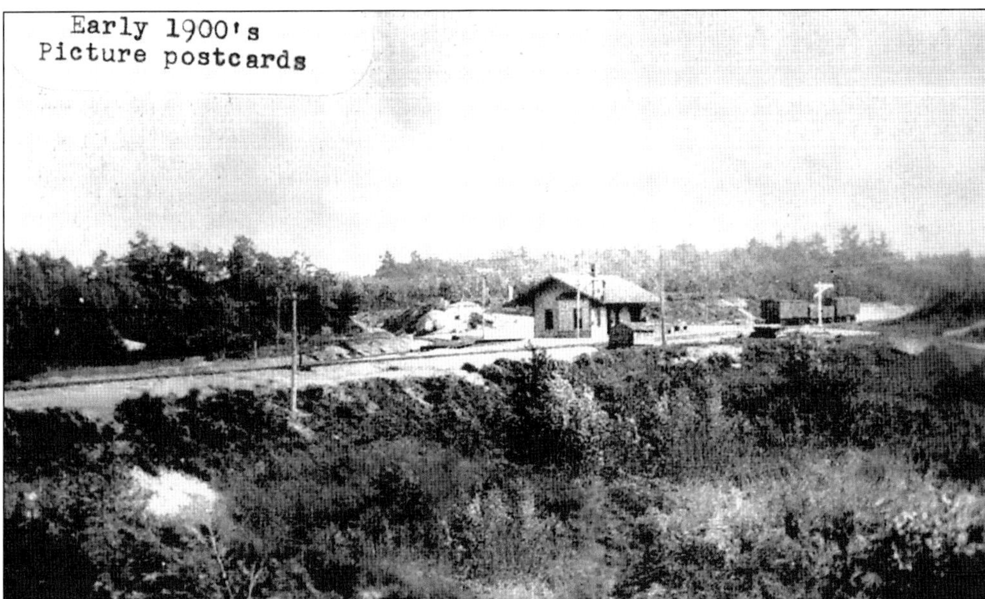

The Bellingham Junction station was built in 1852. The Woonsocket division of the New York, New Haven, and Hartford Railroad, plus the Charles River Railroad, used this station. Part of the Bellingham line was known as the Skunk Hollow Express. In 1902, the Sears Roebuck catalogue listed Bellingham Junction as a freight and express station. Even though the station is gone, one line running from Franklin to Milford remains. This station, known as the Milford Depot, was located at the corner of Riverbank Road and Depot Street.

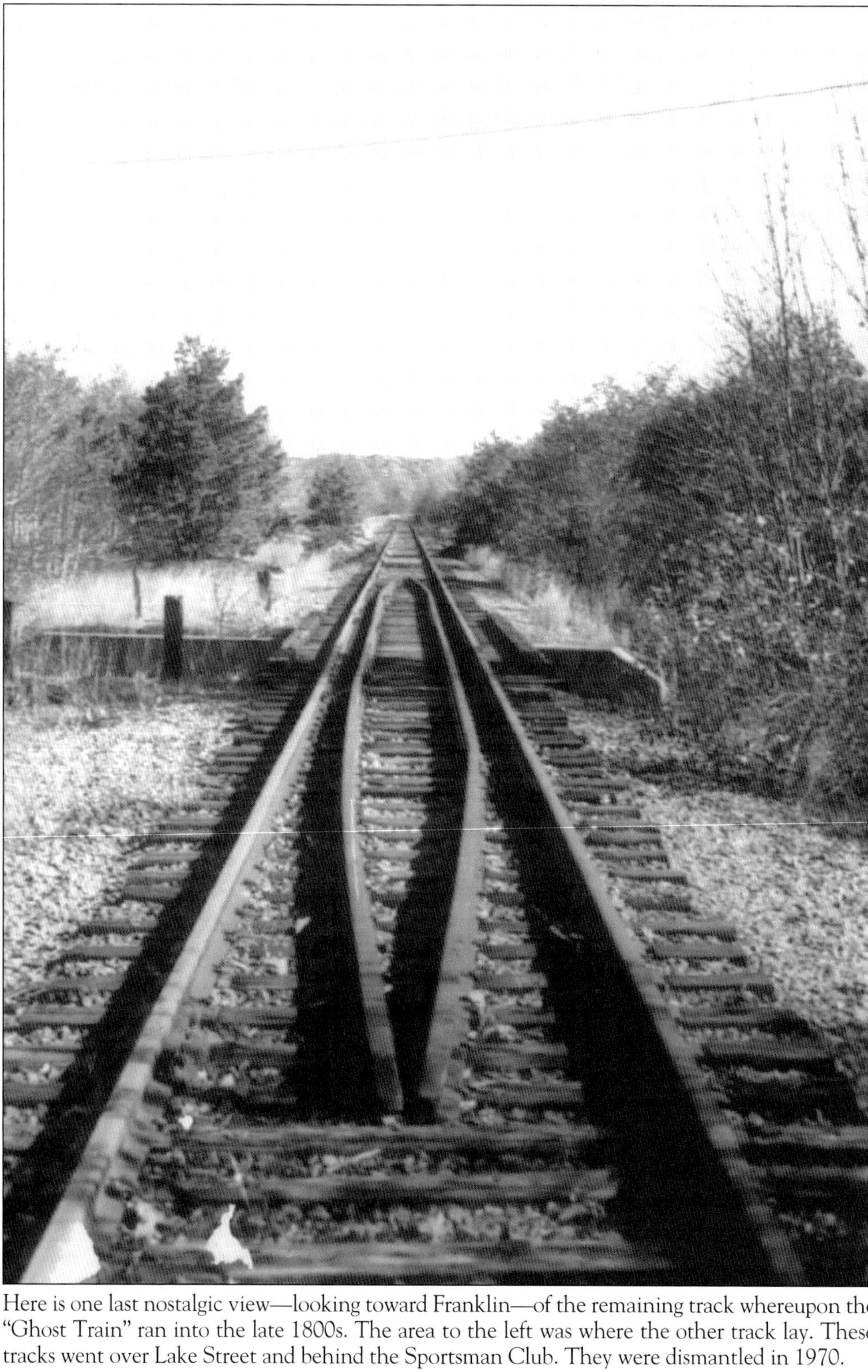

Here is one last nostalgic view—looking toward Franklin—of the remaining track whereupon the "Ghost Train" ran into the late 1800s. The area to the left was where the other track lay. These tracks went over Lake Street and behind the Sportsman Club. They were dismantled in 1970.

Five

Homes and People

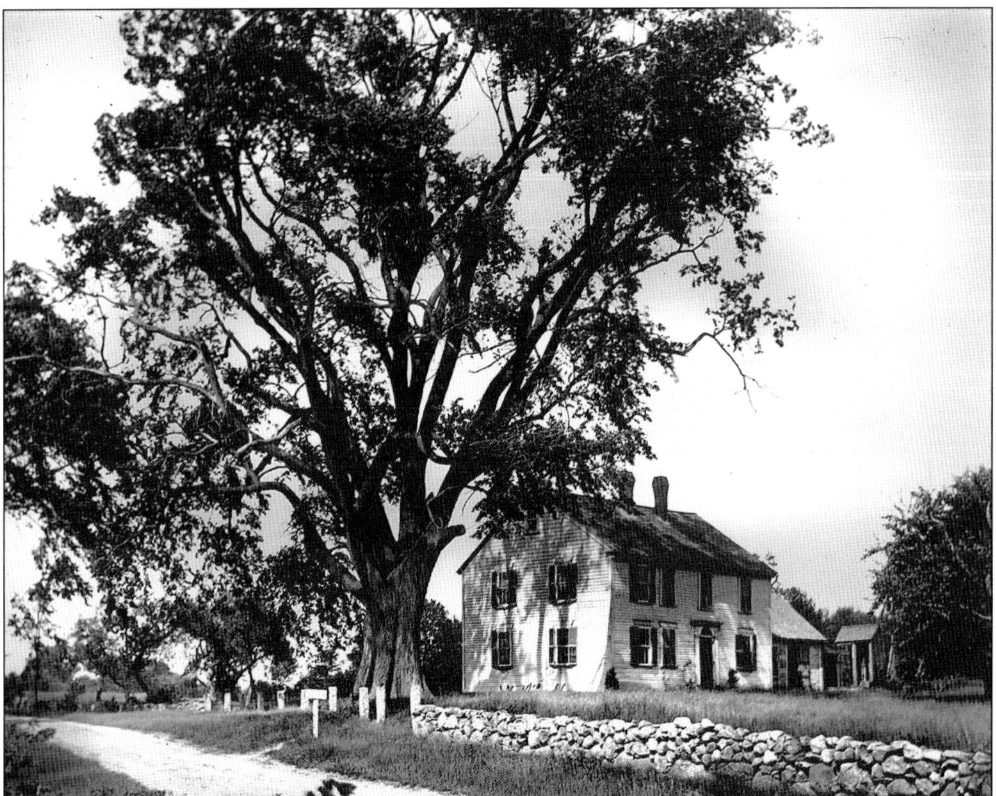

When this photograph was shot in 1903, this tree was known as the largest tree in Massachusetts. The home is located at 1010 North Main Street.

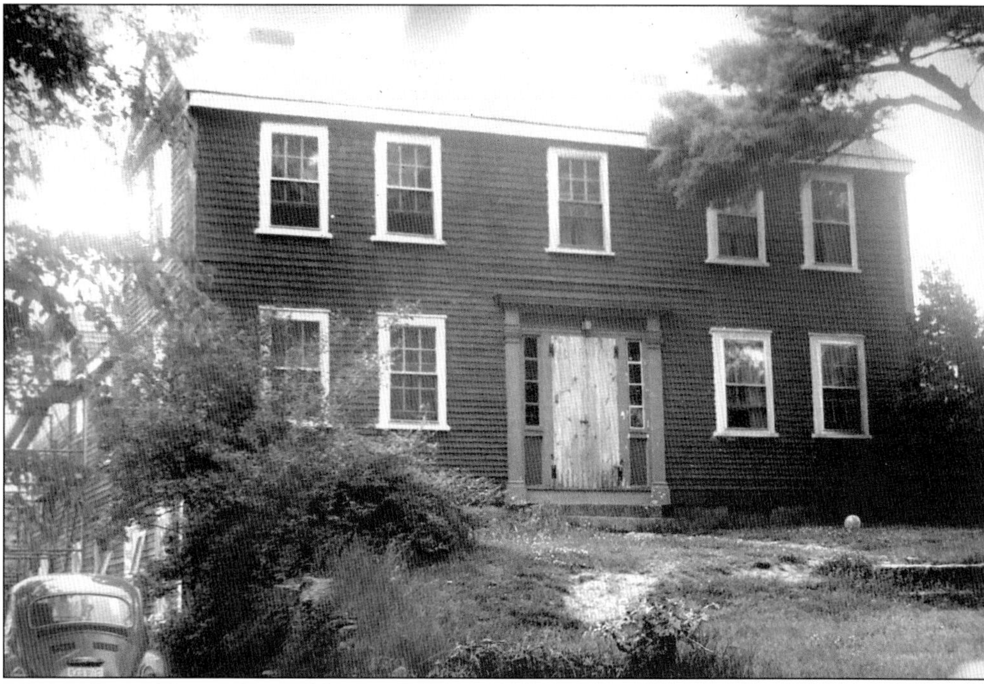

The Rockwood house, located by the railroad tracks on Hartford Avenue, may have been built in 1699. John Rockwood obtained this house in 1703, and the house remained in possession of the same family until 1955.

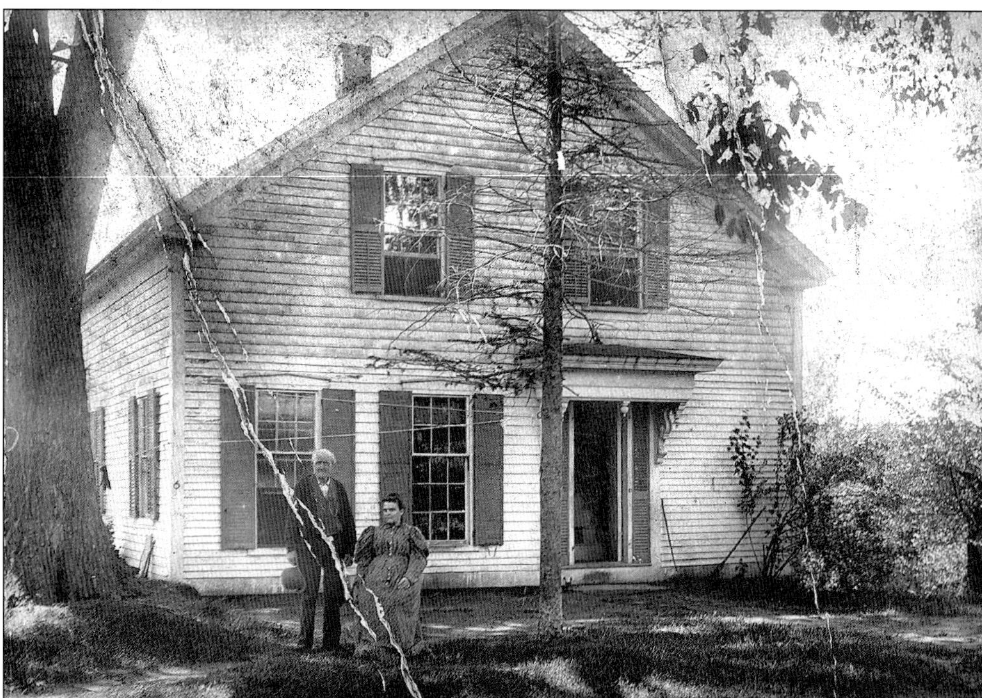

The Nathaniel Weatherby house stands at the corner of Taunton and North Main Streets. Weatherby was one of the petitioners of the Bellingham charter. The house was built in 1702.

Henry A. Whitney was born in Bellingham on July 1, 1842. He was known as the town historian and served as town clerk from 1883 to 1915. Whitney served in a variety of other positions: first library trustee, selectman for five years, constable, tree warden, and cemetery trustee. One of his most memorable stories was of the description of the assassination of Abraham Lincoln and the capture of John Wilkes Booth. He died on September 20, 1915, and truly left a void that was difficult to fill.

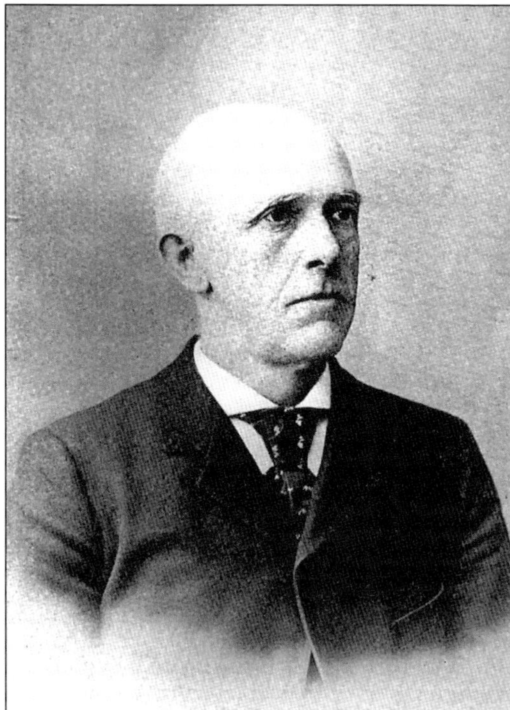

HENRY A. WHITNEY, 1842—1915

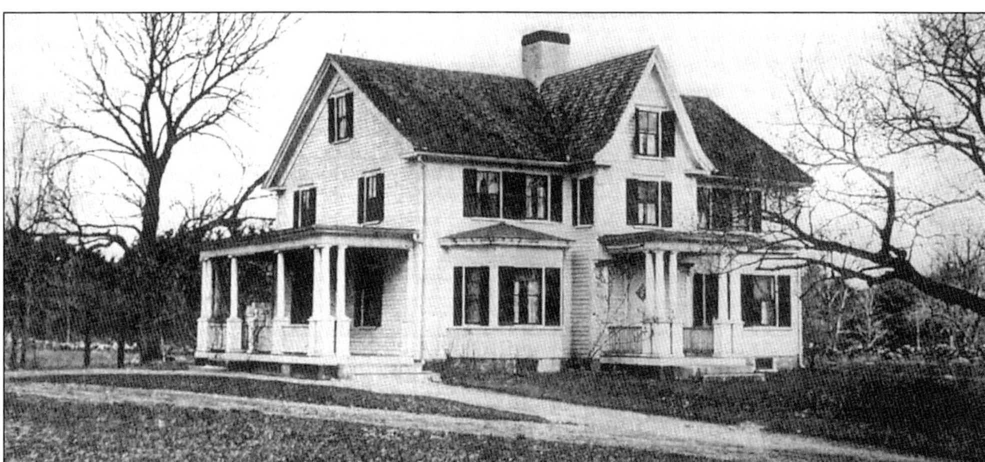

This home was built by Stephen Metcalf in 1777 on Hartford Avenue in Caryville. Metcalf was a prominent member of the community. He was a lawyer and a judge. He also served for seven years as Bellingham's representative, nine years as a state senator, and two years as a member of the governor's council.

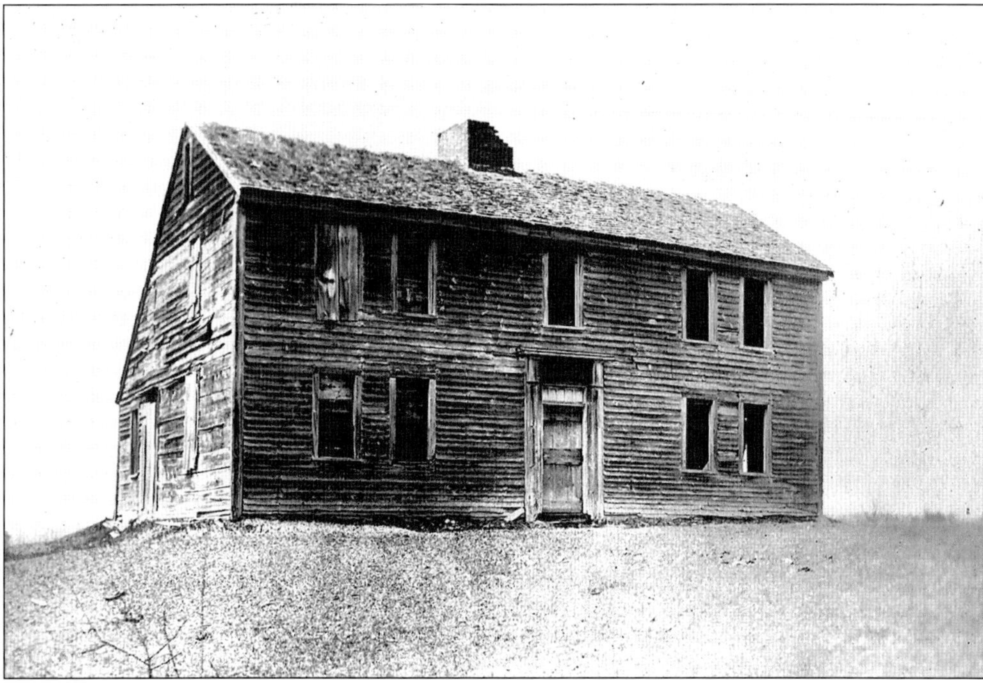

The Asa Burr farmhouse was built on Maple Street in 1767 in a saltbox design. For many years, it stood vacant and was torn down in the late 1930s.

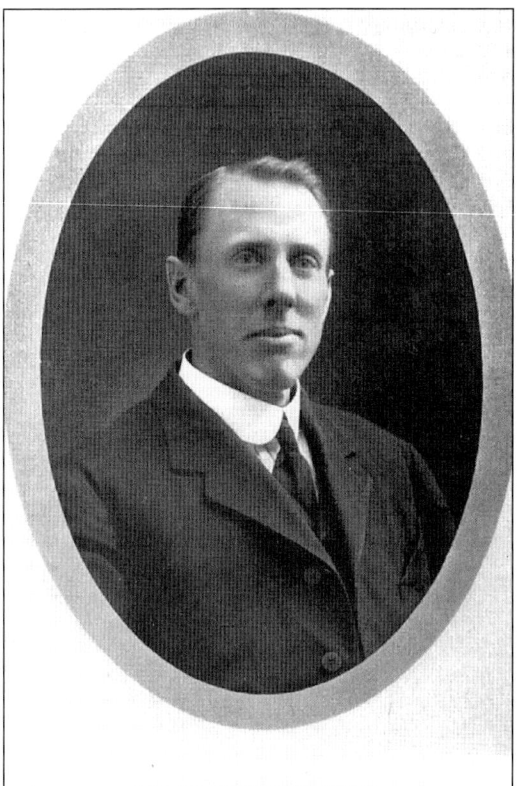

Percy Clifton Burr was born on September 9, 1868, at the Capt. Lathan Burr place (also known as the Asa Burr farm). Percy was a trolley man for the Milford, Attleboro and Woonsocket Street Railway Company for 25 years. He served on the board of selectman from 1913 to 1914 and as clerk of the board from 1916 to 1926. He also served as overseer of the poor from 1916 to 1926 and town clerk from 1915 to 1926. He was extraordinary in his devotion to Bellingham. He collapsed after a re-count of election ballots in March 1926. He never fully recovered and died on July 21, 1926.

In the summer of 1909, the *Boston Post* newspaper distributed to 700 New England towns a specially produced gold-headed cane. They were given to the eldest resident of the community "as a tribute to honored and useful lives." The Bellingham Historical Commission still retains this historic artifact and continues the annual, traditional presentation of the Boston Post cane to its eldest resident.

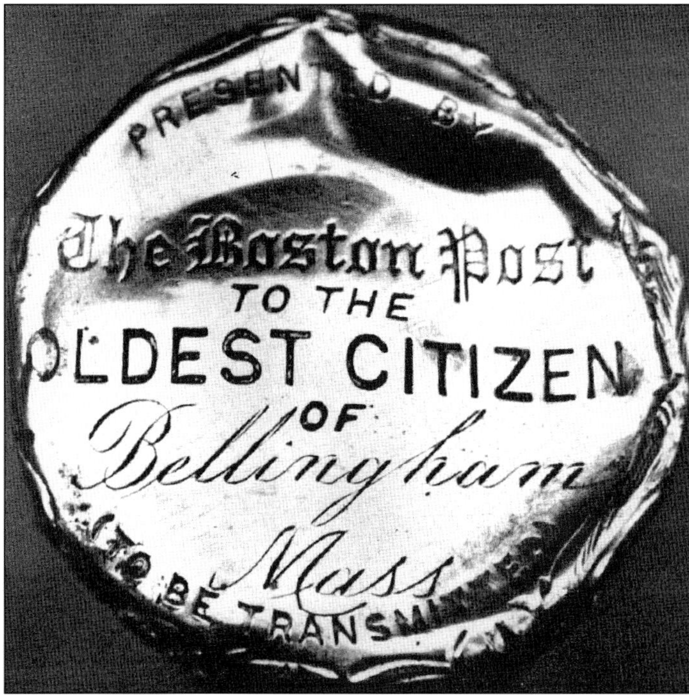

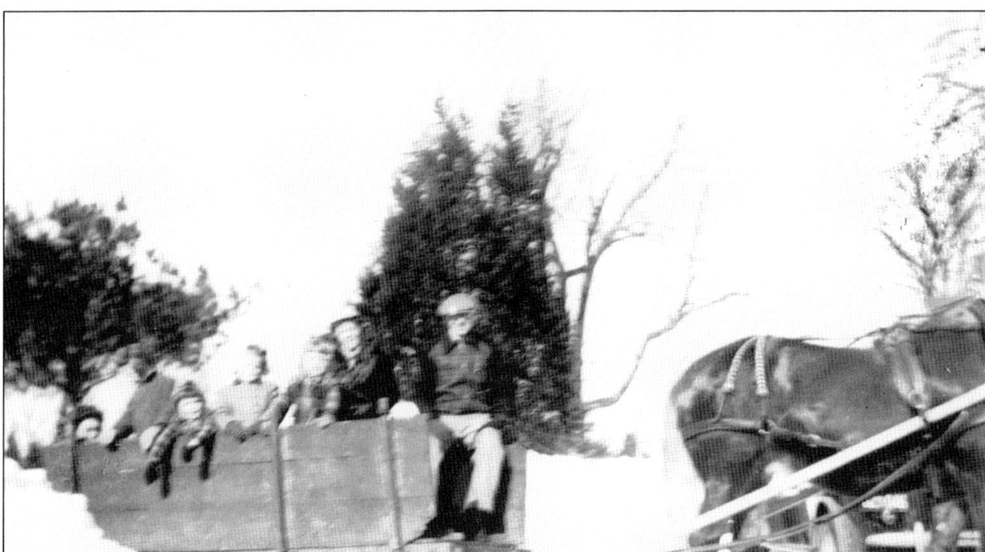

Captured is one of the many sleigh rides that Ruel Thayer would give the children of the neighborhood on Depot Street many years ago.

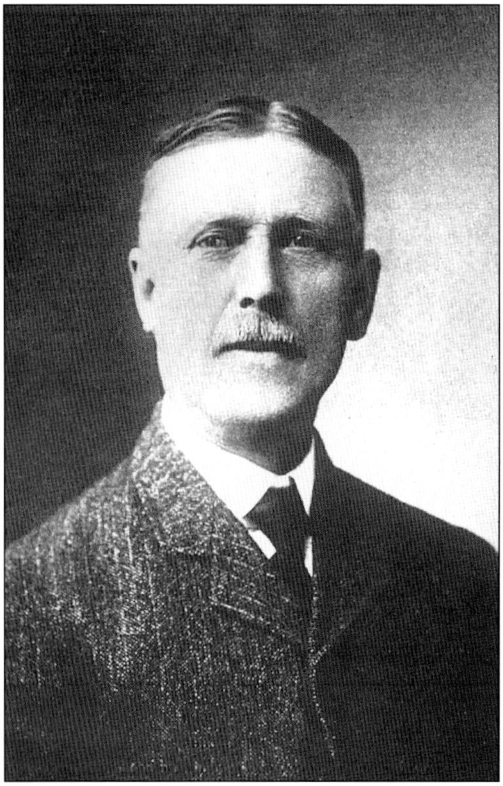

Elijah B. Stowe was a very successful Caryville merchant. He lived on Pearl Street, where he also kept a village store in the combined railroad station. He served as postmaster and station agent. He was a member of the state legislature in 1889 and also held some town offices. He was a lover of music and managed many concerts and oratorios in Milford. For 23 years, he was a member of the Worcester Music Festival Chorus. E.B. Stowe's sleigh that he used to make winter deliveries is on display at the historic commission museum.

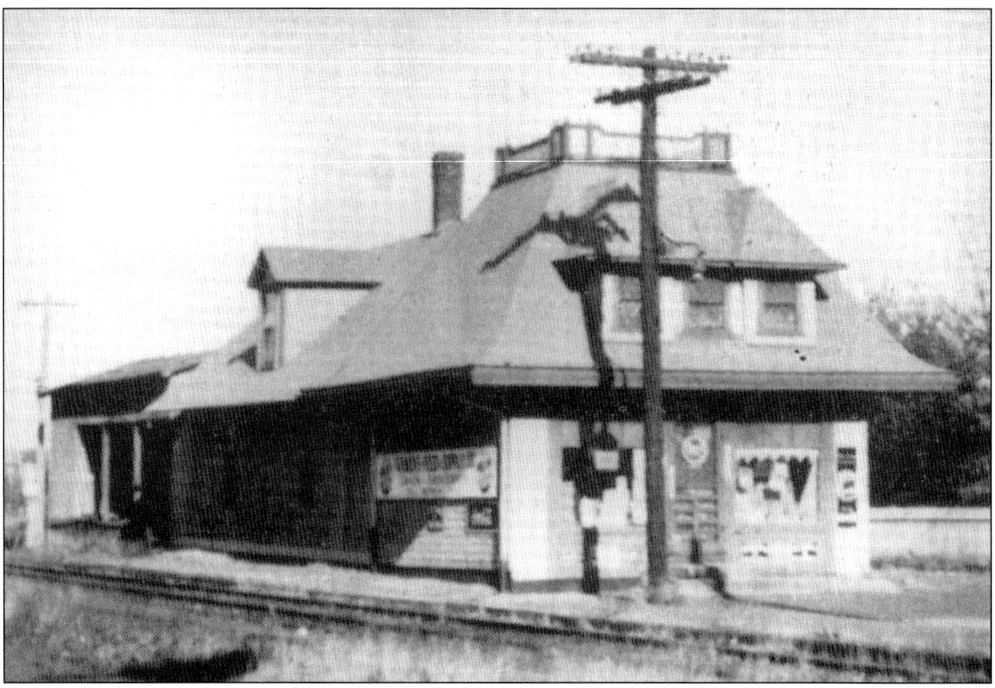

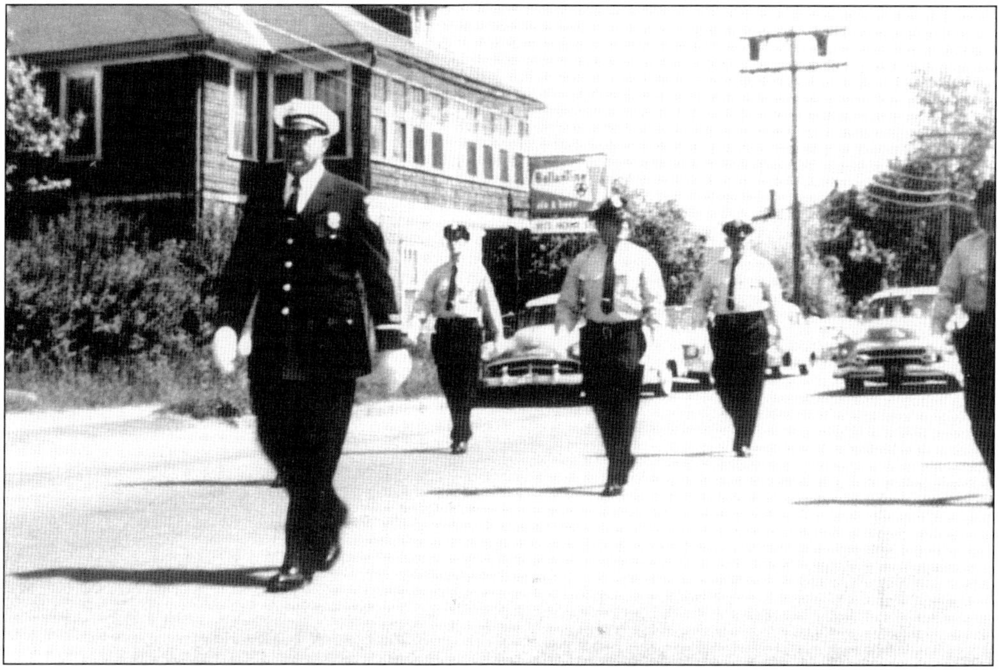

Police Chief Euclide Fleuette and his police officers marched in the 1955 Memorial Day parade. This photograph was taken on South Main Street, almost across from Vets Package Store. (Note that the original Vets Package once stood across the street.) Marching with the chief are, from left to right, P. Thomas McCluskey, Albert Grenon, Norman MacLinden, and Herb Chaplin.

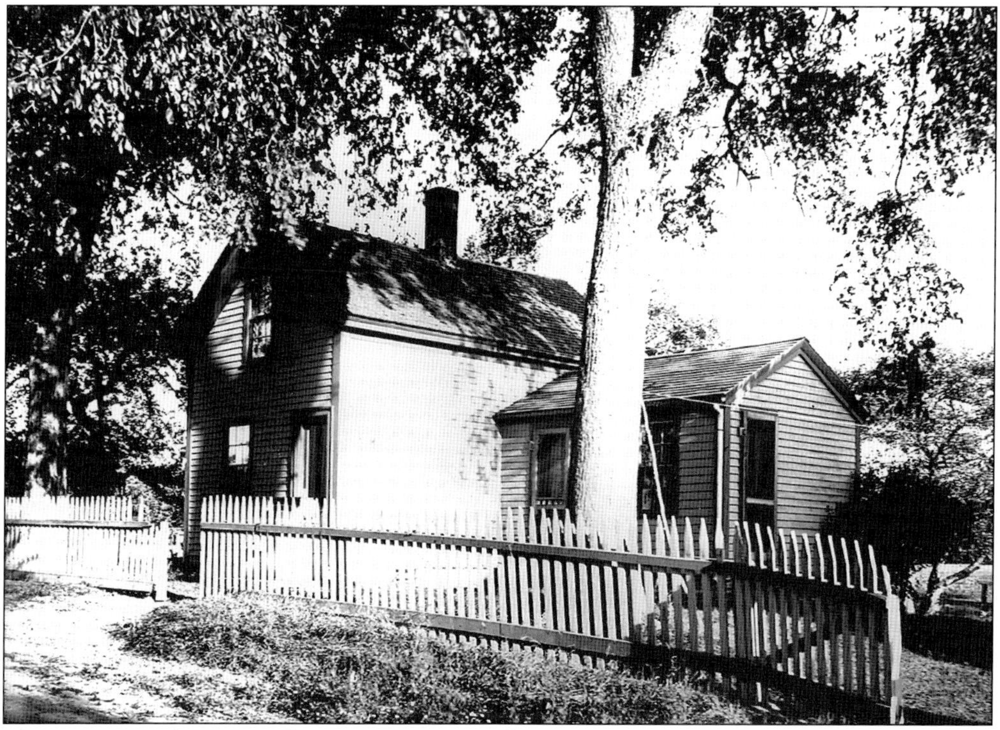

The James Carr home on Plain Street in Caryville is shown here in September 1900.

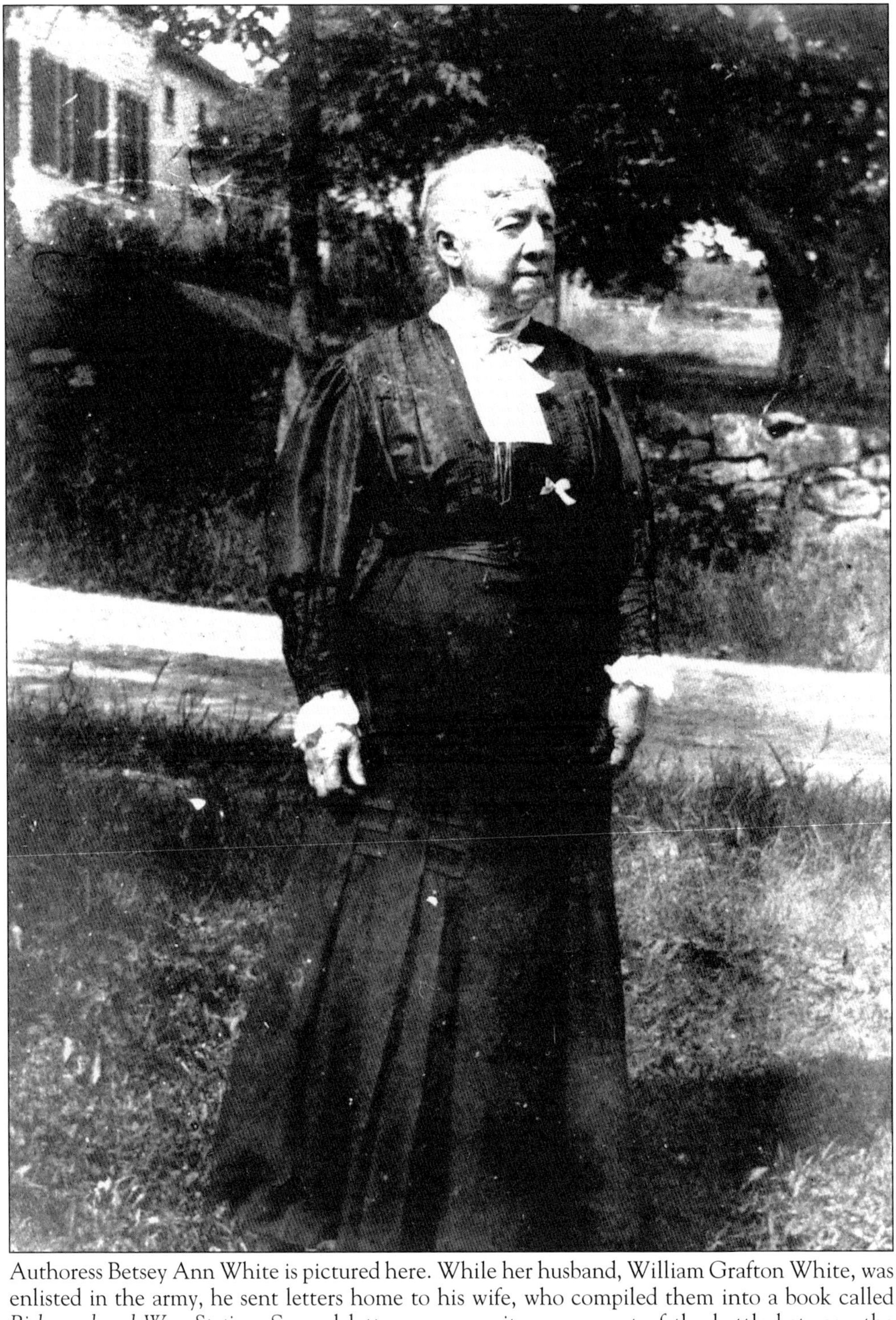

Authoress Betsey Ann White is pictured here. While her husband, William Grafton White, was enlisted in the army, he sent letters home to his wife, who compiled them into a book called *Richmond and Way Station*. Several letters were a witness account of the battle between the *Monitor* and *Merrimac* on March 9, 1862. Betsey Ann White also wrote another book, *Three Holes in a Chimney*, under the pen name Didama.

William Grafton White enlisted in the army on July 27, 1861, and served with the 16th Regiment, Massachusetts Volunteers, in Company A. He served for three years.

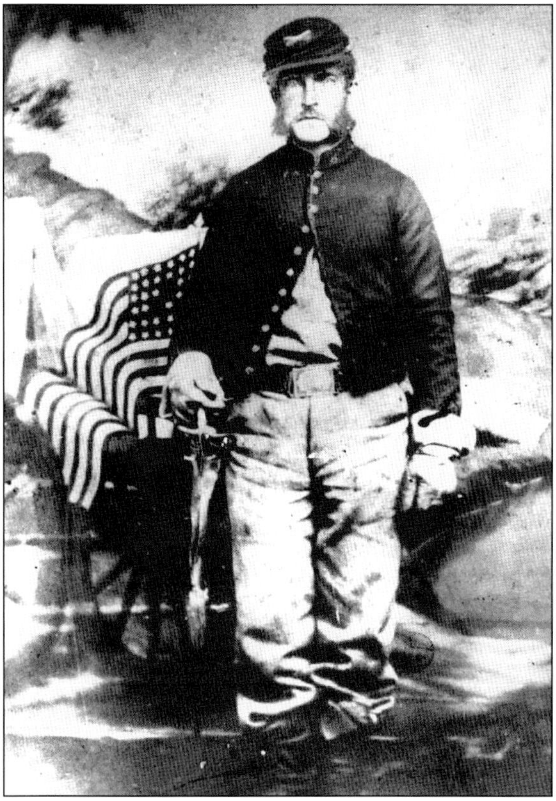

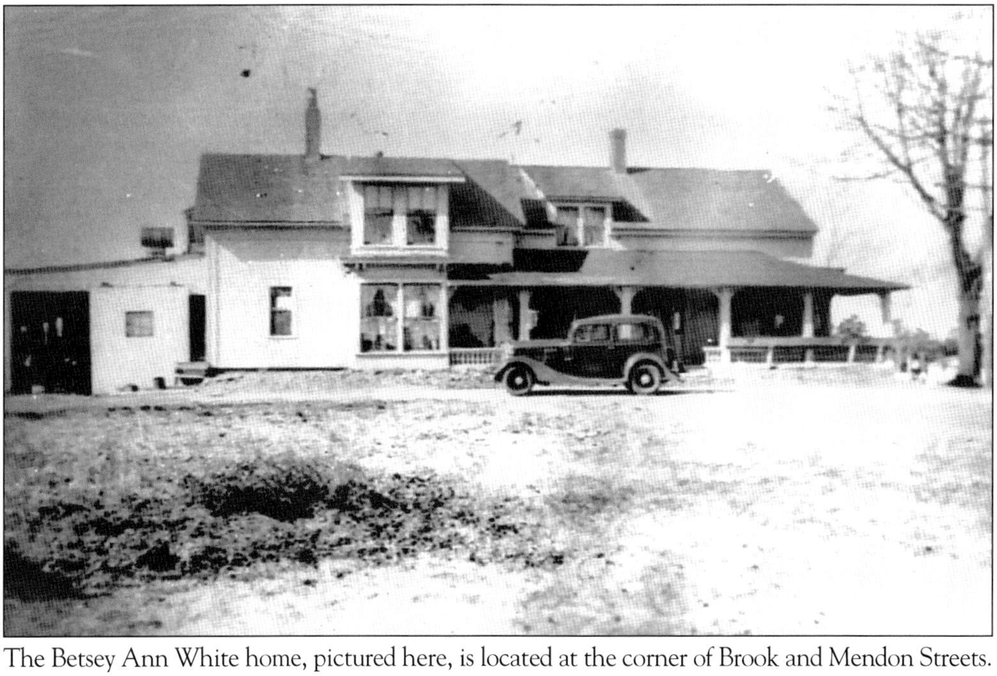

The Betsey Ann White home, pictured here, is located at the corner of Brook and Mendon Streets.

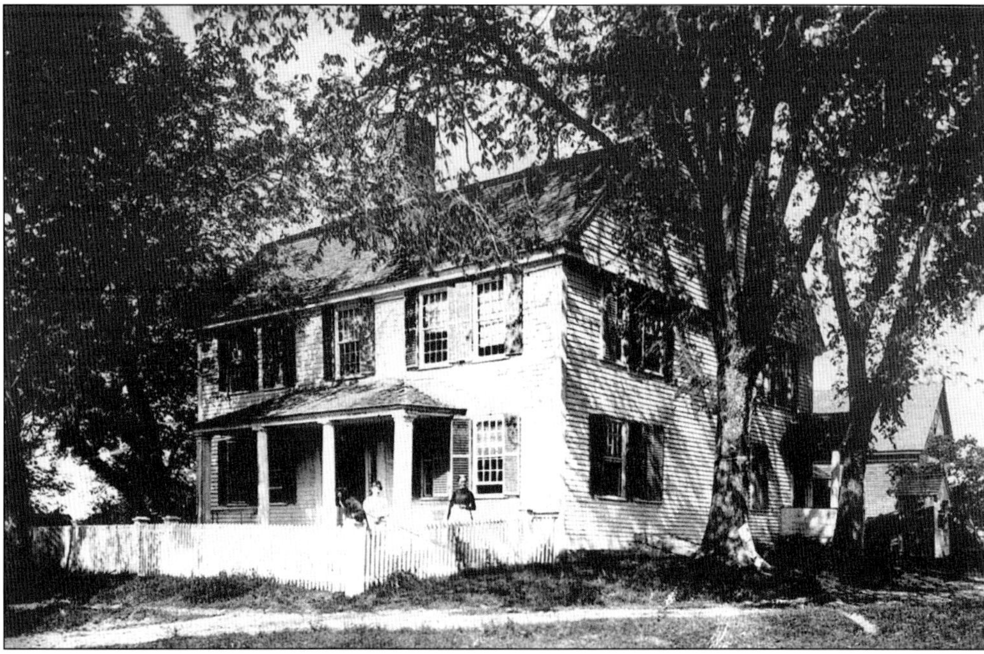

The Fairview house, once located at the corner of Hartford Avenue and Grove Street, was described in a newspaper article as the "healthiest and most beautiful resort in Mass." Built in the early 1700s, it was also known as the Tavern House, Toll House, and Corbet-Scammel House. Pictured in photograph are Ray Howard and Clara Thayer.

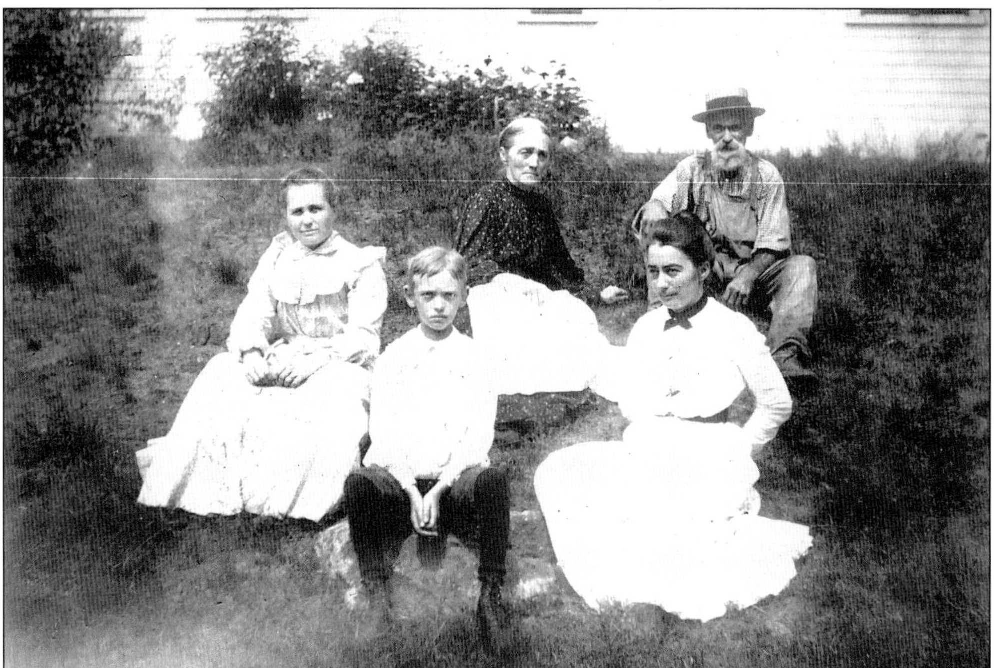

This photograph was taken on the western lawn of the Corbet-Scammel House. From left to right are Harriet (Warfield) Thayer, Merrick Thayer, Ella (Thayer) Howard, Clara Thayer, and Ray Howard.

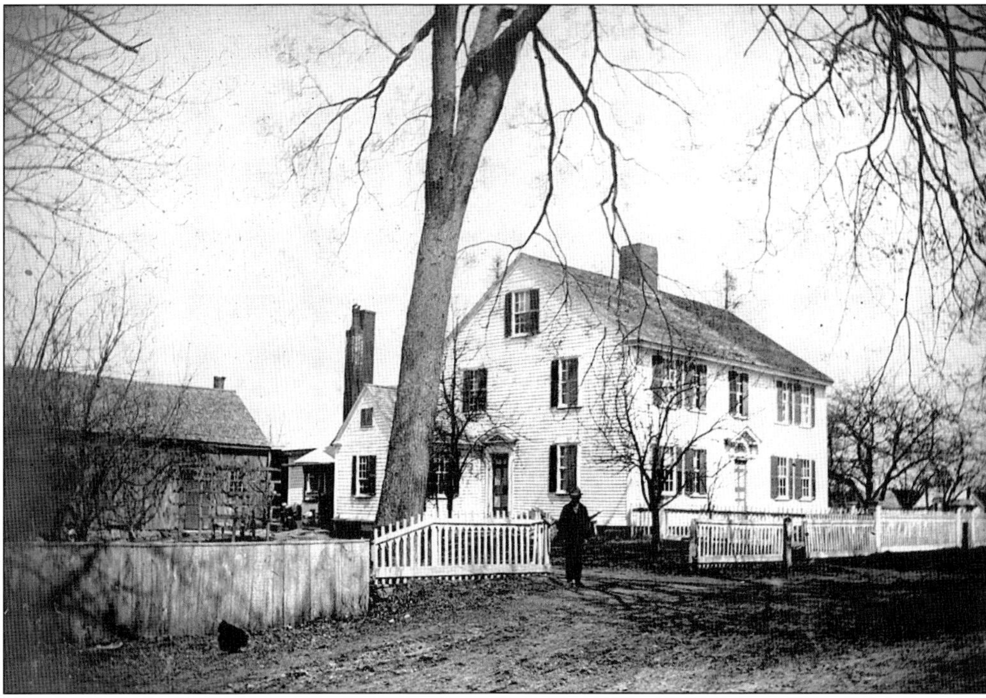

The Fairbanks house is located at 462 Hartford Avenue. Joseph Fairbanks, who owned and operated the Caryville Mill, built this home in 1803.

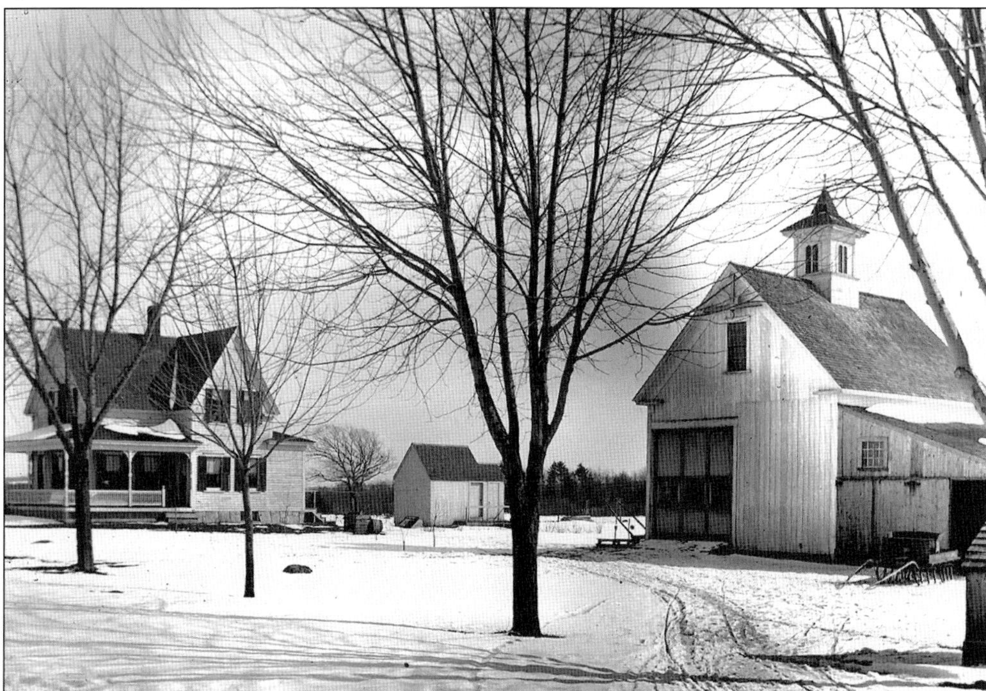

This is a 1907 view of the Francis H. Dawley estate. Margaret C. Crocker owned the place in 1921. In 1931, Anna and Emerick Olson owned the property at 207 Hartford Avenue.

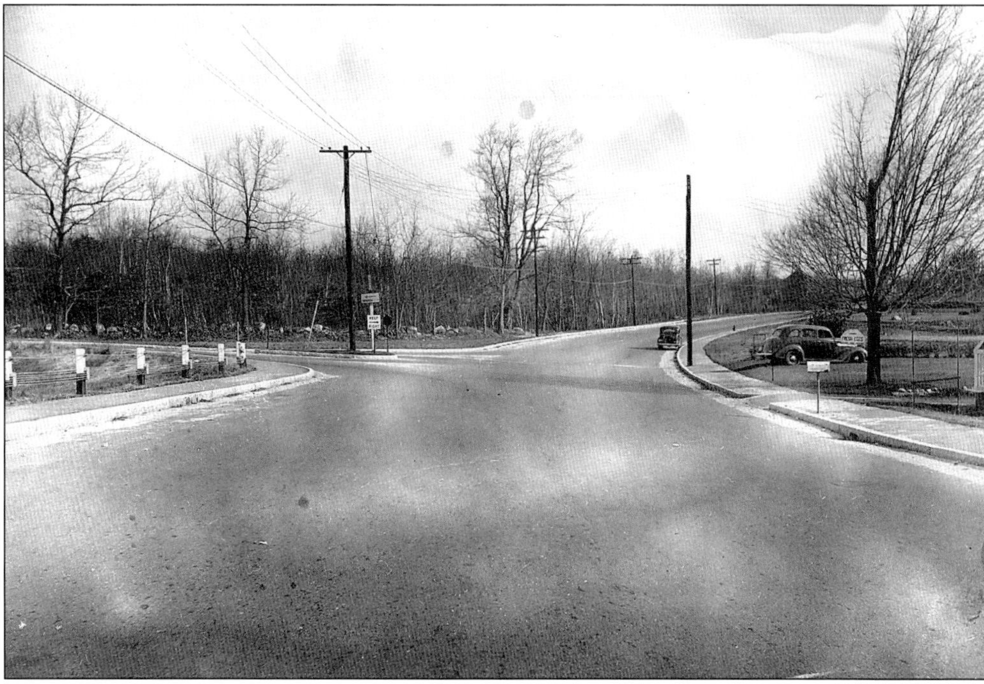

This view of South Main Street, with Elm Street to the left, was taken in 1940.

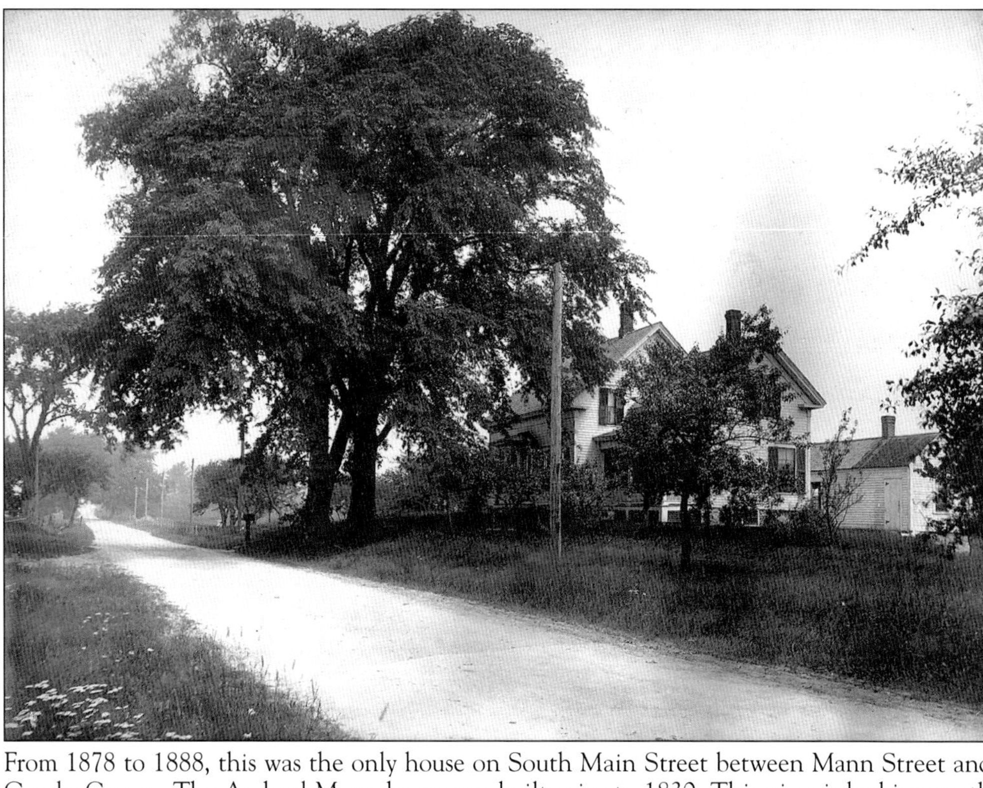

From 1878 to 1888, this was the only house on South Main Street between Mann Street and Crooks Corner. The Aashael Mann home was built prior to 1830. This view is looking north toward Old Elm Street from near Mann Street.

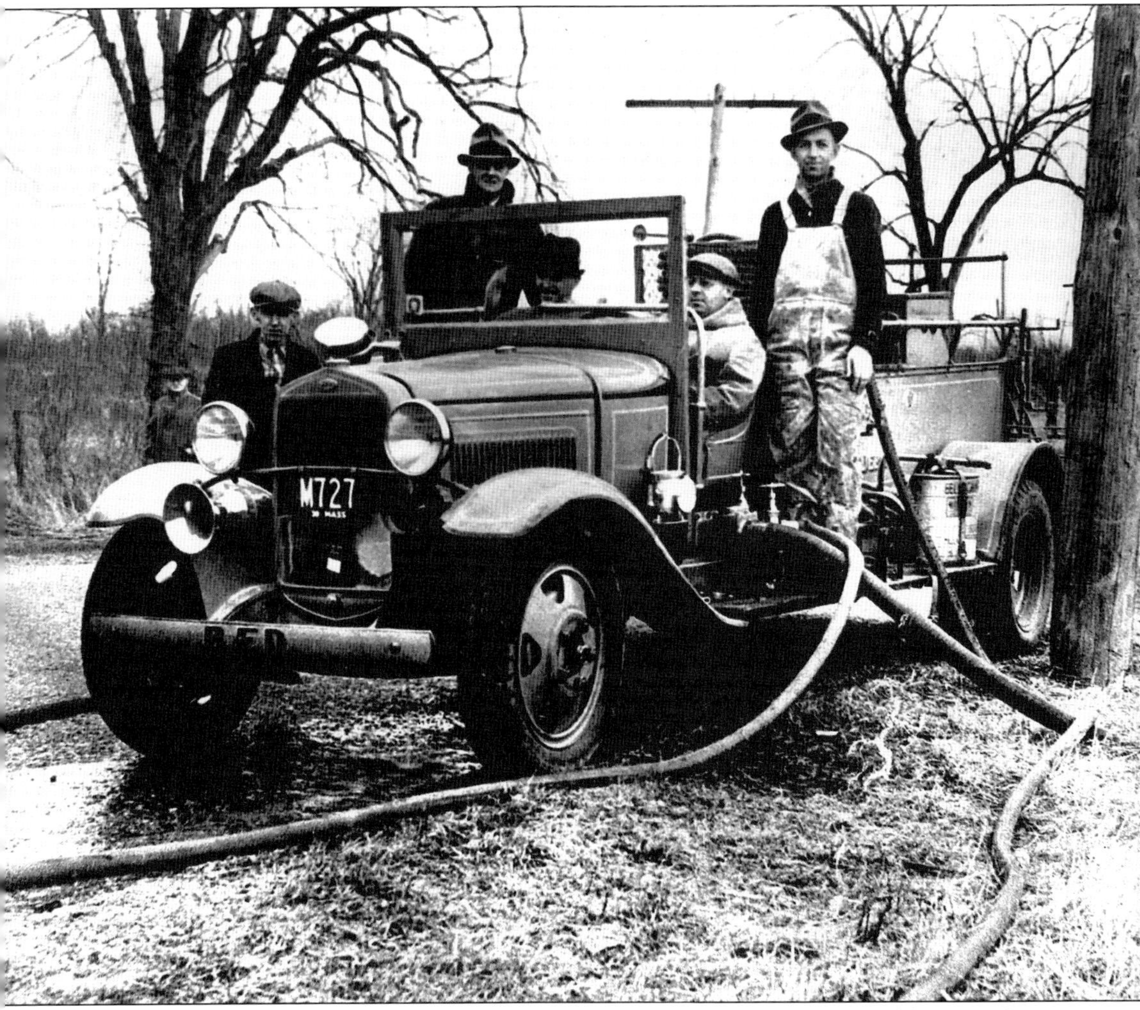

A 1931 Ford Model A was Bellingham's first fire truck. It was nicknamed "Double O" and is still housed at Station No. 1 in South Bellingham (at the Murray Community Building). The town fire chief was George Grant. Chief Grant only served six months. He died of pneumonia that he contracted by riding in the Double O, an open-cab truck, in sub-zero weather on his way to a chimney fire in North Bellingham. Seen here are, from left to right, unidentified, Clifford Mowry, Lionel Trudeau, unidentified, and Arthur White.

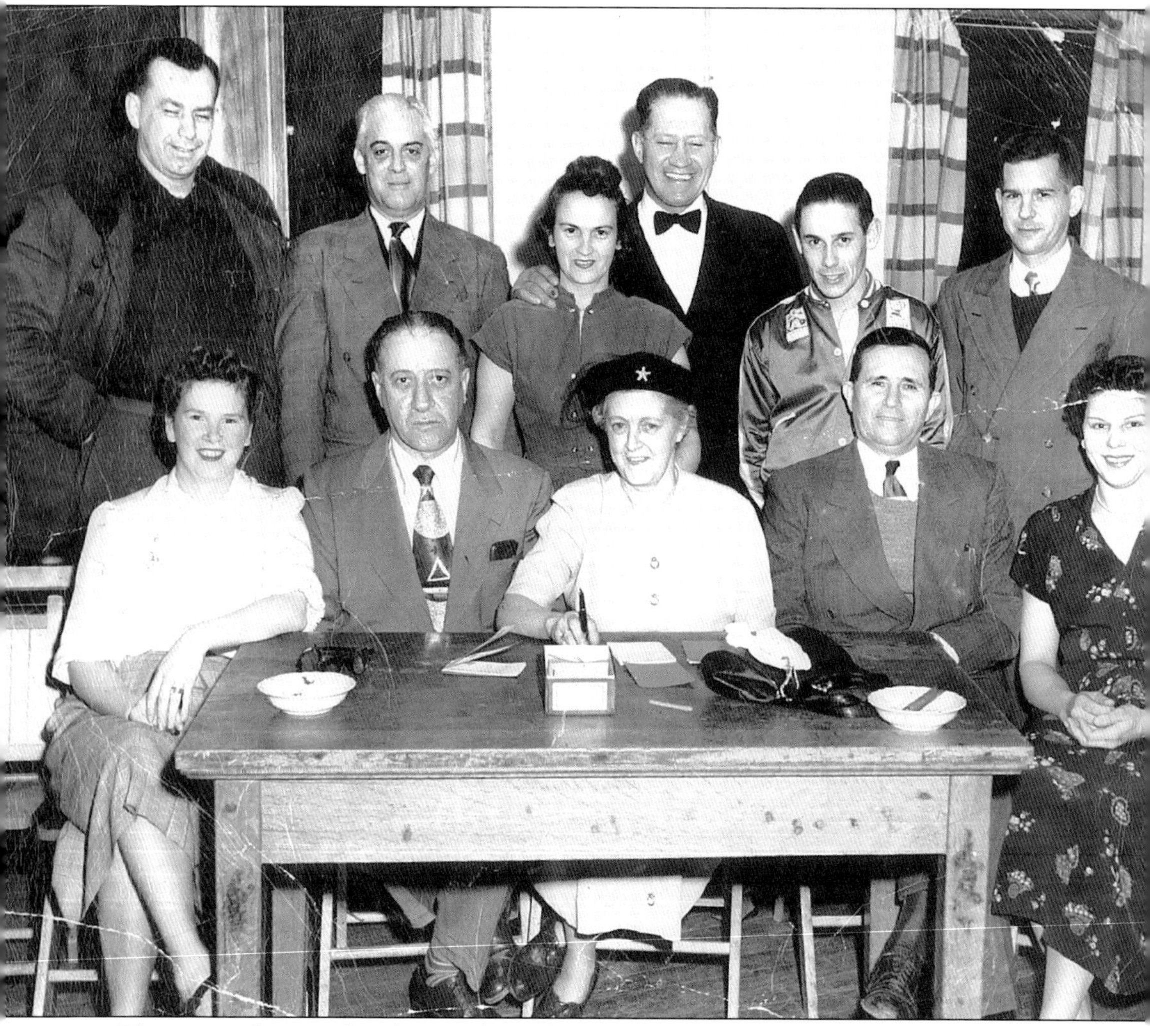

This group photograph, taken in the early 1960s, shows the testimonial committee for Chief Fleuette. Seen here are, from left to right, the following: (front) Maggie Frances Cook, Joe Fleuette, Sarah Wrenn, Lee Smith, and Gloria Meotti; (back) Donat LaPlante, Francis Locklin, Tina Cook, Euclide Fleuette, ? Laferriere, and Richard Clouart.

Six

Mills and the Charles River

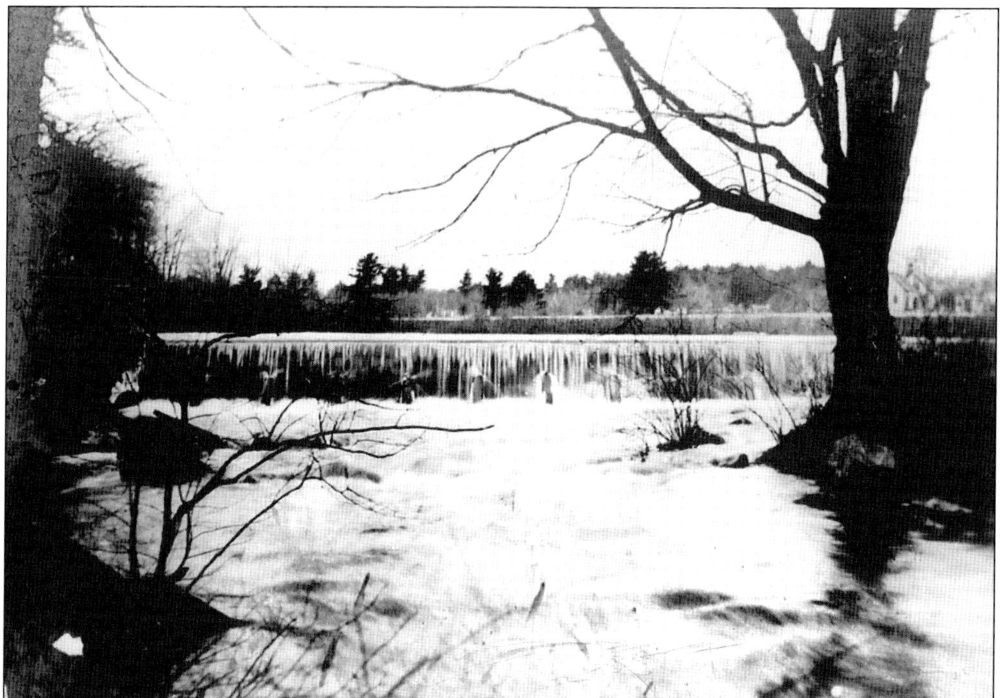

This Charles River-North Bellingham dam was built in 1810 to retain the water during the dry summer season.

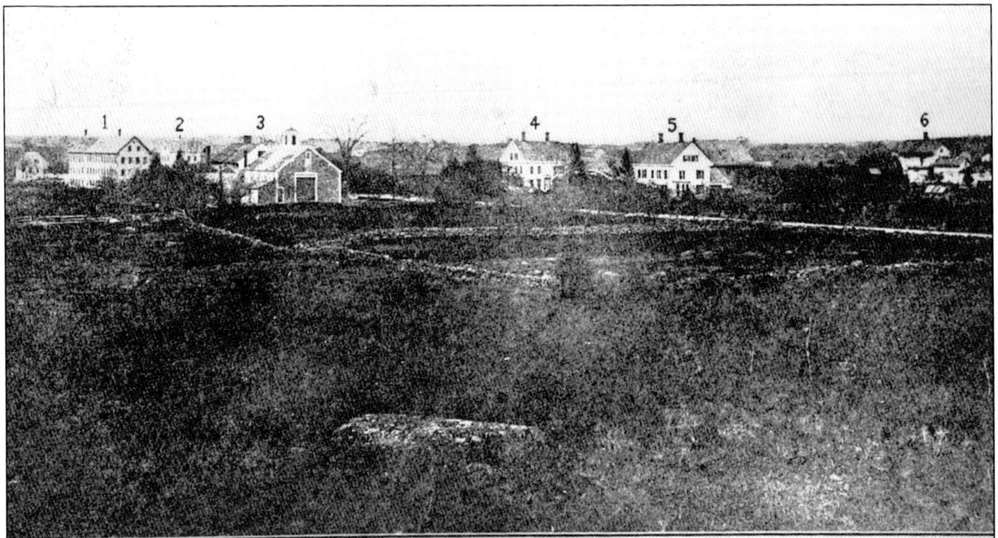

CARYVILLE ABOUT 1870

1 Boot Shop
2 Francis Metcalf
3 Calvin Fairbanks
4 Edwin Fairbanks
5 William Fairbanks
6 C. H. Cutler
7 Mill

Caryville, the northern section of Bellingham, originated in 1866, when a post office was established and given that name in honor of William H. Cary, who had operated the mill on Pearl Street from 1848 to 1864.

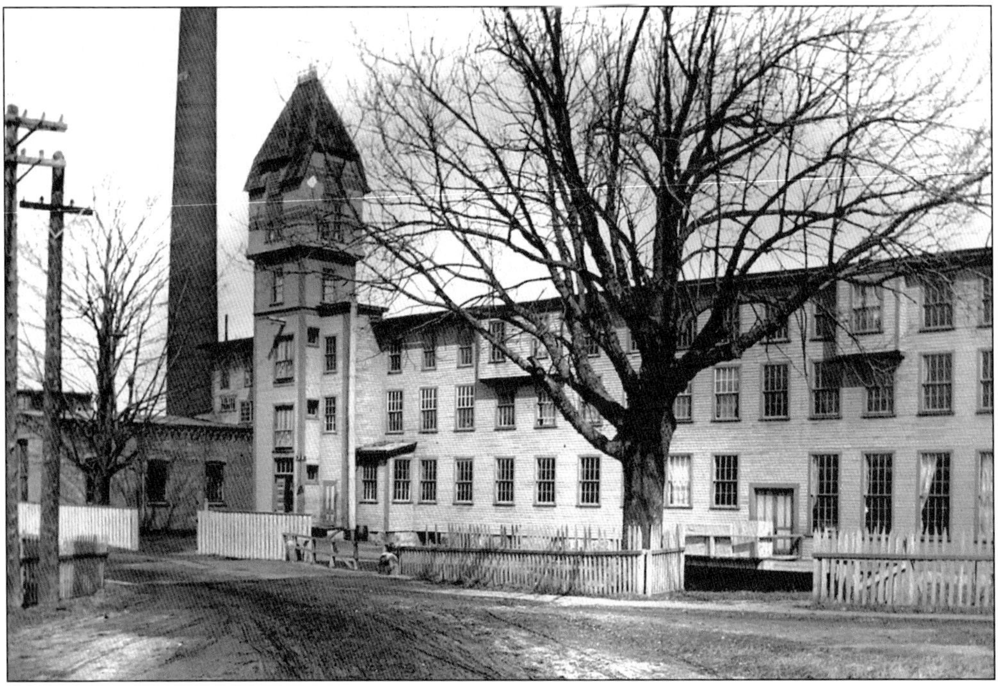

The Caryville Mill was the second textile mill to be built in Bellingham. It was built in 1813 and owned by Stephen Metcalf. The original mill burned in 1824 and was rebuilt by Alexander Wright and Royal Southwick. The town currently owns this site and may soon develop this old mill into senior housing units.

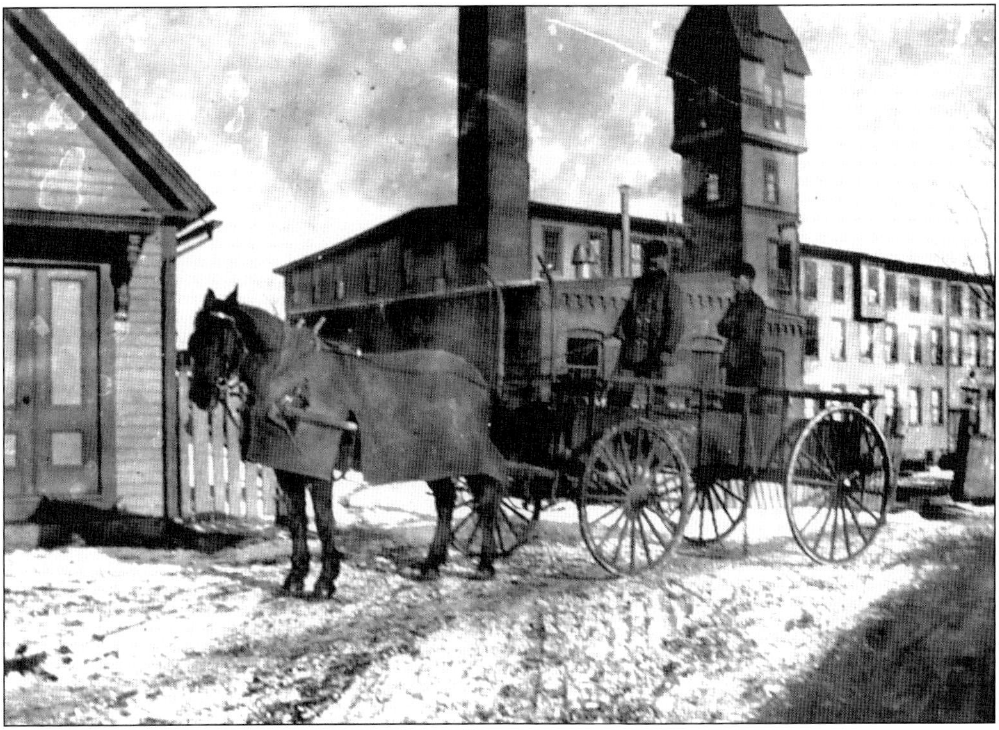

Above is a winter scene at the Caryville Mill.

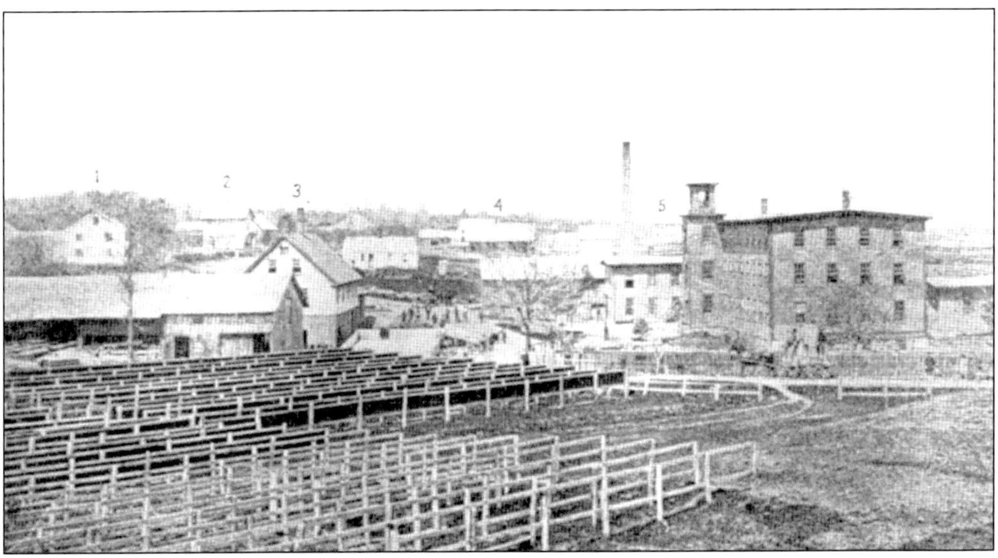

The Caryville Mill is show here in May 1871. Tenter bars, used for stretching and drying cloth, are in the foreground. In the background are the Jonas Fairbanks House (1), the C.H. Cutler home (2), the old sawmill (3), the Calvin Fairbanks house (4), and the boot shop (5).

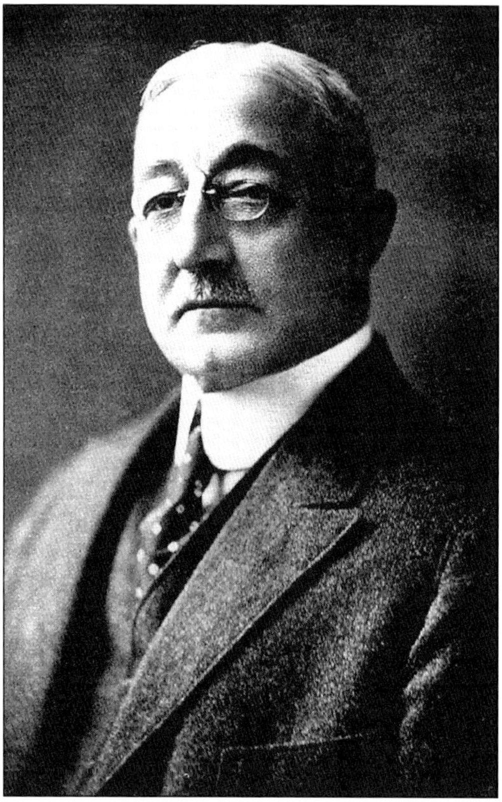

Addison E. Bullard, a very prominent Bellingham citizen, was born March 7, 1855, and died on December 9, 1938. The following is a list of his contributions to his hometown and country: school committee 1883–1886, selectman 1895–1899, state representative 1906–1907, chairman of the Liberty Loan Drive in World War I, and sponsor of the Bellingham town history in 1919. In 1912, Addison E. Bullard bought the American Woolen Company mill complex on Maple Street and formed the Bellingham Woolen Company.

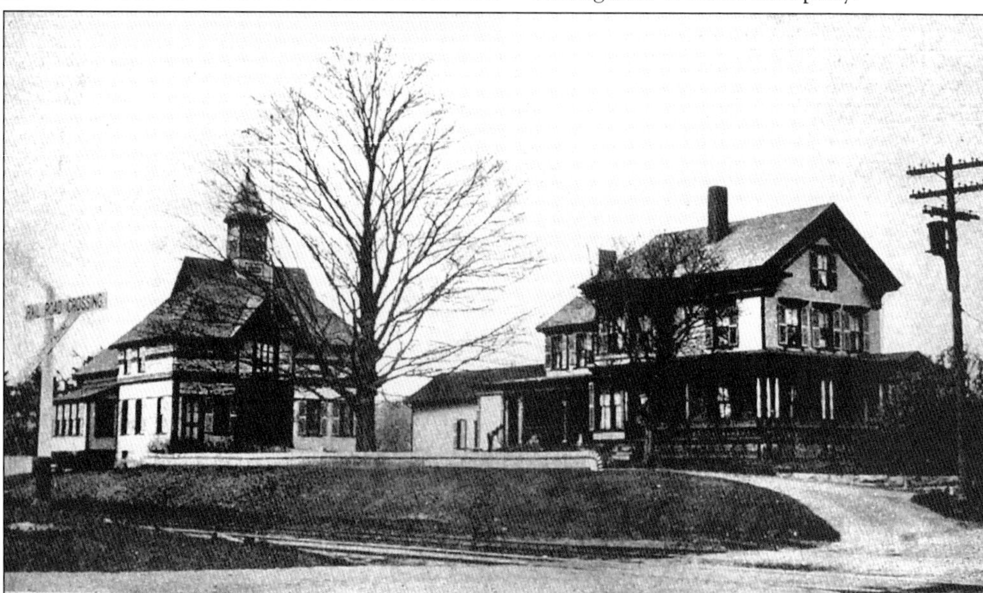

W. H. CARY 1855-64, C. H. CUTLER 1864-78, W. A. McKEAN 1878-99, A. E. BULLARD 1899-1919

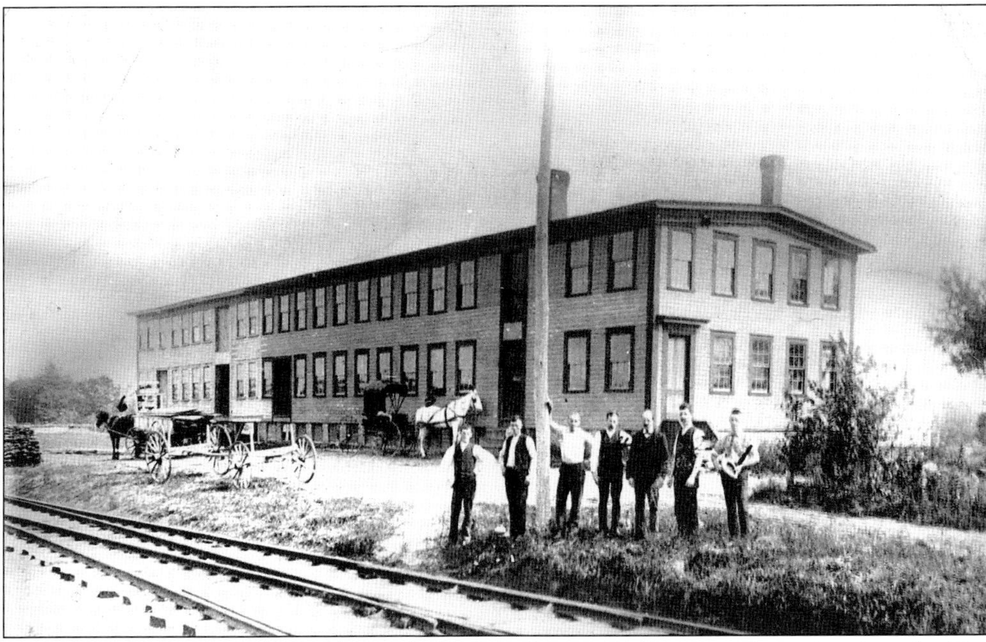

The American Toy factory was located off of Pearl Street, adjacent to the railroad tracks. This photograph was taken in 1910. The two horses are Black Bess and Old Whitey. The men in the photograph are, from right to left to right, Fred Claflin, George Williams, Frank ?, and Ed ?. The others are unidentified.

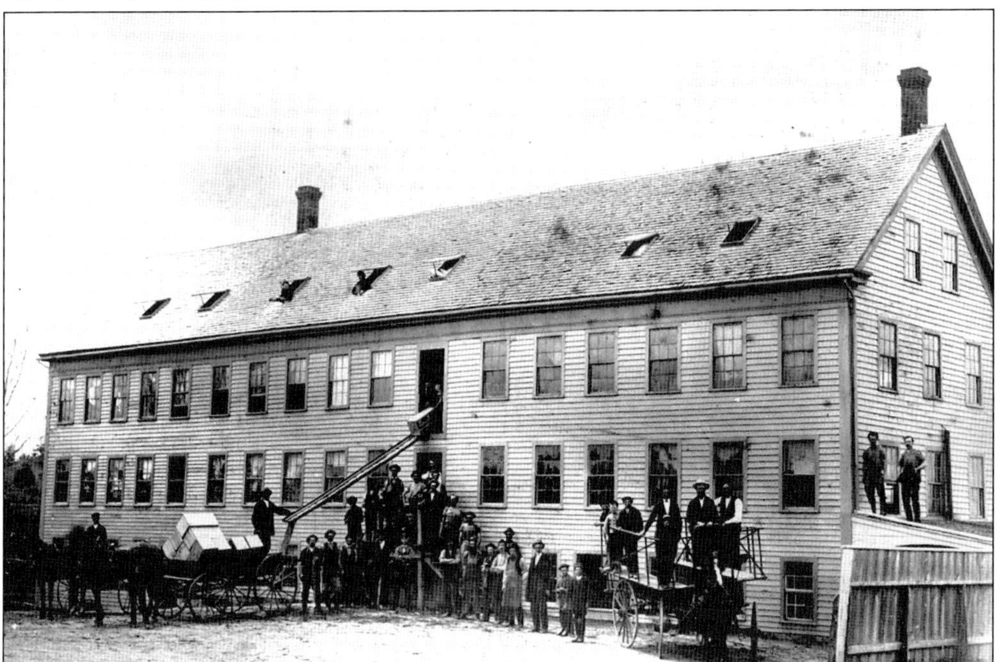

Here is the Caryville Boot Factory as it looked in 1871. It was located on Hartford Avenue at the corner of Stone Street. About 90 men were employed here and they made heavy boots for the army and for the miners out west. The factory was built *c.* 1851 and burned down in 1876.

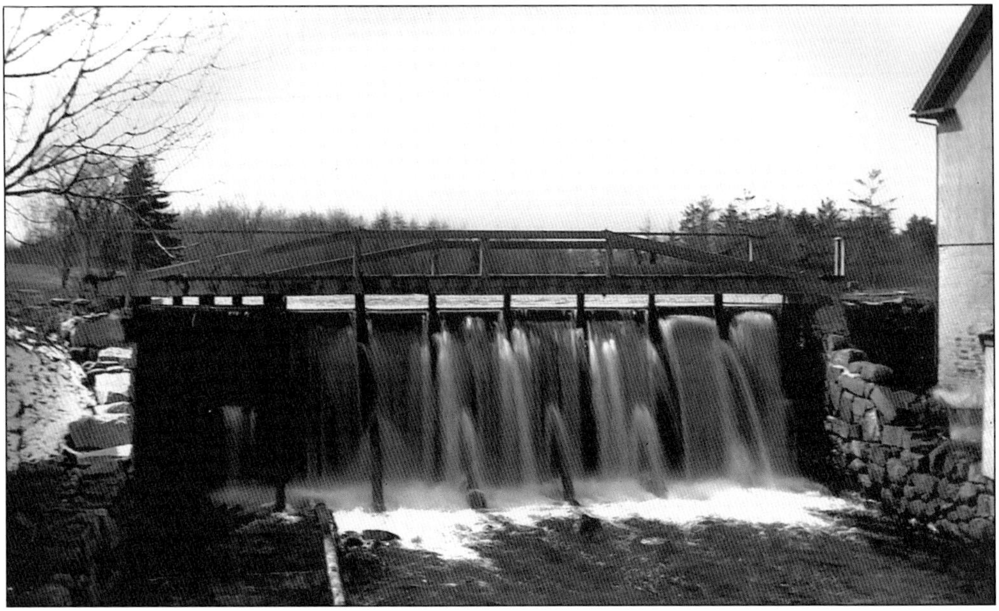

The first Caryville dam, located off of Pearl Street, was built in 1735. The dam shown in this photograph is a more modern replacement. At one time, there were five dams on the Charles River in Bellingham at different locations. Numerous early Native American artifacts have been found in this area.

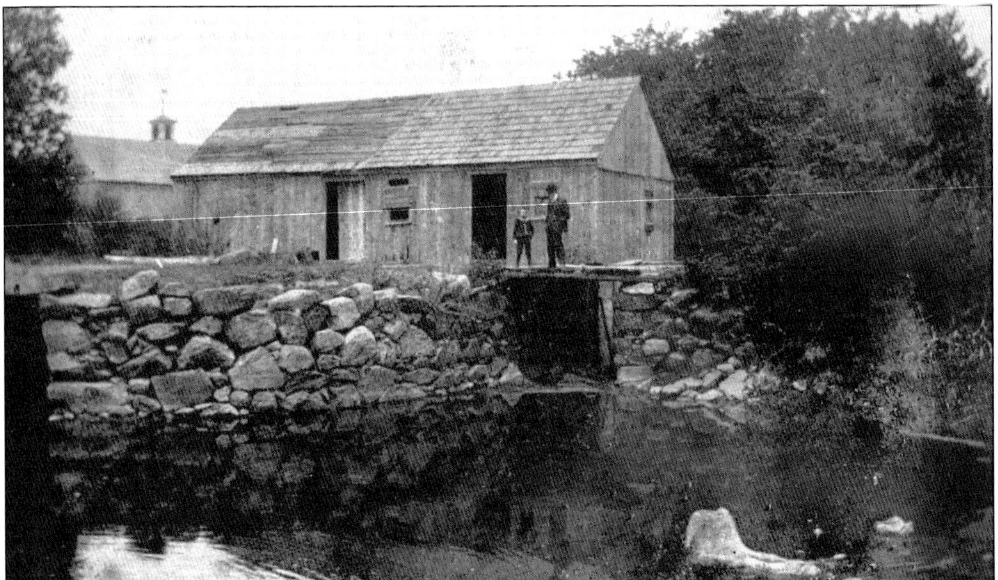

The Stall Brook was first dammed up in the 1700s. The first mill to harness the water for power was a sawmill. It was a short running stream before it reached the Charles River but was very useful. It flowed over Hartford Avenue, where the brook appeared to stall and linger. There was no bridge over this stream. The wagon wheels could be submerged in the water to allow the wood to expand and thus tighten the spokes again after drying out from the hot and dusty roads. The water also refreshed the hooves of the horses. The mill shown in the photograph is the gristmill. Later, a second floor was added (see page 98).

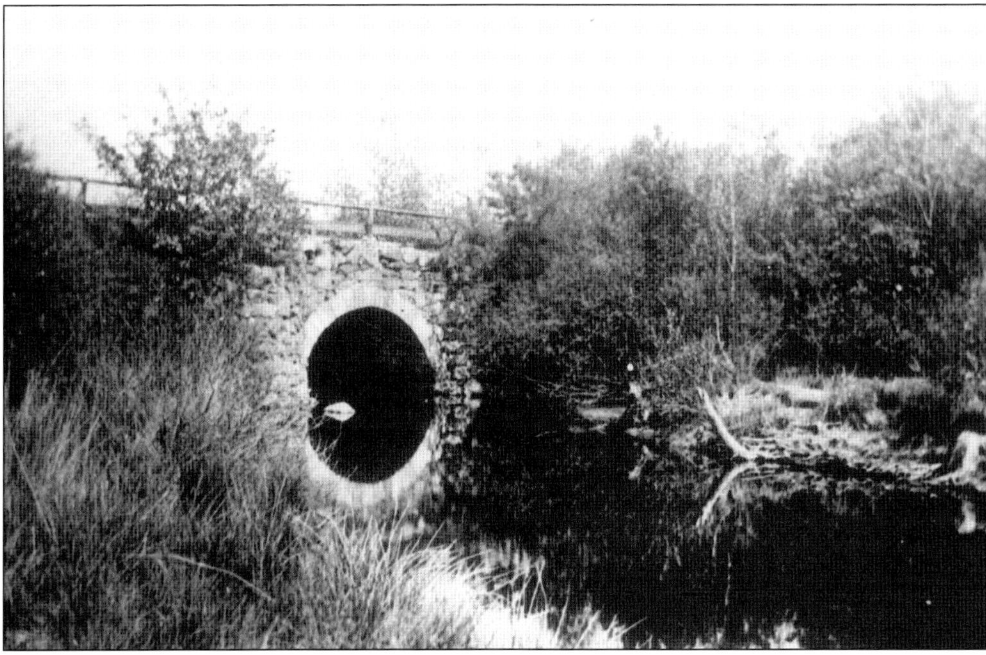

The Depot Street Bridge, spanning the Charles River, was built in 1829 to provide easier and quicker transportation from the turnpike to the meetinghouse in the center of town. Aaron Thayer is credited with building the bridge. This keystone bridge was dismantled several years ago to make room for a newer bridge.

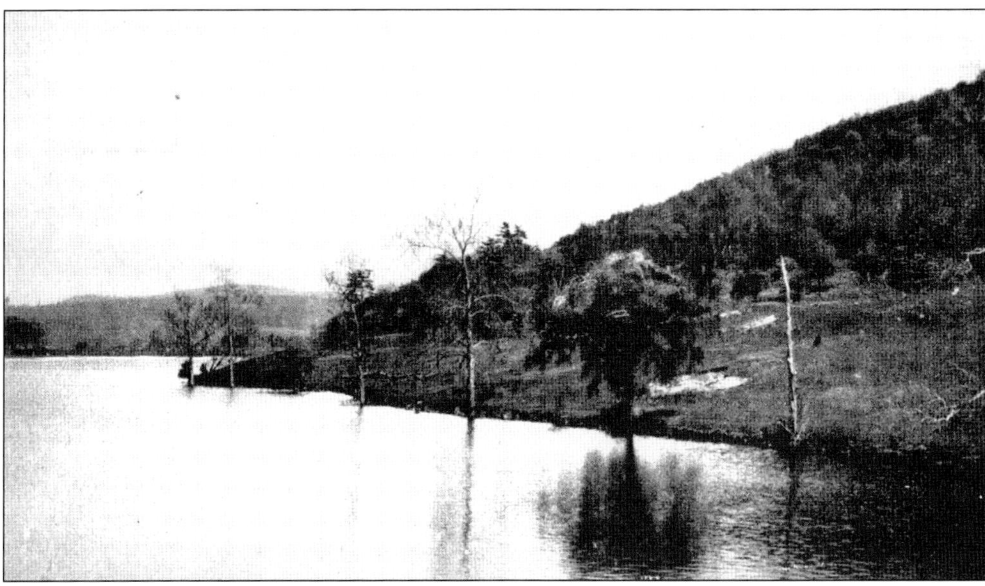

The Charles River was named after King Charles of England. It has always been called a river, but it has no rushing currents and its natural width is no wider than a stream. It has been dammed up in so many places that it gives the appearance of being as wide as a river. In Bellingham alone, four dams are known to have existed. This view of the Charles River is opposite of the Charles River Grove. The Red Mill Dam created the wideness of the river. The dam was created in 1800 and was breached by a flood in 1927.

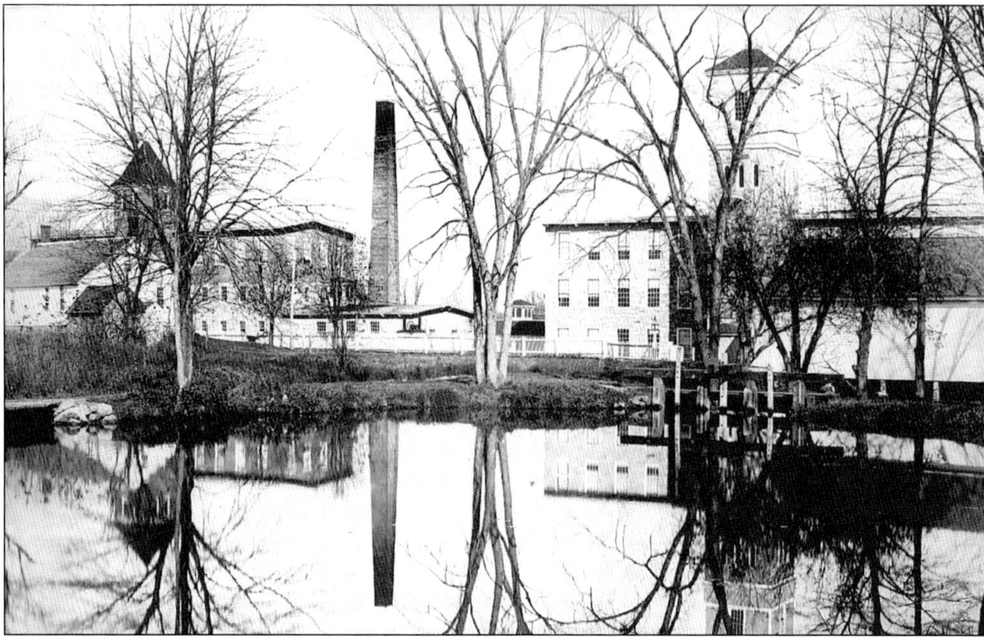

The North Bellingham Woolen Mills are located on Maple Street. Joseph Ray built the first mill, pictured on the left, in 1810 out of granite and brick. The second mill, adjacent to the first, was constructed entirely of granite in 1899. During the World War I, both mills operated 24 hours a day, filling government contracts.

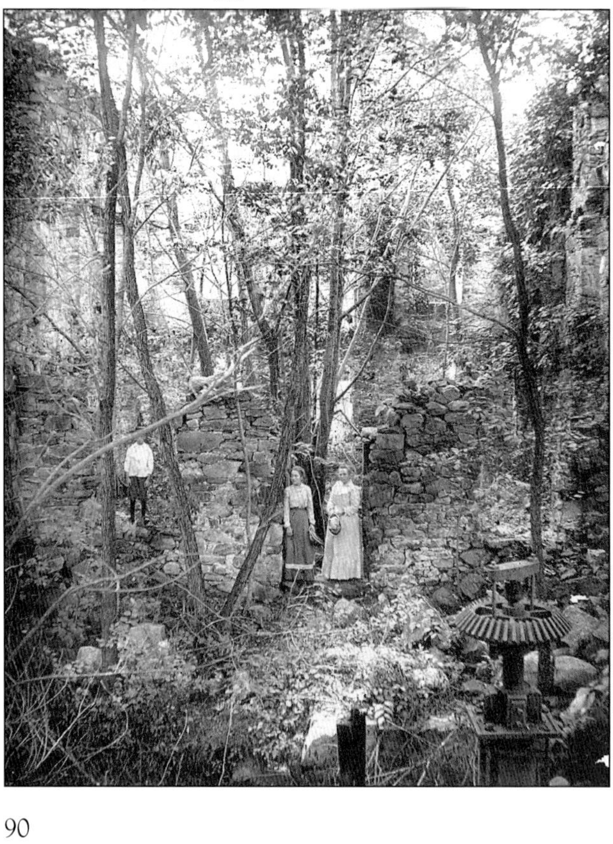

Remains of the Holbrook, or South Milford, Mill located off of Hartford Avenue are pictured in this 1900 photograph. This cotton mill made ladies' bonnets. Seen here are, from the left to right, Ray Howard, Clara Thayer, and Ella Thayer. The mill burned in 1868.

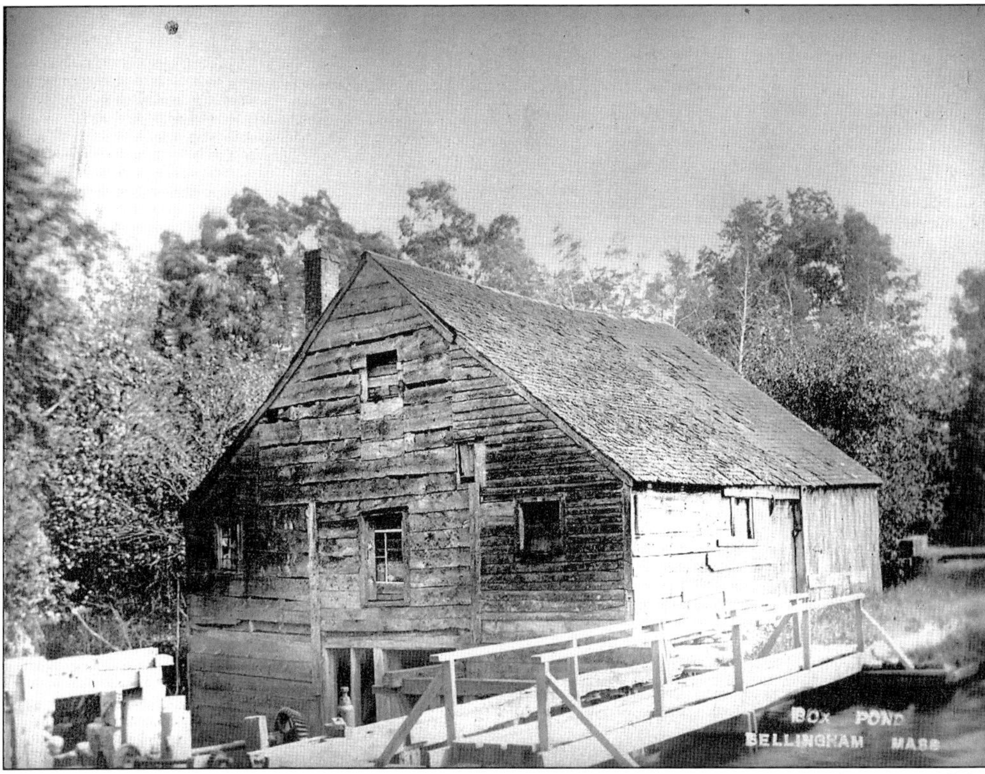

A millpond was created in 1821, when Thomas Thayer built a dam to capture the water of the Charles River to power his mill, a sawmill and gristmill.

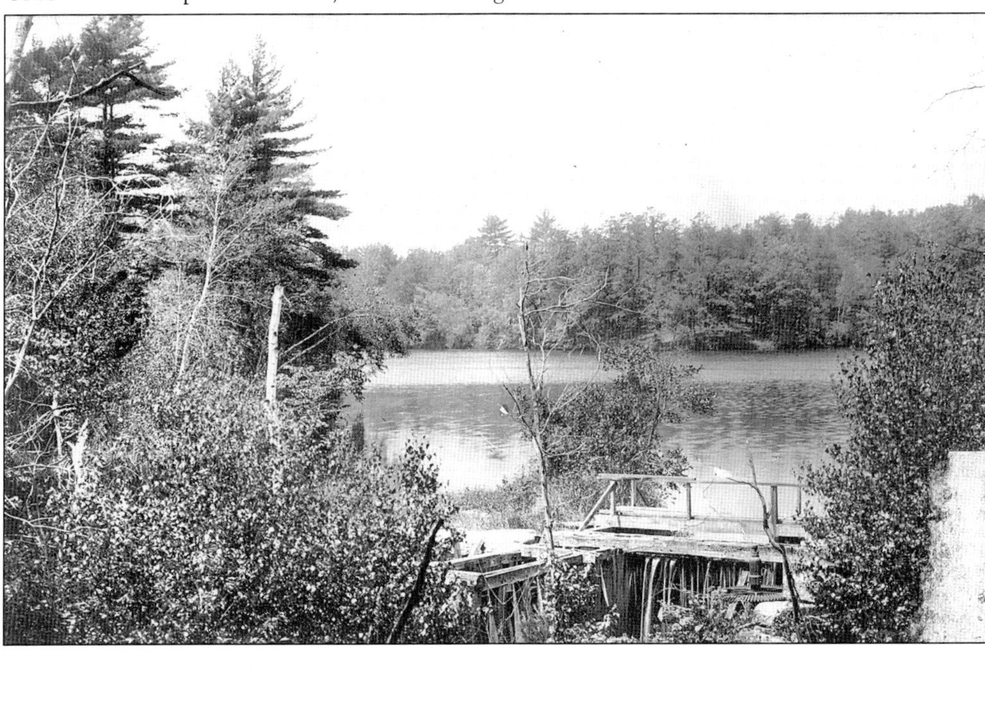

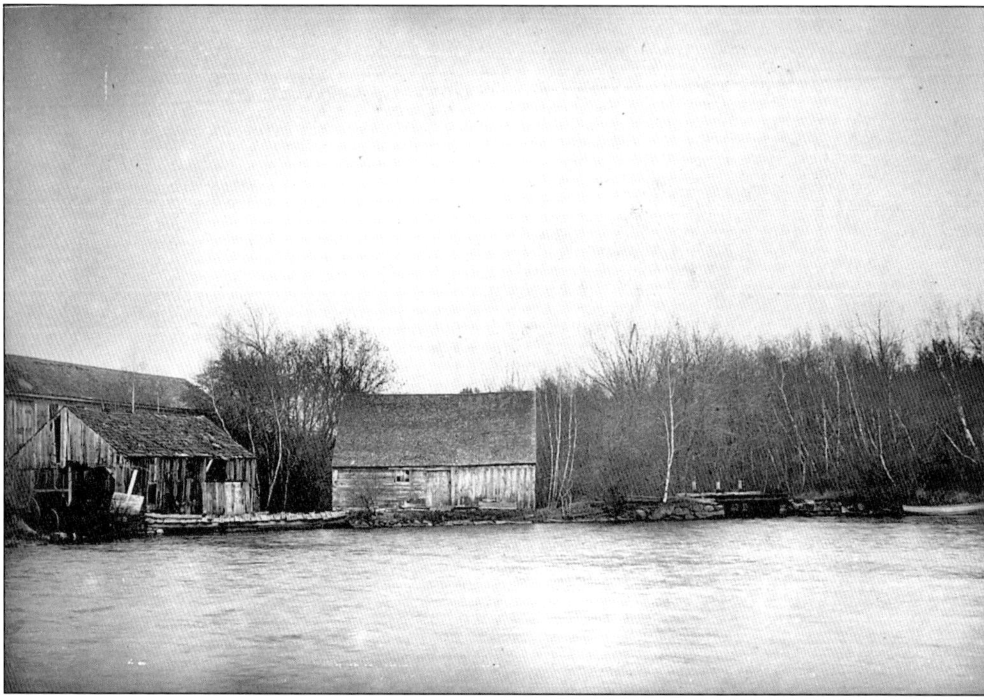

In 1844, this mill harnessed the water of the Charles River to produce boxboard. Shortly thereafter, this millpond became known as Box Pond.

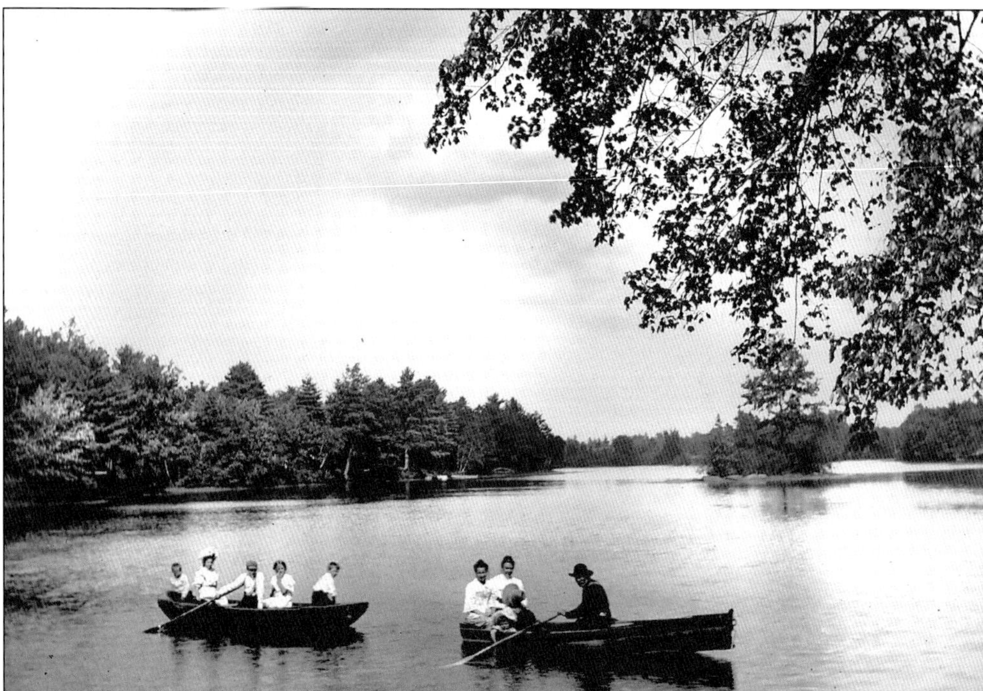

Box Pond became a favorite fishing and recreation area during the early 1900s. This photograph was taken in 1904, when there were numerous summer cottages. Today, no cottages remain.

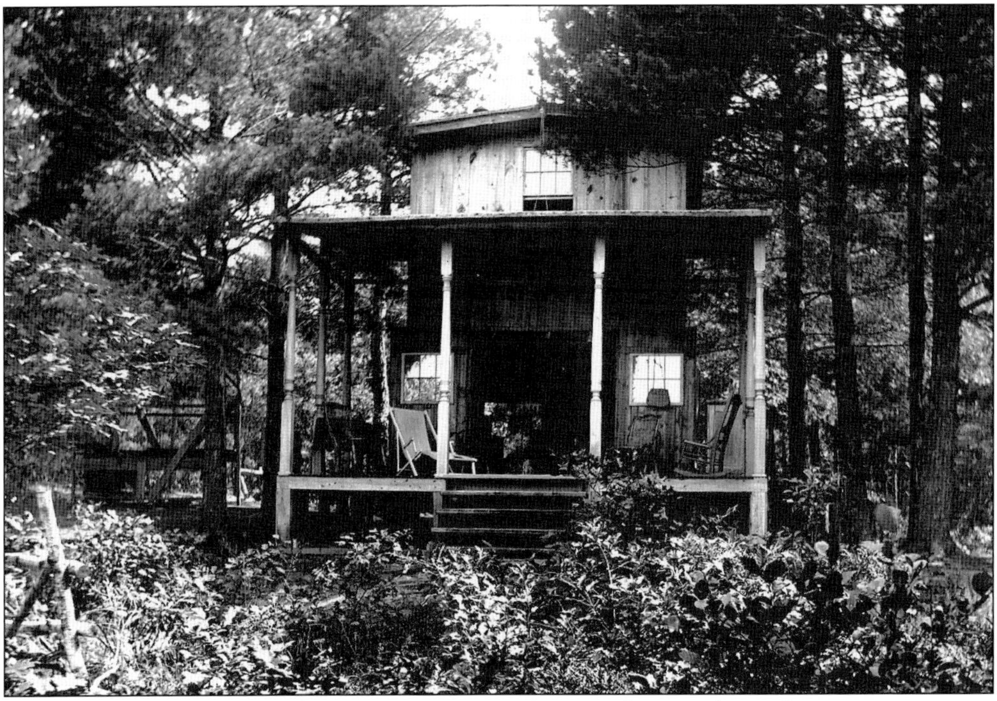

This is a 1904 photograph of a summer cottage at Box Pond. Note that only women are sitting on the front porch. This cottage was known as the Women's Club.

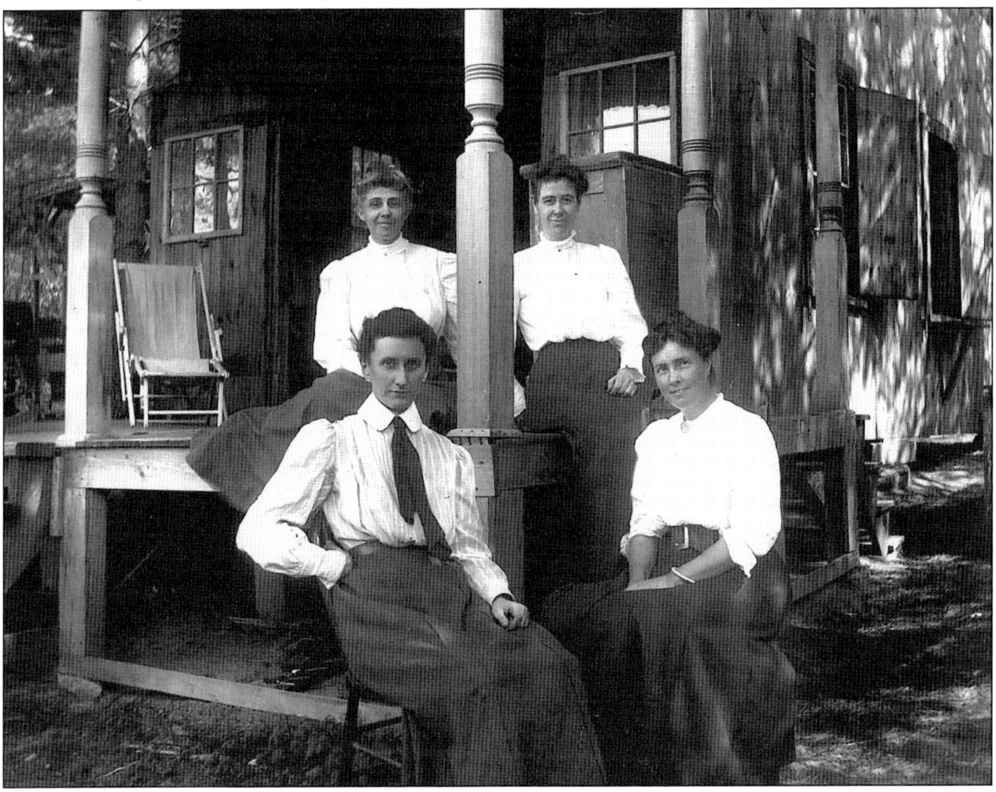

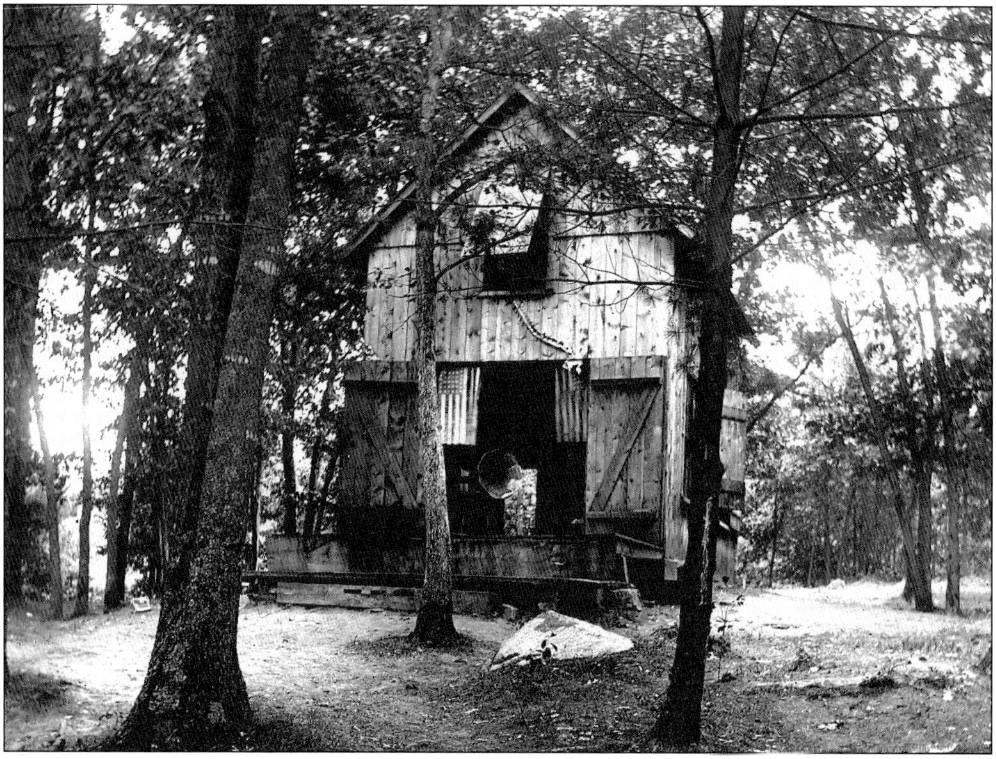

This summer cottage was known as the Men's Club. It was also located at Box Pond, adjacent to the Women's Club. Note the large Victrola and horn in the doorway of the cottage.

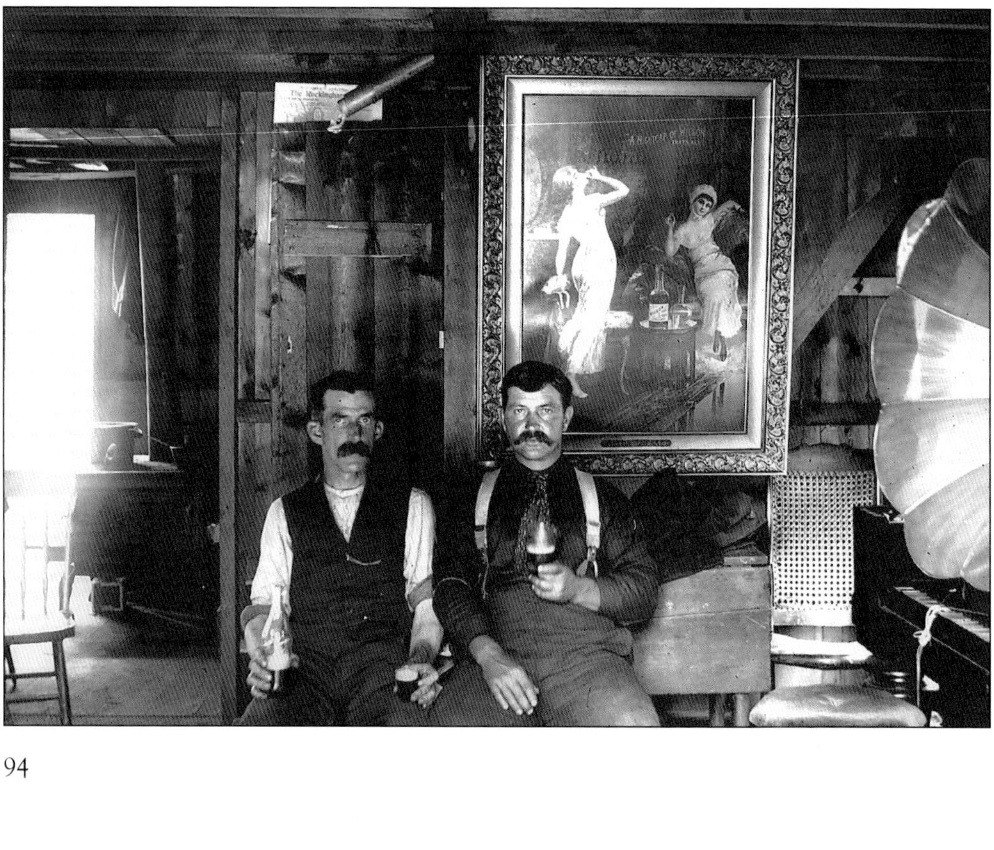

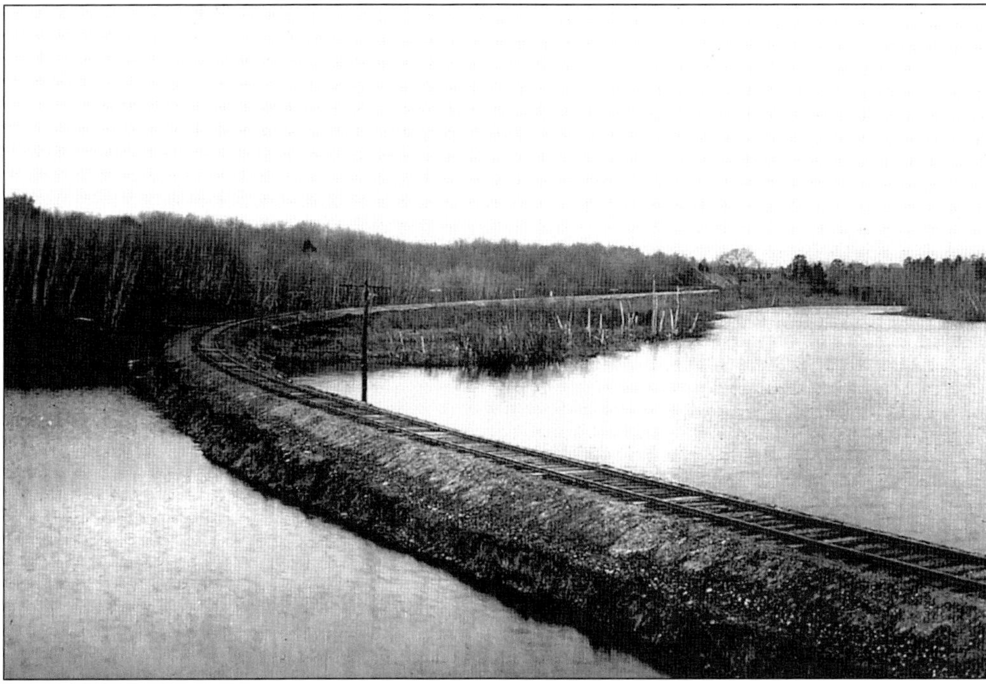

The dam at the Red Mill gives the impression that the Charles River is extremely wide at the Charles River Grove location. In actuality, at certain times of the year, the Charles is little more than a slow-running stream.

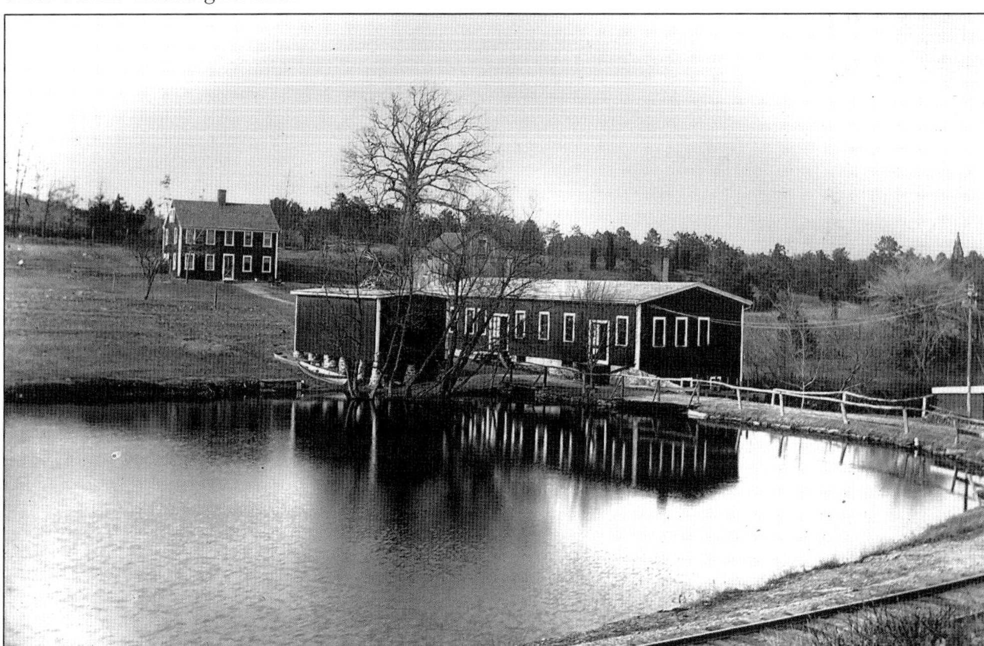

The Red Mill, located on Mill Street, had a variety of functions. It harnessed the water from the Charles River to run its sawmill and cotton and wool manufacturing machines. It also housed a boot-making shop. The business, which began in 1852, ended in 1927, when a flood breached the dam and washed it away.

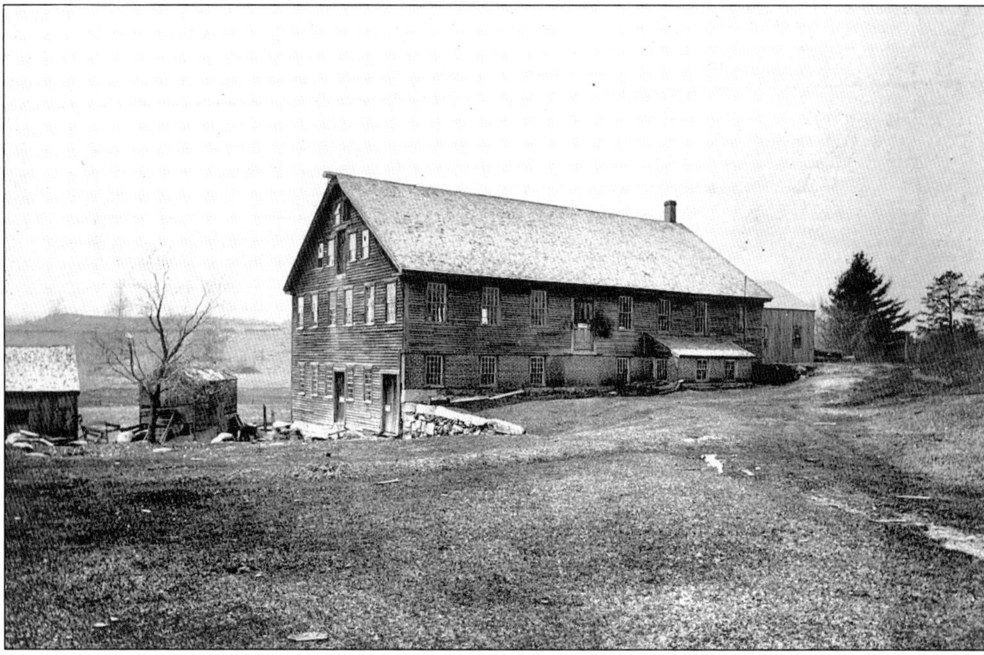

The Wilcox rake shop was located on Wrentham Road near Lake Street. Jerald D. Wilcox began his agricultural tool-making business here in 1848. This factory was destroyed by fire in 1905. This section of town, for many years, was known as Rakeville.

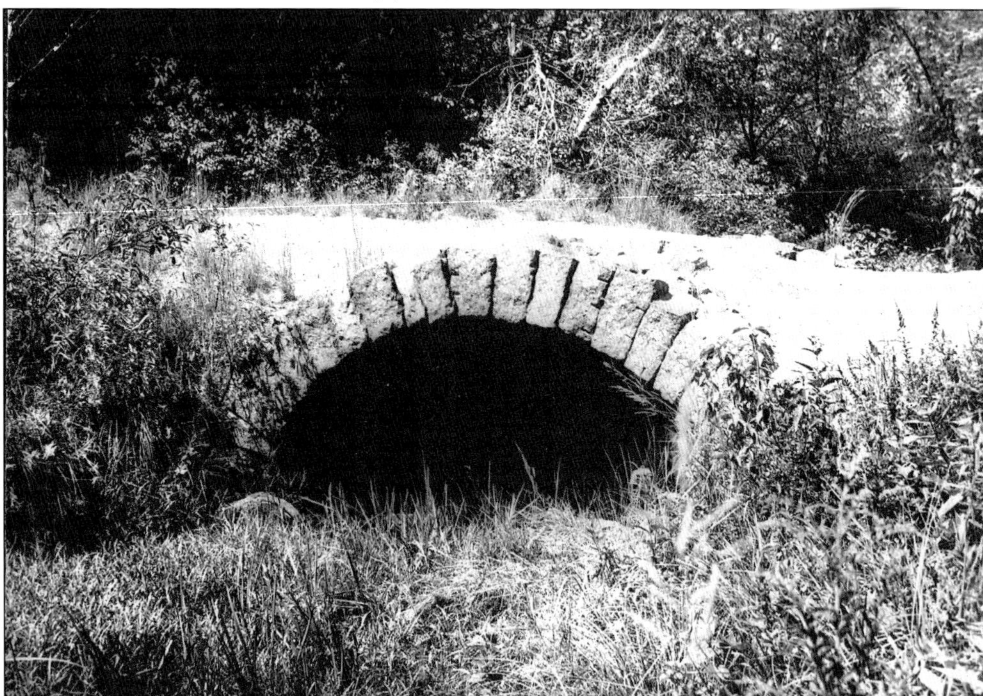

In 1835, the town appropriated $100 for building a keystone bridge over Peter's River in South Bellingham on the old abandoned Franklin Street, now known as Pulaski Boulevard. The bridge can be found at the entrance to Arcand Park.

The first organizational meeting of the Most Ancient and Honorable Society of Free and Accepted Masons was held at Bellingham's town hall on April 27, 1939. The original members decided to name this Masonic group the Bellingham Navy Yard, after a Bellingham legend. Edwin F. Tuttle was chosen to head this fraternal organization and was also named admiral.

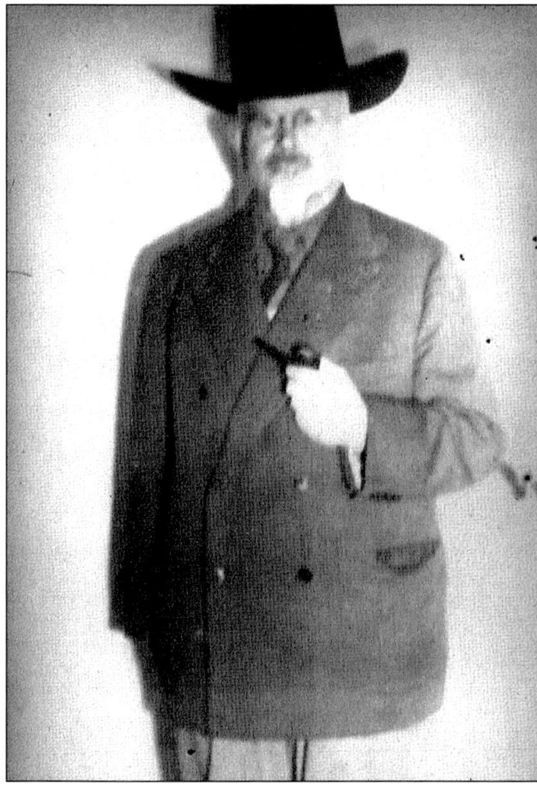

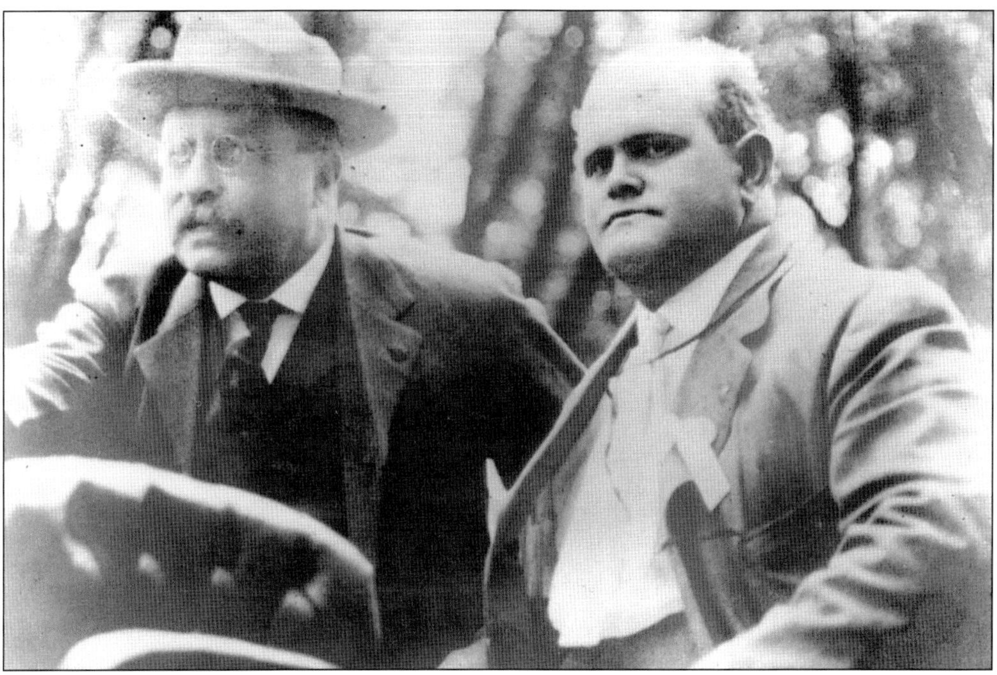

A founder and prominent member of the Bull Moose party of 1912, Edwin F. Tuttle led the Rhode Island campaign for Teddy Roosevelt. This photograph of Tuttle and Roosevelt was taken in Boston c. 1912.

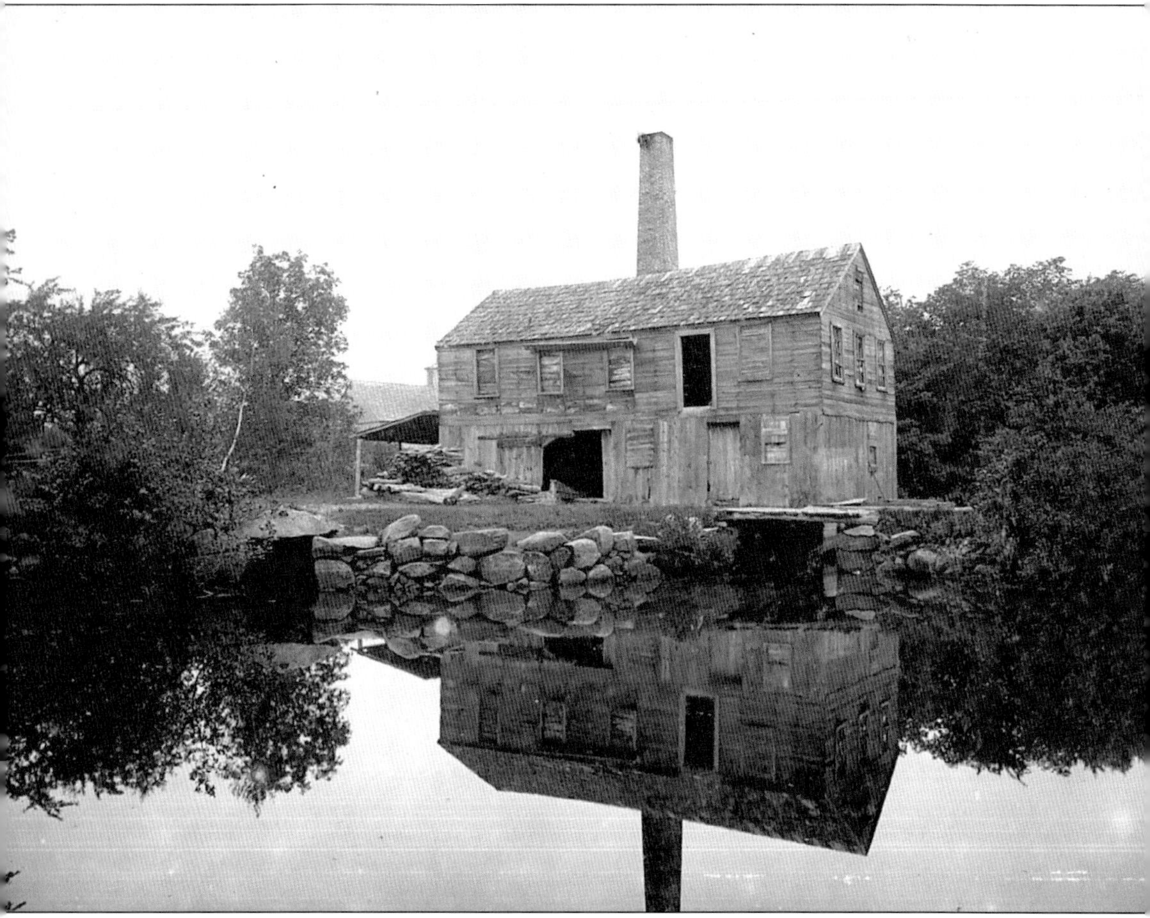

Shown is the Stall Brook Mill, with a second floor, in North Bellingham.

Seven

SCHOOLS AND STUDENTS

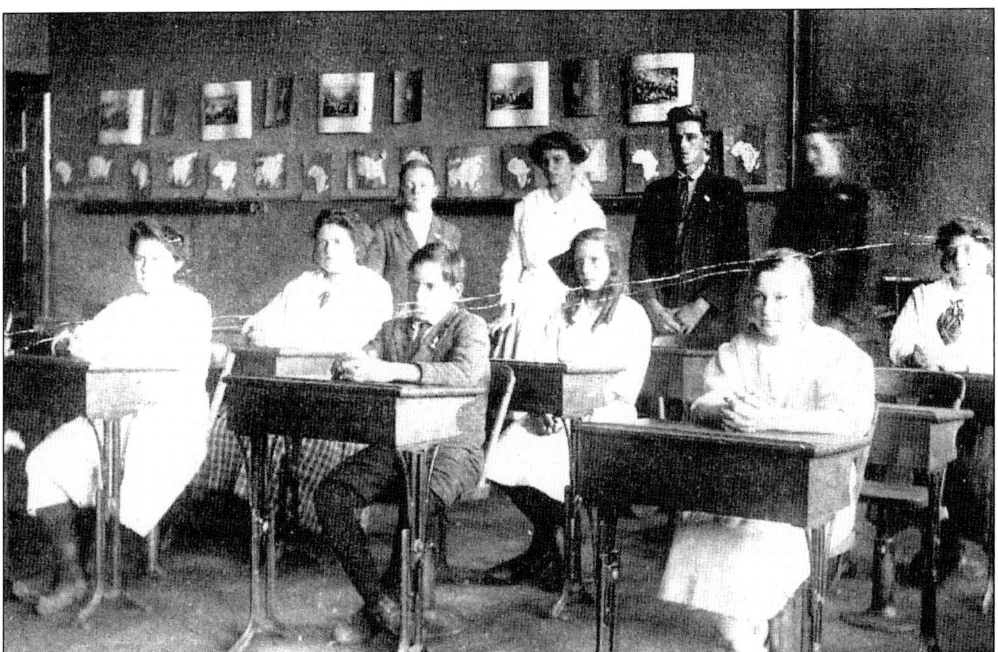

Pictured are Charlotte Rhodes, Albert Paquin, Mildred Unwin, Irma Crooks, Elise Rhodes, Harriet Whiting, Clarence Leland, Laura Richards, Raymond "Bud" Mowry, and Harold Burr.

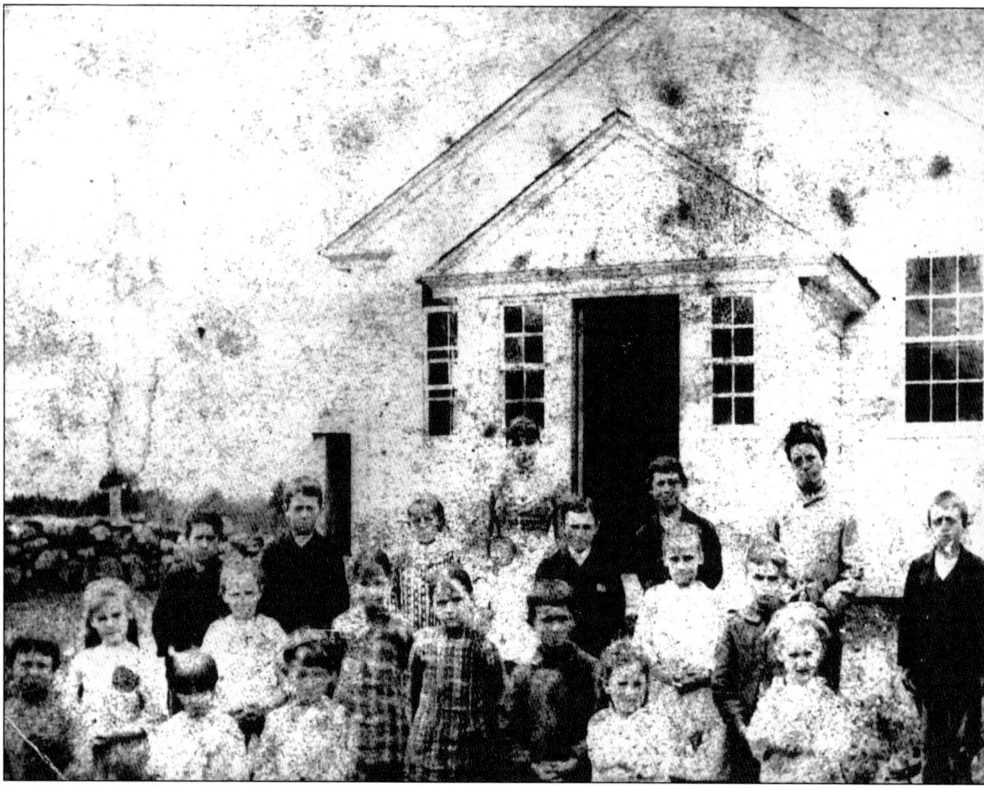

District School No. 3 was located on North Main Street at the junction of Horseshoe Drive. In 1829, the selectmen ordered the town to establish a school here. In 1889, the school was named Quinobequin School. It closed in 1897. In 1902, part of the building was moved, and the rest was torn down.

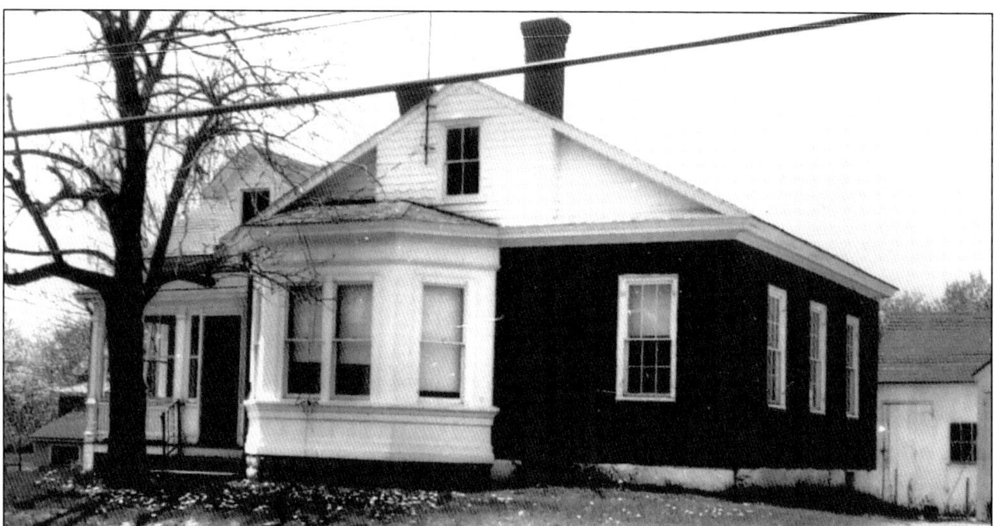

In 1889, this brick building, located on South Main Street, became the new District School No. 8. At this time, it was known as the City School. In 1896, this old brick building was closed as a school and put up for sale. In 1898, it sold for $132.

District School No. 1 stood on Hartford Avenue at the approximate site of the Varney Brothers office. This school first appeared on the 1830 map. In 1889, it was named the Beaver Pond District School. The school closed in 1897. In 1902, the building was sold but burned before it could be moved.

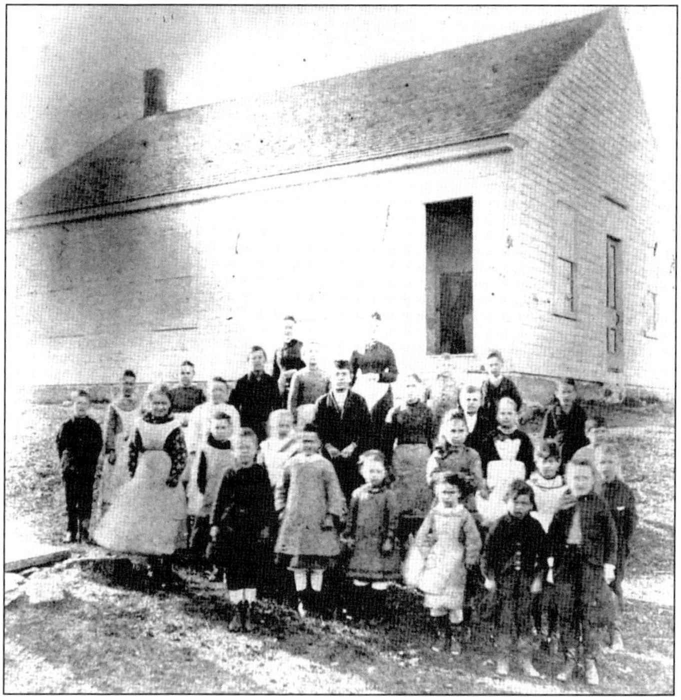

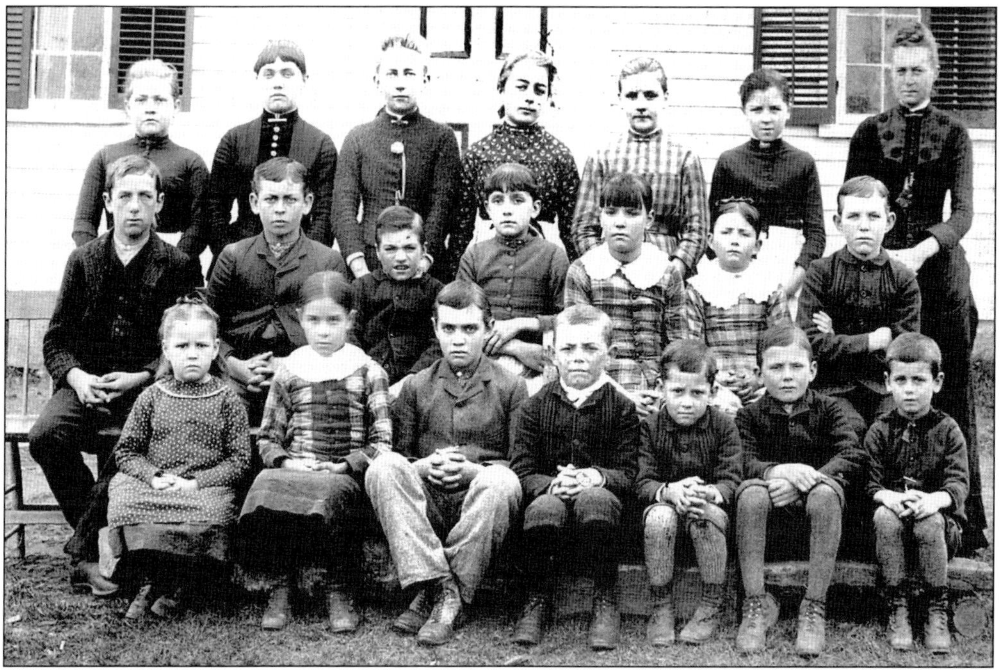

Teacher Effie E. Worthen is pictured with her students at the Beaver Pond District School c. 1887. Seen here are, from left to right, the following: (front row) Rubie Wales, Mabel Tingley, Fred Tingley, Charles Hixon, Herbert Grant, Willie Davis, and Arthur Shannon; (middle row) John Woodbury, Frank Albee, Ernest Johnson, Jennie Tingley, Cora Tingley, Clara Davis, and George Baxter; (back row) Bertha Albee, Amelia Gardener, Hattie Williams, Clara Thayer, Jennie Davis, Jennie Daniels, and teacher Effie E. Worthen.

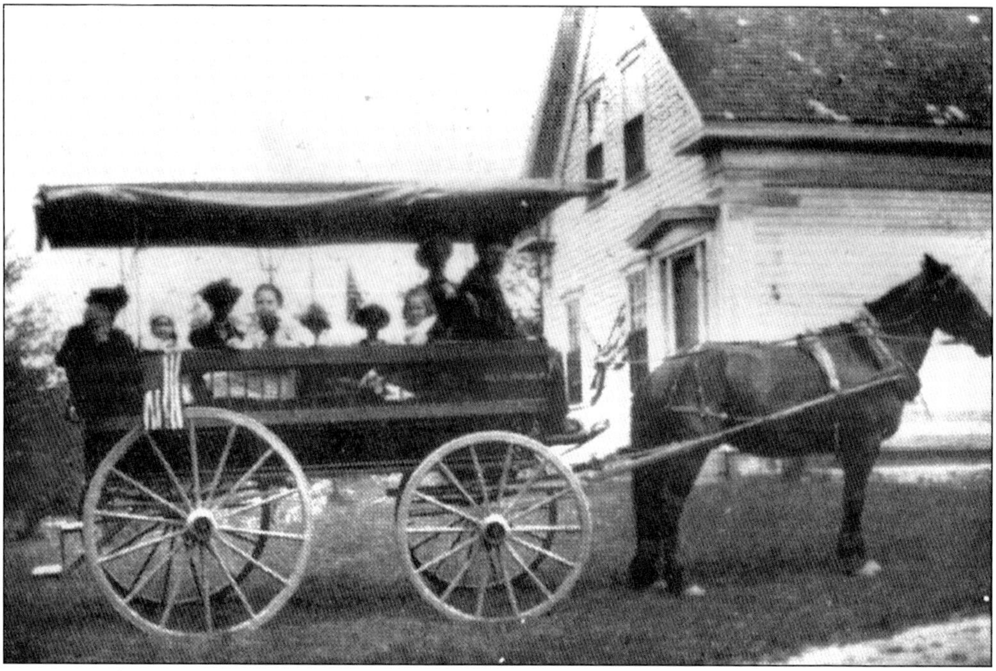

Imagine riding to school like this on a snowy day. Eldred Wentzel drove this school barge from Hartford Avenue to Center School.

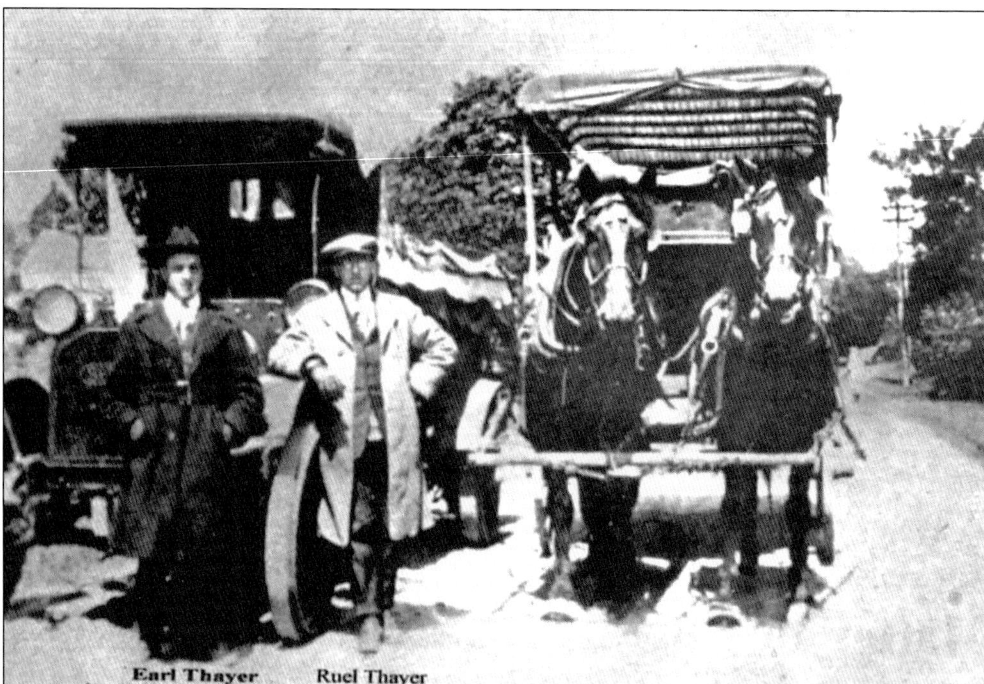

Two different modes of transportation were available during 1920. The horse-drawn wagon is the old Bellingham school barge, which was owned by Francis Thayer.

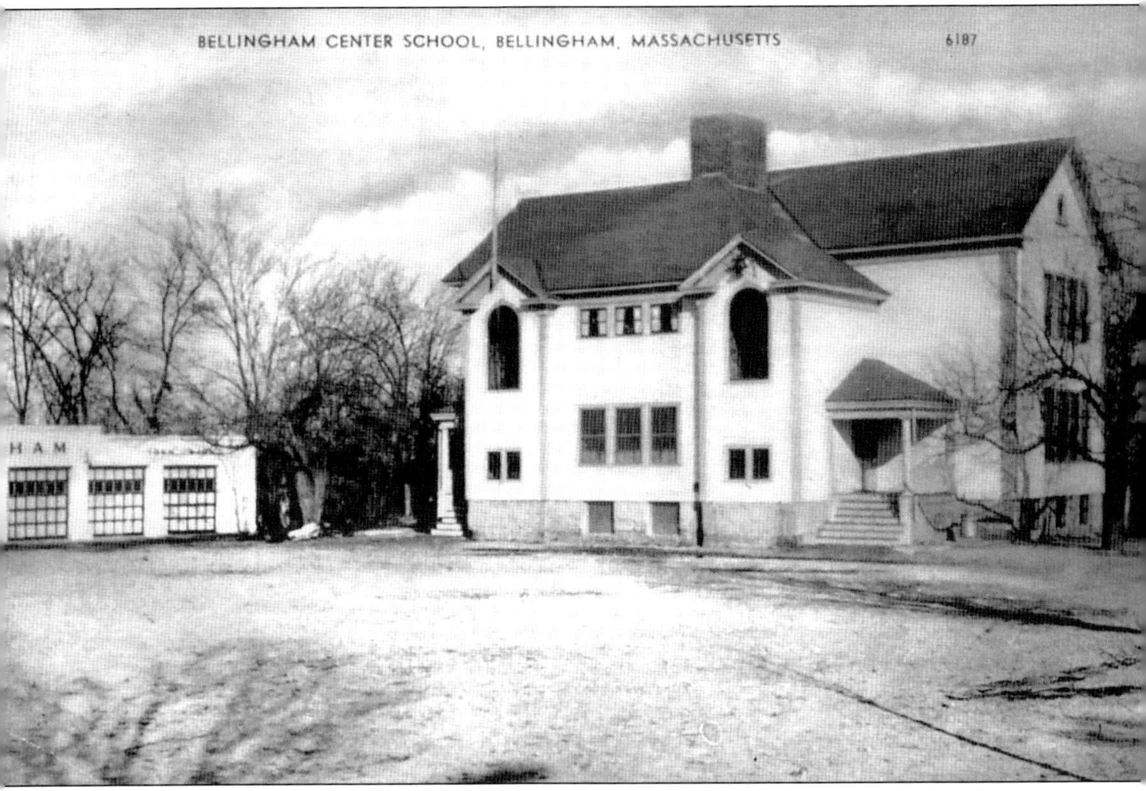

In 1873, the Center School was built as a two-story, two-room structure. It was listed as a grammar or primary school. In 1887, the school was named the Massey in honor of Rev. Joseph T. Massey, pastor of the First Baptist Church. From 1895 to 1899, the upper floor was used as a two-year high school. In 1901, the school was remodeled into a four-room school. The town public library existed here from 1905 to 1928. The original school bell that once called students to class is on exhibit in the town hall annex. This 1955 photograph shows the Center District School No. 10 and the town barn. The town barn was built in 1942 as a Works Progress Administration (WPA) project and was used by the highway department and the fire department. Both buildings were located on the old town common. When the combination fire-police station was built in 1965, the barn was used exclusively by the highway department. In 1973, a new barn for the highway department was built on Blackstone Street. In 1974, the old garage was converted into office space and has since been known as the town hall annex.

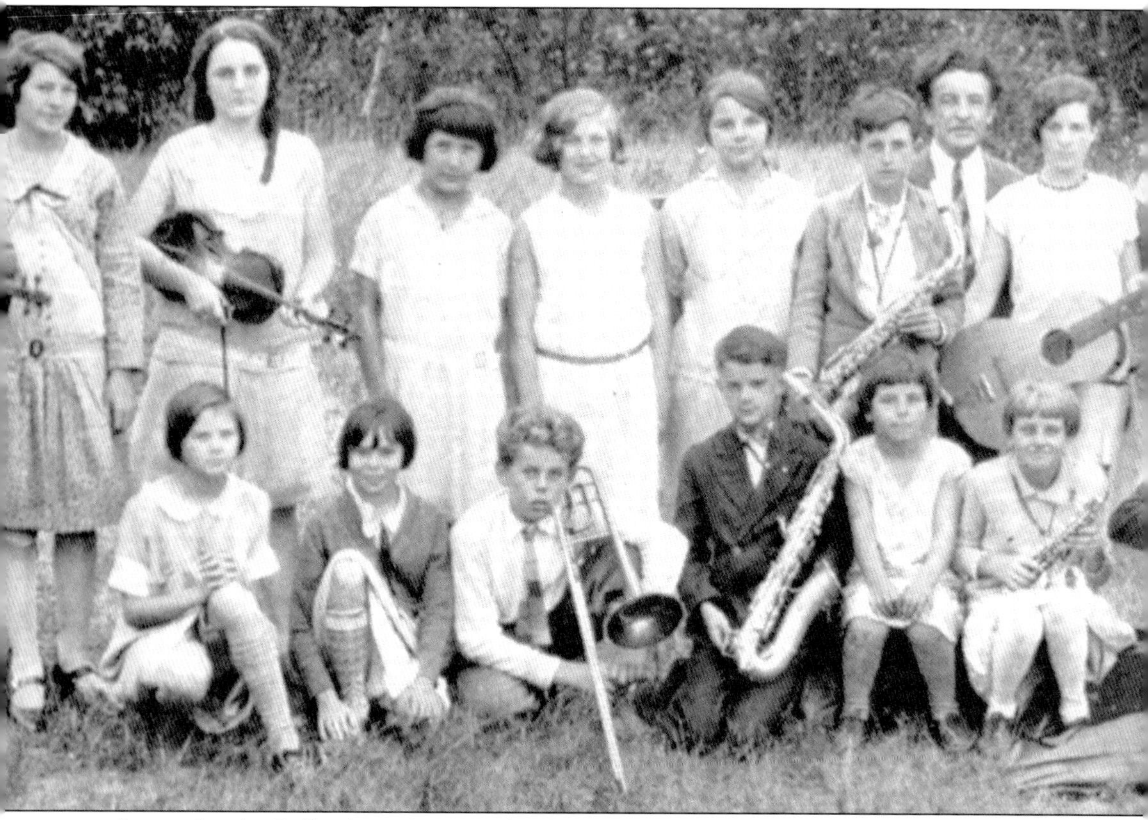

Pictured is the Bellingham Center School Orchestra *c.* 1926–1928. Seen here are from left to right, the following: (front row) Ida Estes, Susan Estes, Arthur Curtis, unidentified, Pauline DiPietro, Rita Guerin, Leo Garneau, Raymond Guerin, Gabriel DiCalmutier, and Orland DiPietro; (back row) Louise Southwick, Jeanette ?, Sophie Petrosky, Zina Cranzaw, Filomena

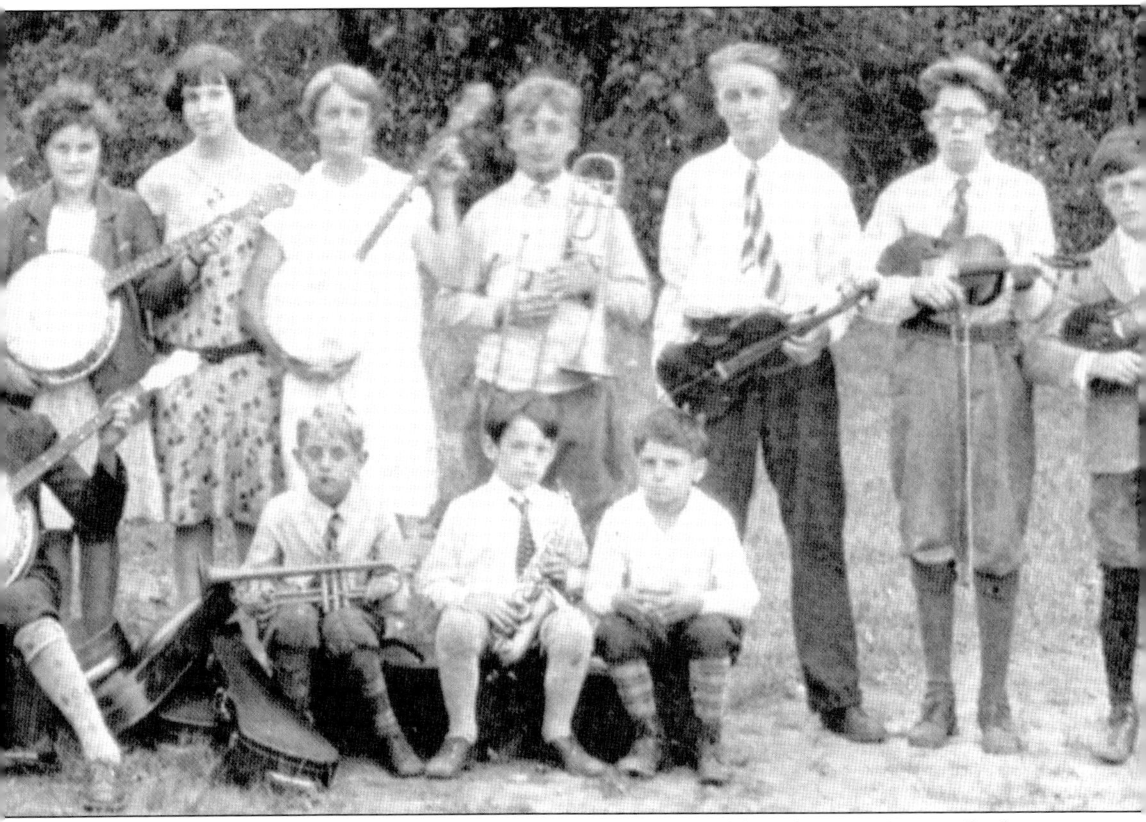

DiPiettro, Alfred Garneau, Professor Di Calmutier, Dorothea Ambler, Florence Guerin, Evelyn Cormier, Bertha Garneau, Irene Guerin, Henry Guerin, Bertram Guerin, George Southwick, and Eugene Garneau.

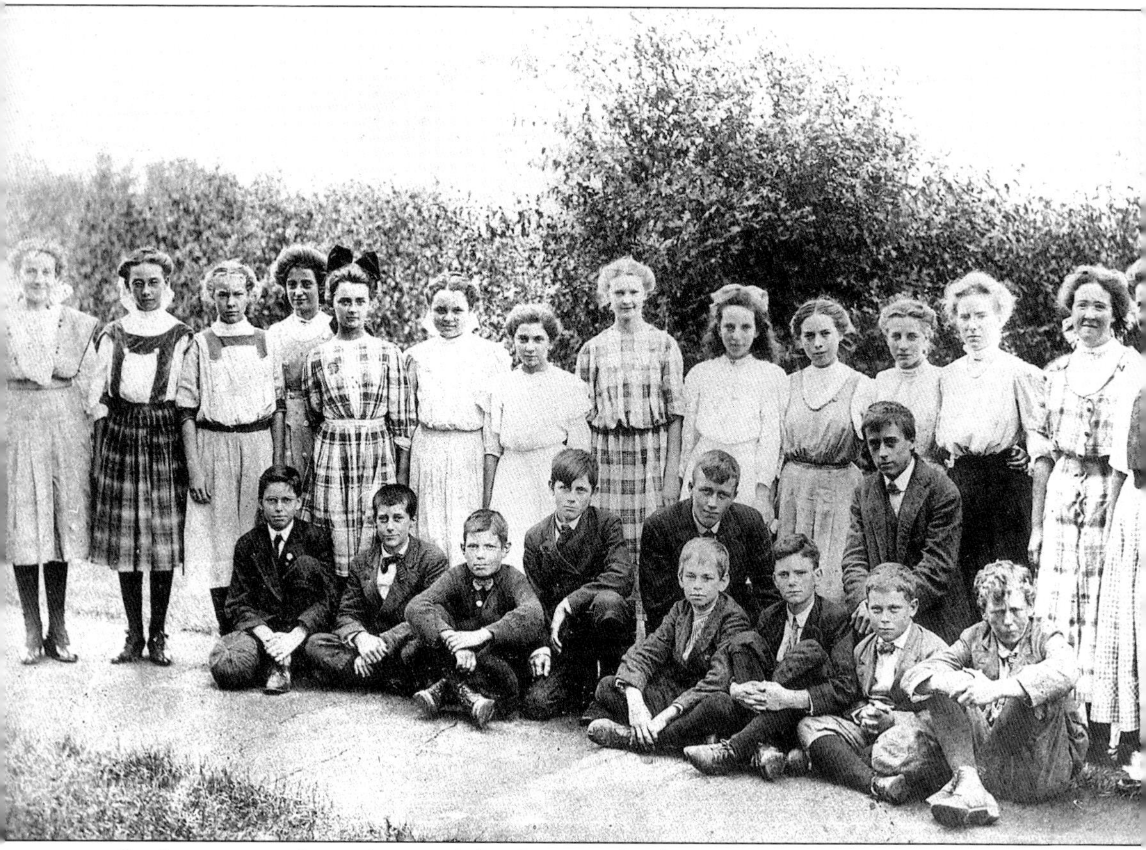

Grades seven, eight, and nine of the Center School are pictured in 1910 with their teacher, Eva M. Jackson. Seen here are, from left to right, the following: (front row) William Allison, Frederick Hunter, Harland Cook, George Melrose, Roland Chamberlain, Ralph White, C. Peao, Chester Davis, Chester Rouse, and Henry Ratti; (back row) unidentified, Mary Goodwin, Ruth Haskard, Bertha Arnold, Charlotte DeJony, Emily Migneault, Matilda Brothers, Eva Symmes, Doris Hutton, Myrtle Spencer, Elizabeth Sears, Eva M. Jackson (teacher), Anna Grant, and Rosina McLaughlin. The graduating class of 1910 included Myrtle Spencer, Rosina McLaughlin, Anna Grant, the Matilda brothers, Bertha Arnold, and Mary Goodwin.

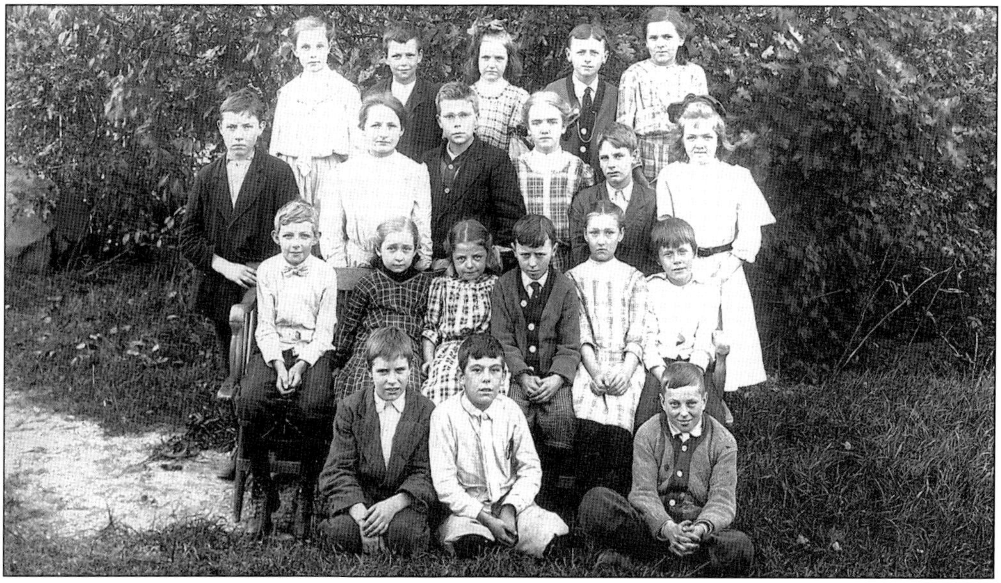

Grades four, five, and six of the Massey grammar school are pictured in 1911 in Bellingham Center. Seen here are, from left to right, the following: (first row) Elmer Moore, Francis Lemire, and Earl Thayer; (second row) Arthur Haynes, Edith Aldrich, Lois Dean, Carlton Gaskill, Grace White, and Ernest Davis; (third row) Harry Boone, Carrie Iby, Wellman Graves, Dorothy Symmes, Alvin Moore, and Audrey Symmes; (fourth row) Rilla Sanderson, Clifford Lemire, Beatruice Symmes, Chester Gaskill, and Myrtle Migneault.

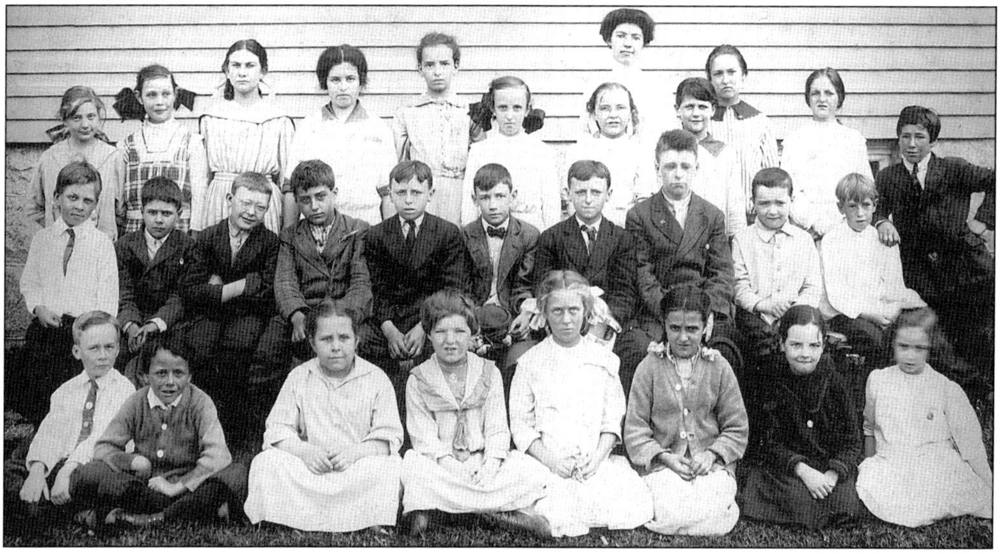

Grades four, five, and six of Center School pose for a picture in June 1914 with their teacher, Gertrude Rockwell. Seen here are, from left to right, the following: (front row) Martin Calkins, Roy Davis, Esther Wentzel, Gladys Symmes, Elizabeth Dawley, Irene Ratti, Mamie Byron, and Eva Lantz; (middle row) Evan Roberts, LeRoy Moore, Benjamin Stusse, Napoleon Ratti, Carleton Gaskill, Alfred Brothers, Chester Gaskill, Fleming Calkins, Reginald Wakeman, Clarence Bourcier, and Roy Prentiss; (back row) Cecile LaForce, Rilla Sanderson, Bessie Nash, Mildred Willows, Virginia Wakeman, Alice Sanderson, Lillian Johnson, unidentified, Grace White, and Beatrice Symmes.

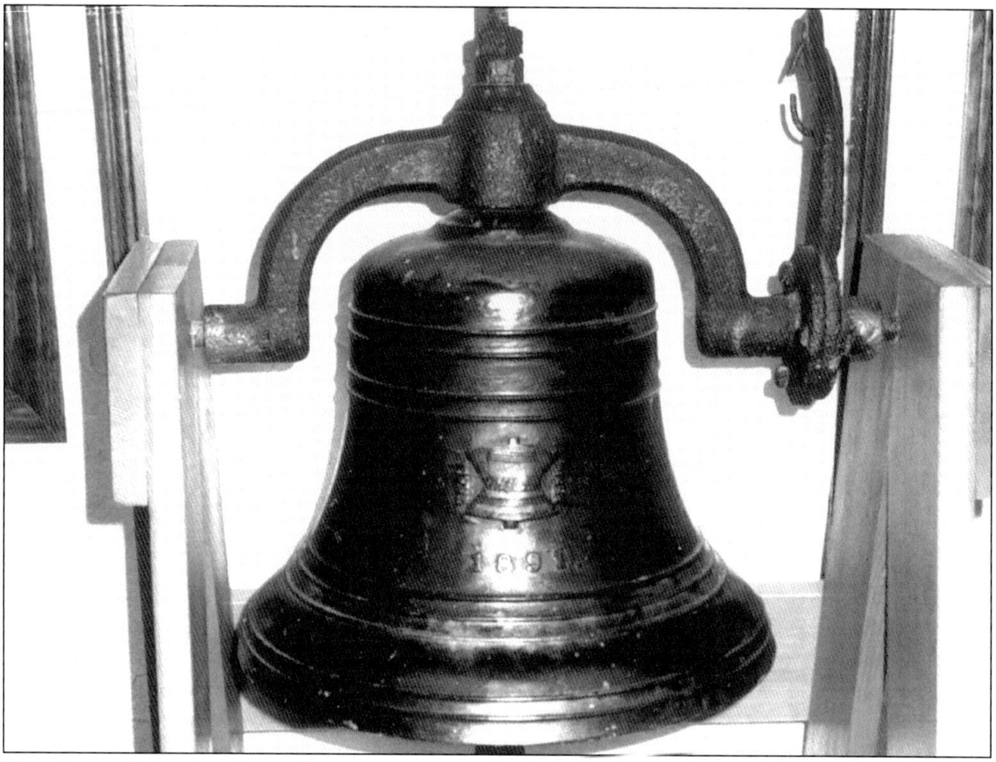

The Center School bell once hung on the outside of the building. It was rung to call the students to class. It is now on display at the town hall annex.

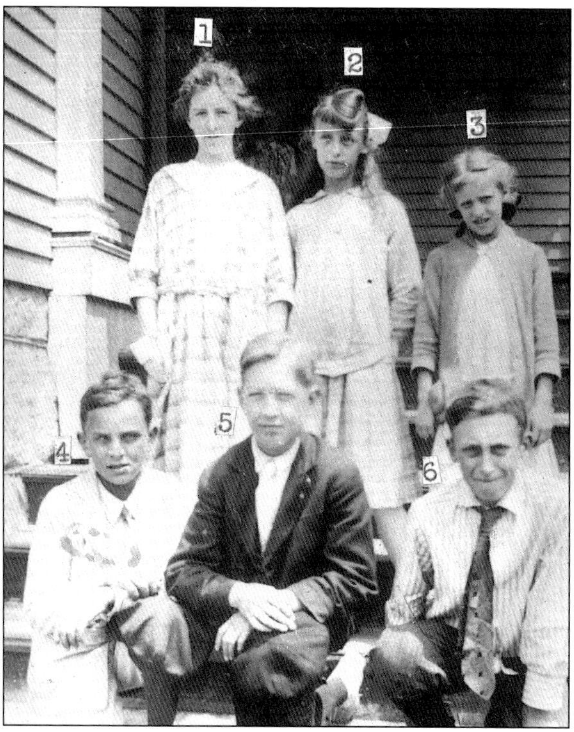

Grade six of the Center School is pictured in June 1918. The students' teacher was Ruth Haskard. The students are, from left to right, as follows: (front row) Alfred Migneault, John Lundvall, and Ashley Felton; (back row) Victoria Soule, Elsie Hobbs, and Florence Bourcier.

Shown is the 1930 graduating class of Center School. Their teacher and principal was Lucy Hill. From left to right are the following: (front row) Alice Allaire and Claire Farley; (middle row) Filomena DiPietro, Minnie Petrosky, and Amy Smith; (back row) Oscar Robillard, Vincent Thayer, and Arthur Curtis.

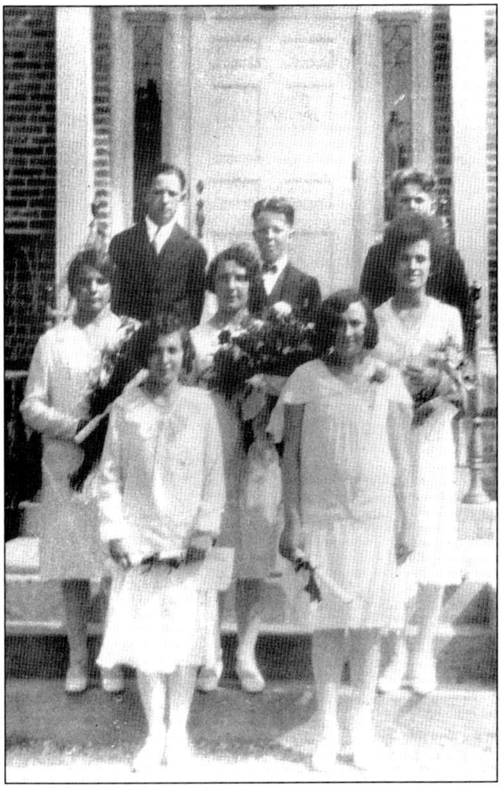

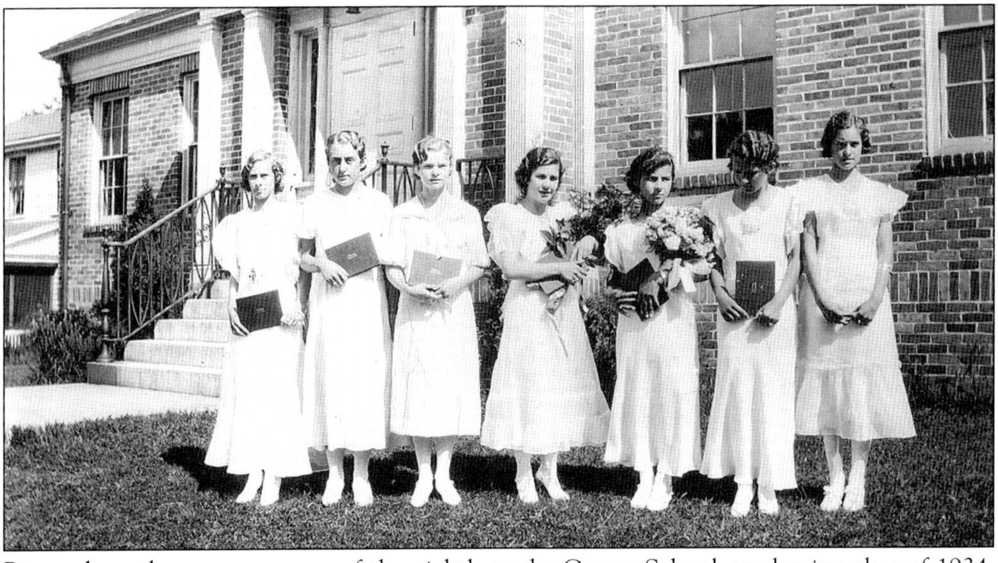

Pictured are the young women of the eighth grade, Center School, graduating class of 1934. This was the last graduating class of which Carroll H. Drown was superintendent. From left to right are Laura Southwick, Irene Pouliot, Lillian Binks, Edith Bates, Pauline DiPietro, Olga Petrosky, and Phyllis Hughes.

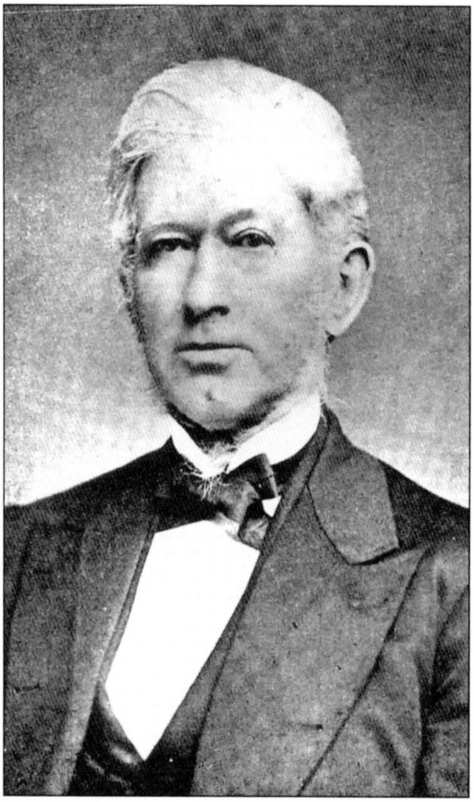

Rev. Joseph T. Massey was ordained in Bellingham in 1834 and served intermittently until 1880. Loved by church parishioners and townspeople, he was the driving force behind a parsonage house on Mendon Street for the First Baptist Church and Society. He served as town treasurer from 1859 to 1868 and as both town clerk and treasurer from 1870 to 1979. A southern Virginian gentleman who made Bellingham his home, he is buried in the Center Cemetery, and the Center School (Massey School) is named in his honor.

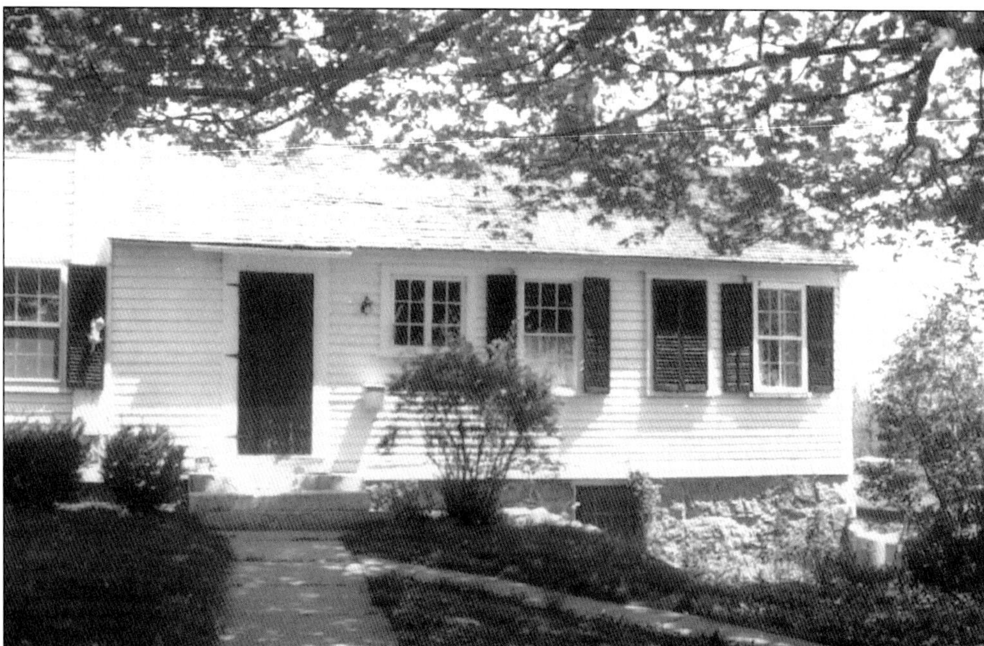

In 1889, District School No. 8 was moved to this location from Crooks Corner. It took 20 oxen to move this structure up Scott Hill to Scott Street. It is now part of the Whiting home.

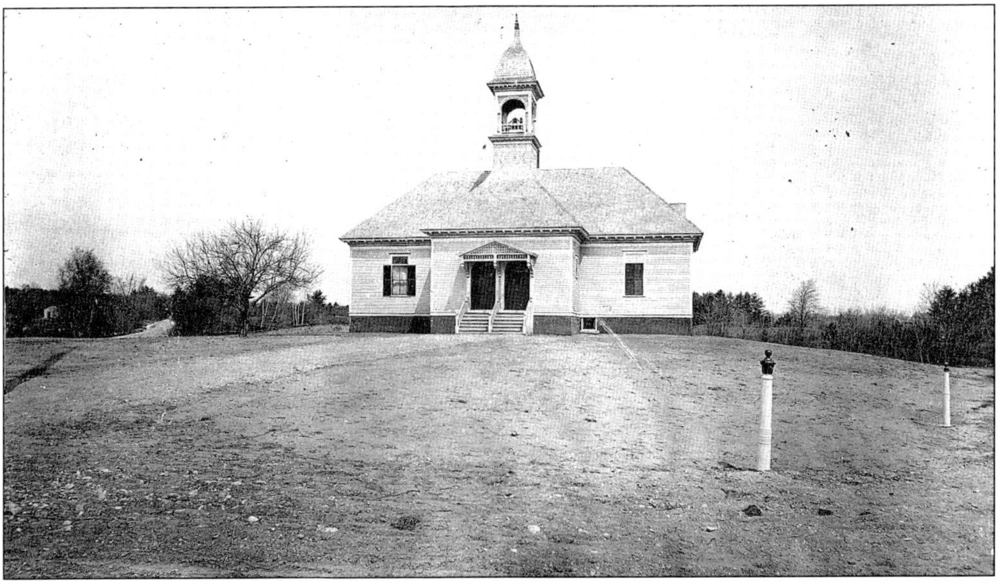

In 1896, on a small wedge of land between Pulaski Boulevard and South Main Street, the South School was built. Originally built as a two-room schoolhouse, the building was jacked up in 1902, and two more rooms were added on the bottom level. On May 24, 1920, the building was expanded again to eight rooms (below). It was torn down in 1998 because of unsafe conditions, and a small park, called Crooks Corner Common, was built upon the site.

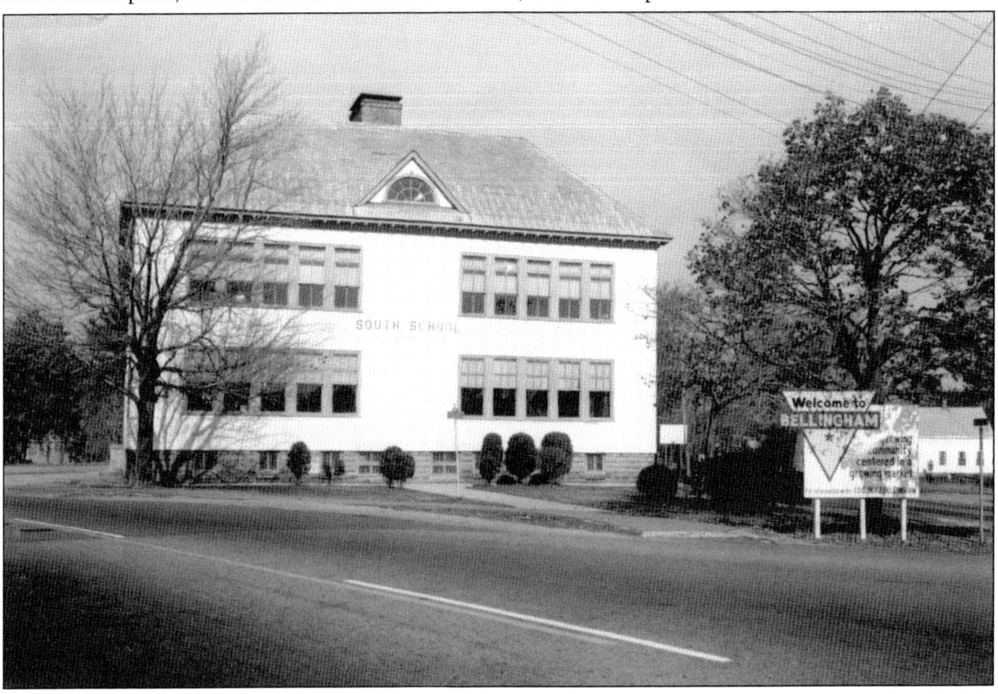

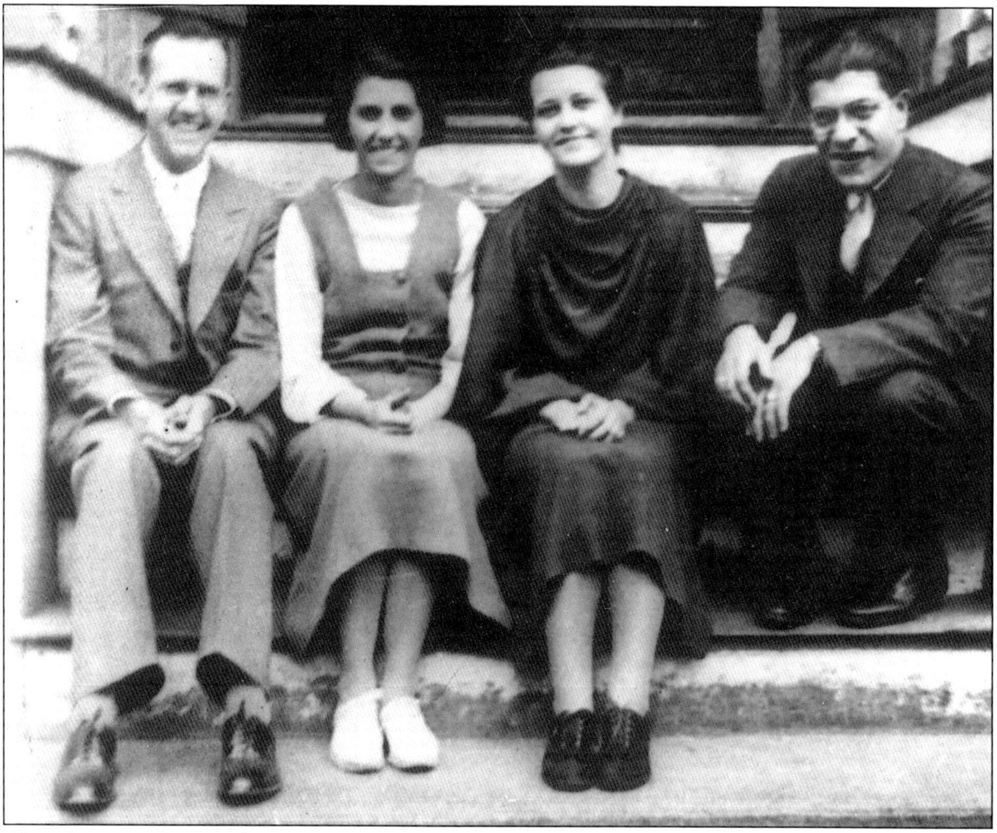

This photograph was taken in South Bellingham in 1936. From left to right are Maurice Adams, principal; Chilistine Negrotti, seventh-grade teacher; Marguerite Dubois, eighth-grade teacher; and Mac McDonald, eighth-grade teacher.

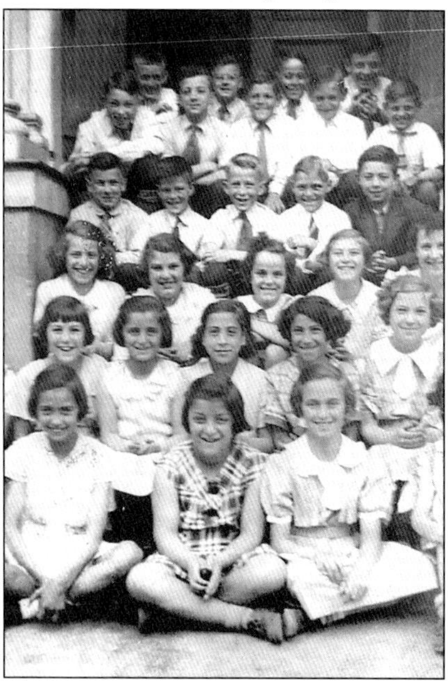

Pictured is the South Bellingham Grammar School's fifth grade in 1936. Students seen here are Janice Whiting, Lea Rotatori, Bertha Richards, Cecile Bernier, Theresa Houde, Rita Boucher, Luigi Cubellis, Filameno Campano, Rita Levesque, Alice Blanchard, Marcella Gagnon, Beulas Rhodes, Florence Bernier, Helen Pichie, Theresa Guileault, Clovis Marcotte, Walter Hogarth, Thomas Ponton, Harry Hillsgrove, Norman Arnold, Charles Whipple, Ernest Guilbeault, Russell Nelson, Frank Struzik, Raymond Gagnon, Arthur Leclaire, Roger Marcotte, Normand Dusseault, and Lucian Gagne.

The following South Bellingham teachers are pictured in 1936 from left to right: (front row) Mae Ryan (first grade) and Emilie Bunker (second grade); (second row) Chilistine Negrotti (fifth grade) and Gertrude Rhodes (third grade); (top row) Mildred Trafton (fourth grade) and Marguerite Moran (second grade).

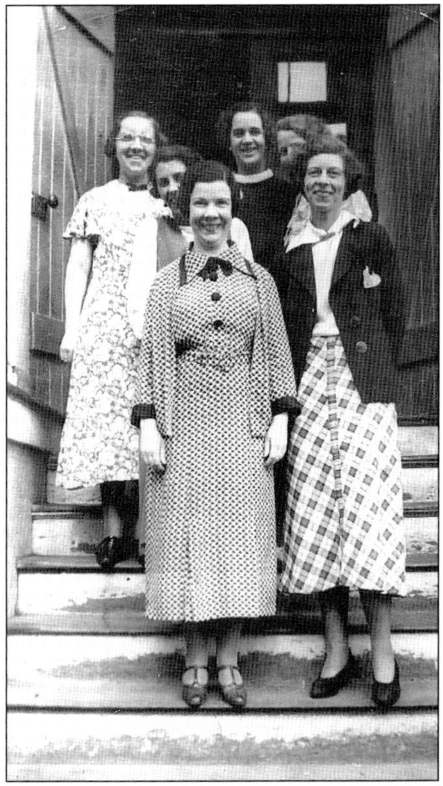

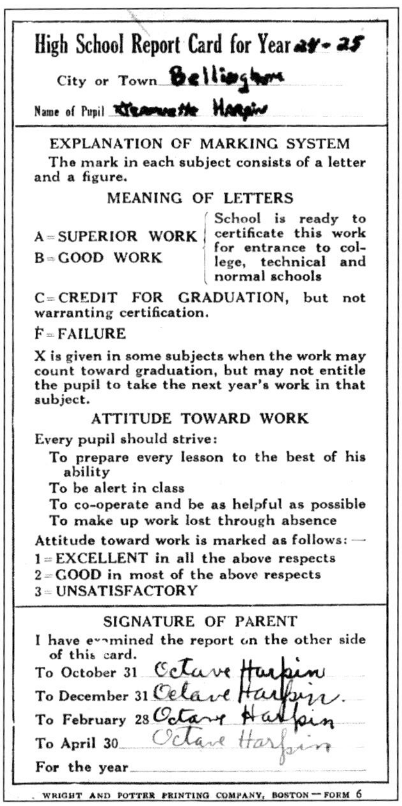

High School Report Card for Year 24-25

City or Town Bellingham

Name of Pupil Jeannette Harpin

EXPLANATION OF MARKING SYSTEM

The mark in each subject consists of a letter and a figure.

MEANING OF LETTERS

A = SUPERIOR WORK
B = GOOD WORK
School is ready to certificate this work for entrance to college, technical and normal schools

C = CREDIT FOR GRADUATION, but not warranting certification.

F = FAILURE

X is given in some subjects when the work may count toward graduation, but may not entitle the pupil to take the next year's work in that subject.

ATTITUDE TOWARD WORK

Every pupil should strive:

To prepare every lesson to the best of his ability
To be alert in class
To co-operate and be as helpful as possible
To make up work lost through absence

Attitude toward work is marked as follows: —
1 = EXCELLENT in all the above respects
2 = GOOD in most of the above respects
3 = UNSATISFACTORY

SIGNATURE OF PARENT

I have examined the report on the other side of this card.

To October 31 Octave Harpin
To December 31 Octave Harpin.
To February 28 Octave Harpin
To April 30 Octave Harpin
For the year

WRIGHT AND POTTER PRINTING COMPANY, BOSTON — FORM 6

Shown is a 1924–1925 report card from South School for Jeannette Harpin. She married Euclide Fleuette, the chief of police.

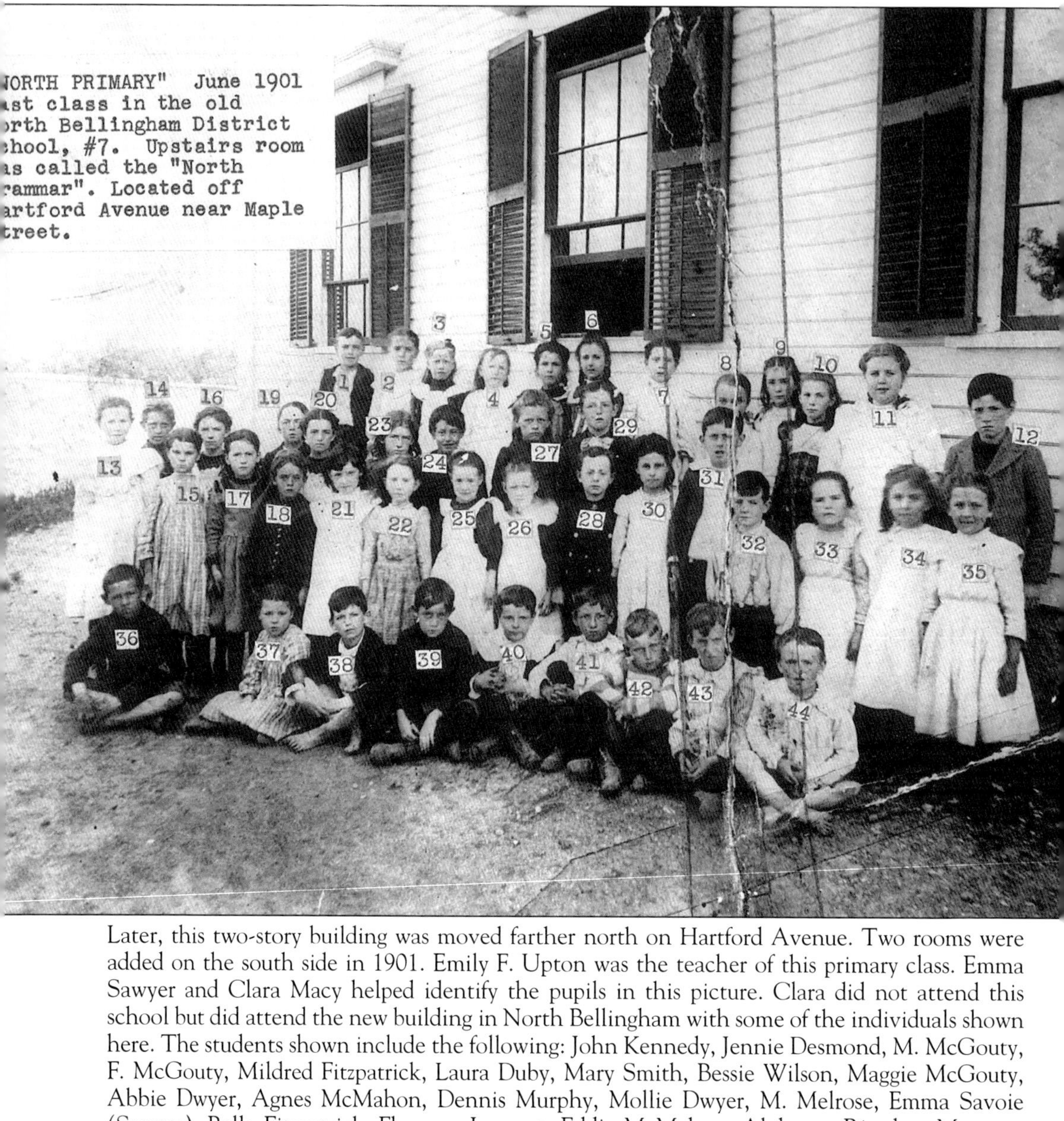

Later, this two-story building was moved farther north on Hartford Avenue. Two rooms were added on the south side in 1901. Emily F. Upton was the teacher of this primary class. Emma Sawyer and Clara Macy helped identify the pupils in this picture. Clara did not attend this school but did attend the new building in North Bellingham with some of the individuals shown here. The students shown include the following: John Kennedy, Jennie Desmond, M. McGouty, F. McGouty, Mildred Fitzpatrick, Laura Duby, Mary Smith, Bessie Wilson, Maggie McGouty, Abbie Dwyer, Agnes McMahon, Dennis Murphy, Mollie Dwyer, M. Melrose, Emma Savoie (Sawyer), Bella Fitzpatrick, Florence Lamont, Eddie McMahon, Alphonse Riordan, Margaret Fitzpatrick, Tessa O'Rourke, Mary Dee, Christine Riordan, George Burns, May Murphy, Ellen Murphy, Christine Melrose, Carleton Grant, William Foley, Mildred Fitzpatrick, Edward Smith, Dan Fitzpatrick, Margaret Desmond, Alice Desmond, Rose Duby, Louis Burns, Agnes Savoie (Sawyer), Bernard Fitzpatrick, Henry Metcalf, John Kennelly, Connie Foley, John Allen, John Smith, and Eugene Riordan.

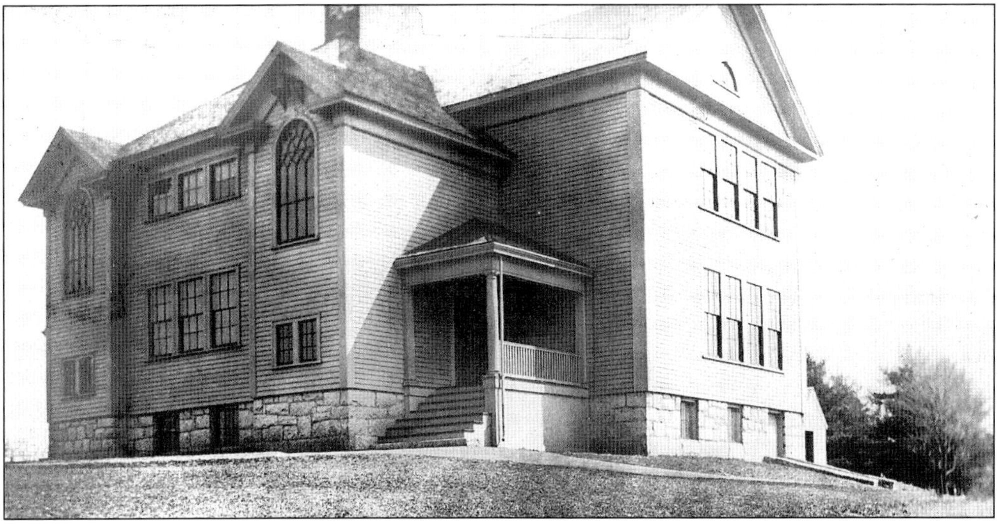

The District School No. 9, known as the North School, was originally located behind the fire station on Hartford Avenue. It was a one-room schoolhouse. In 1881, it was rebuilt into a two-story building. In 1901, the building was moved to its present site across from St. Brendan's Church.

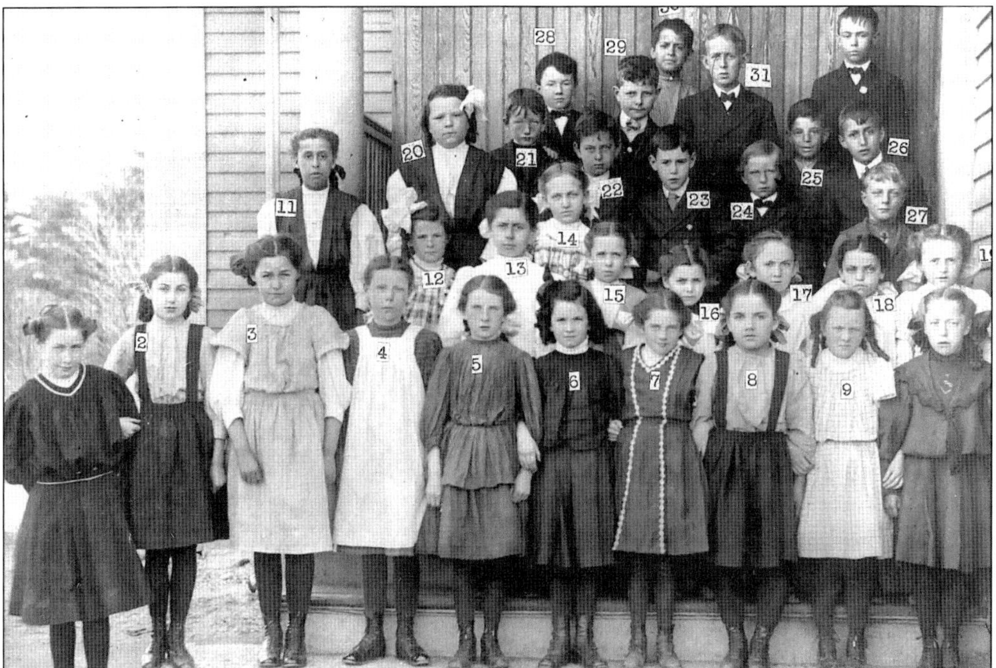

Shown are grades three and four of the North Bellingham School *c.* 1909. The teacher was Miss Sadler of Hopedale. The students include Nellie Connolly, Rita Kennelly, Anna O'Rourke, Mae Diggins, Myra Dee, Mae Flanagan, Lena Fitzpatrick, Mary Kennelly, Mae Allen, Yvonne Hebert, Bertha Jennelle, Mildred Dee, Margaret Smith, Anna Neibor, Edith Lamport, Mildred Barker, Loretta Shay, Lauro Provo, Mae Kelleher, Mary Sawyer, Charles Hume, David Deely, Francis Dwyer, Cornelius Allen, Alec McClean, Ralph Denoyells, Joseph Miner, George Edwards, Waldo Kennelly, Joseph Jennelle, Mark McMahon, and Addison Spear. (Photograph and identification courtesy of Mary Walsh.)

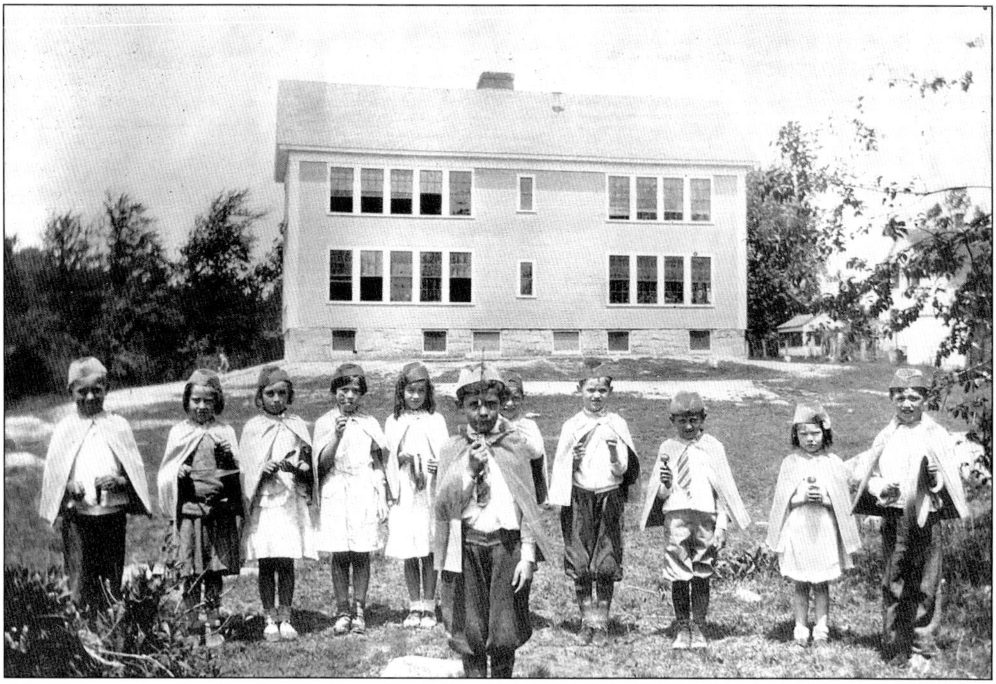

Members of the rhythm band of North Bellingham School are pictured here. From left to right are Danny Nadolny, Janet Brown, Helen Jastrzembski, Helen Marie Buckley, Mary Foley, unidentified, George Melrose (in front), Walter Pratt, Frank Arnold, Claire Fitzpatrick, and William Wright.

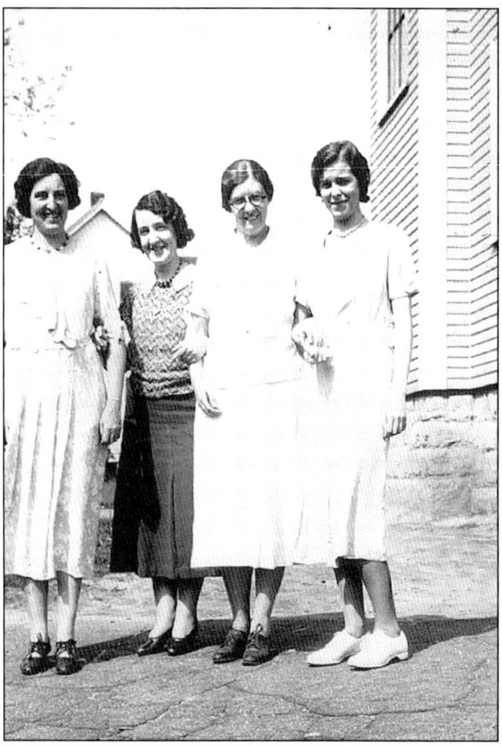

Teachers at the old North Bellingham School pose for a picture. From left to right are Clara Macy, Margaret Lennon, Margaret Drown, and Helen Pickard.

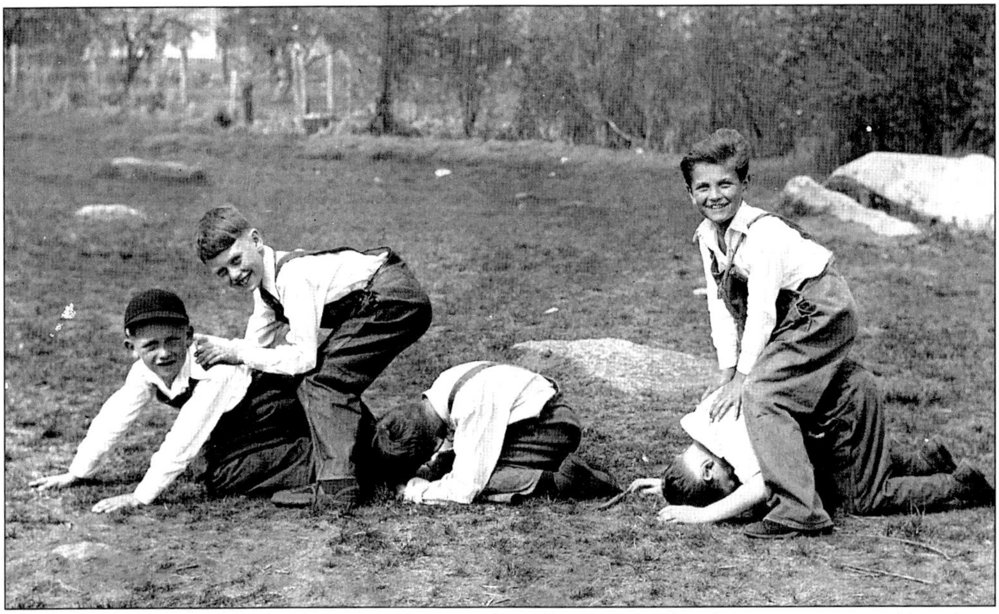

Pupils of Margaret Down, teacher at the North Bellingham School, enjoy a game of leapfrog. This picture was taken at the Mayday Health Program in 1933. The students are Walter Nadolny, Daniel Breen, Warren Lakeman, Edmond Darling, and Joseph Michalowski.

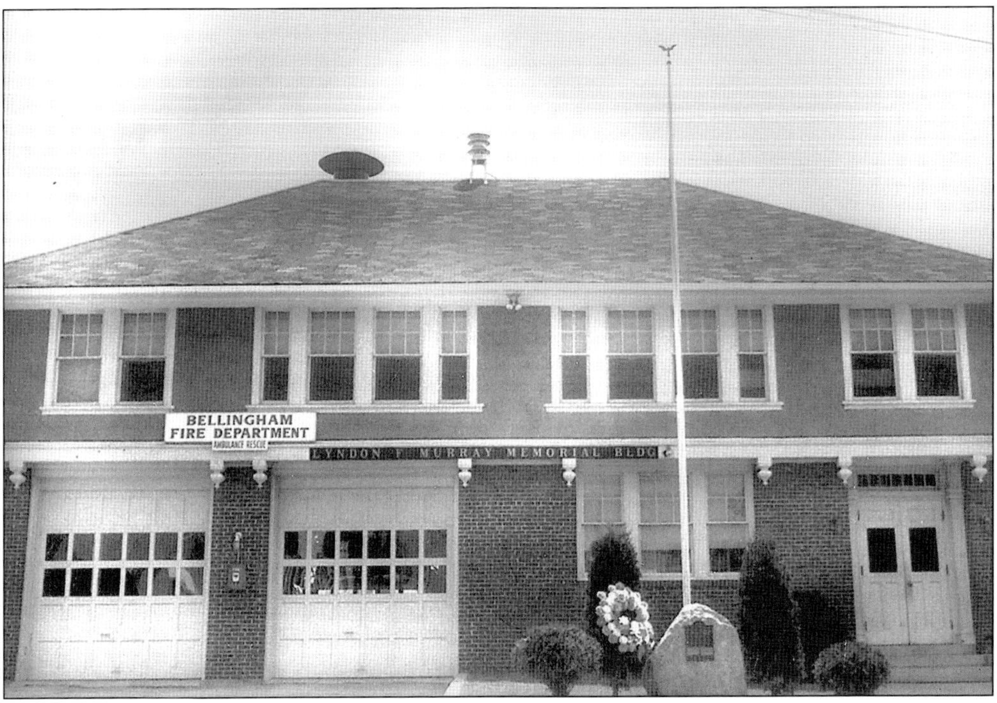

On December 22, 1930, this building was designated as Fire Station No. 1, and later it was dedicated to the memory of Lyndon F. Murray. As a community hall, it had a variety of uses. It was used as a library, and during the 1930s and 1940s, it was used as a classroom. The lower level is still being used as a fire station. Bellingham's first fire truck, Double O, is still stored there.

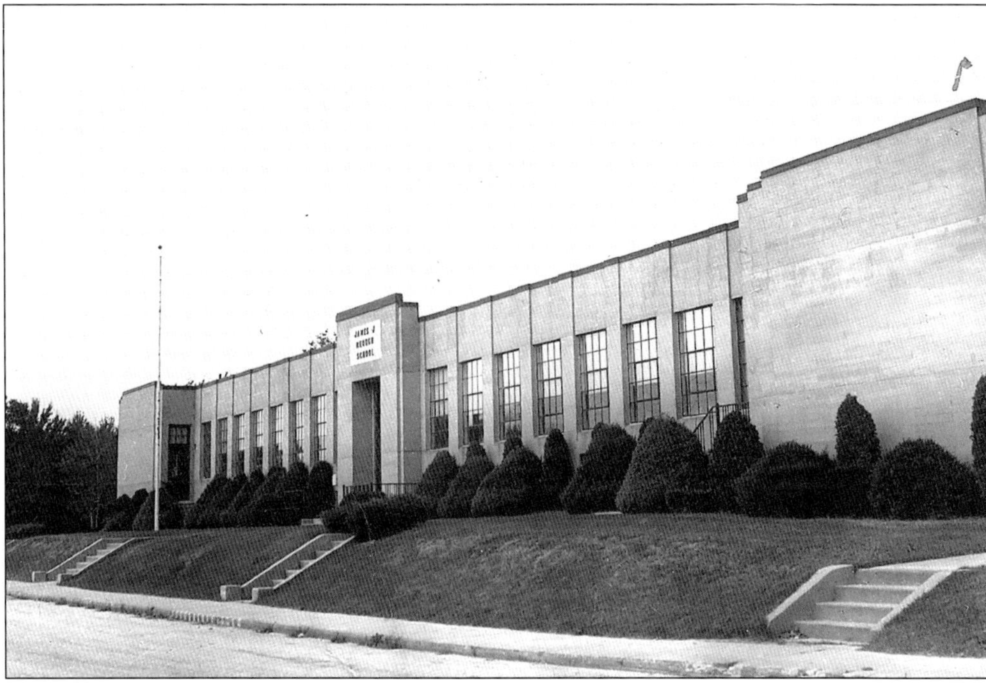

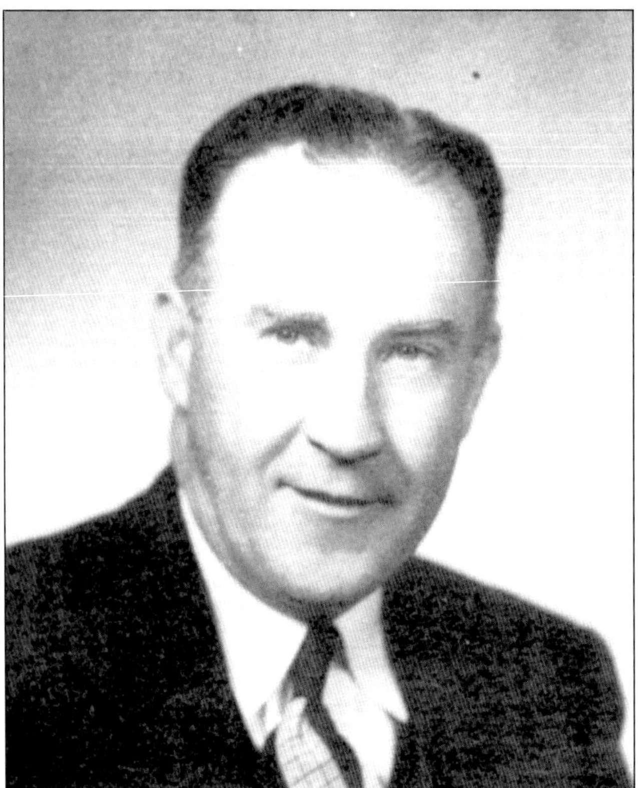

The James J. Keough Administration Building is located at 60 Harpin Street. It once served as Bellingham's high school. The opening day of this new high school was October 24, 1938. Lionel Trudeau was the school's first principal. One hundred and forty pupils were enrolled, seventy boys and seventy girls. The first graduating class was in 1939, and the last class to graduate from the high school was in 1964. To the left is a photograph of James J. Keough.

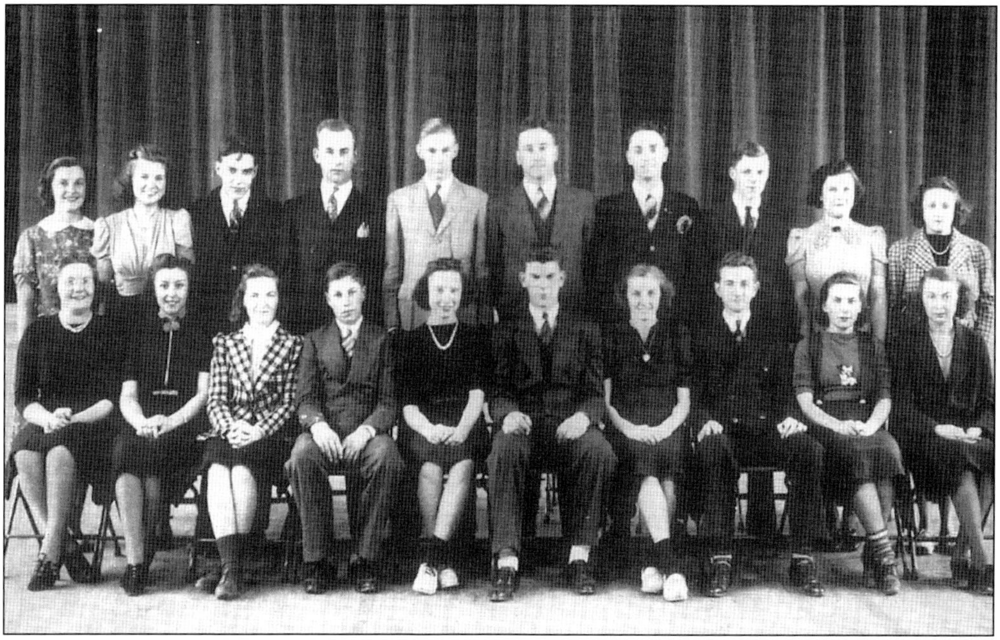

Members of Bellingham High School's Class of 1939 include Windsor Bates, J. Adelard Bernier, Evelyn Boyle, Leo Cartier, Constance Farley, Blanche Fitzpatrick, Ester Foley, Virgilio Forte, Mary Gigante, Rita Guerin, Marion Hogarth, Dante Innocente, Lola Meotti, Helen Mostek, Stephen Nadolny, Edgar Scott, Everlenna Sims, Albert Spencer, George Staples, and Jennie Zhawred.

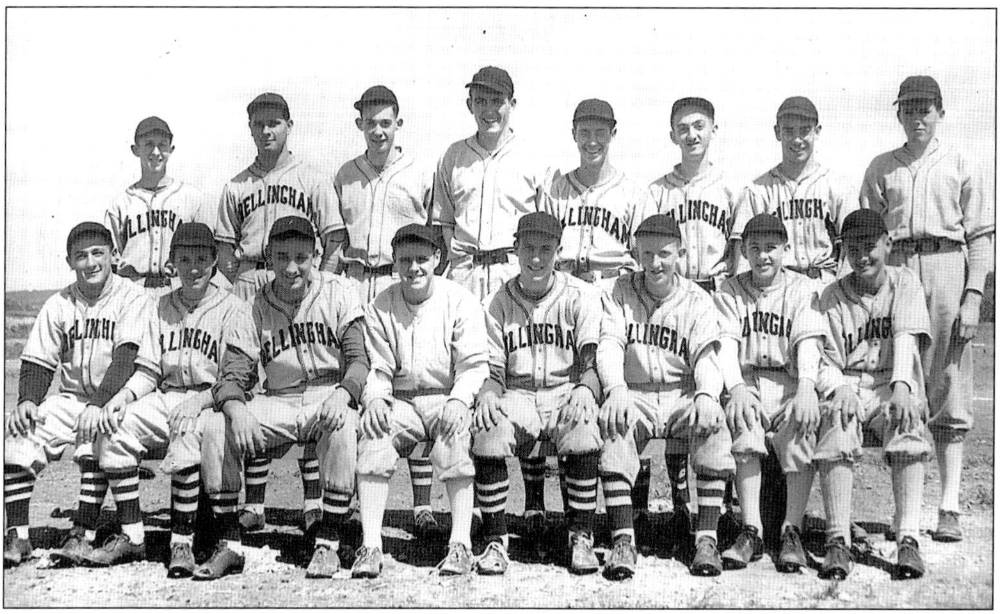

Team members of the Bellingham High School baseball team of 1945 are, from left to right, as follows: (front row) Nicholas Petrosky, Victor Glowka, Walter Nadolny, Bill Hutchinson (the coach), Ted Marchand, Gerard Daigle, Carleton Patrick, and Albert Forte; (back row) Normand Garneau, Chet Lewinski, William Baisley, Jack Tuttle, Michael Berardi, Richard Genereau, Lloyd Rhodes, and Robert Tuttle.

BY-LAWS AND RESOLVES,

Of School District No. 9, in the Town of Bellingham, concerning their School House and School.

ARTICLE I.

Every scholar mu st be cautious against tracking snow or dirt into the School House, spitting about the room, or otherwise soiling it.

ARTICLE II.

No scholar shall be allowed to stand or walk upon the seats or desks.

ARTICLE III.

If any scholar shall cut, or mark the Maps, Seats or Desk, break or crack the glass, deface or otherwise injure the School House, out-house, Pump, or any of the District property, or any way trespass on any of the adjacent lands, said scholar, his parents or guardian, shall pay to the Prudential Committee such damages as he may require.

ARTICLE IV.

If any scholar or person shall feel aggrieved by the damages required of them by the Prudential Committee, he may appeal therefrom to the District at their next legal meeting.

ARTICLE V.

If any scholar shall put wood or coal into the Stove or Furnace, or have any thing to do with it, except those to whose care it be intrusted, or by the request of the Teacher, said scholar, his parents or guardian, shall for each offence forfeit the sum of twenty-five cents, to be paid to the Prudential Committee for the use of the District.

AATICLE VI.

Any of the foregoing By-Laws may be altered or amended at any legal meeting of the inhabitants of the District by a vote of two-thirds of the members present.

RESOLVES.

Resolved, That the Teachers be requested to exert their influence in securing a strict observance of the foregoing By-Laws and Regulations, also that they inform the Prudential Committee of all violations of the foregoing By-Laws, and if possible the names of scholars causing the same, and as the laws of this Commonwealth make it the duty of teachers, in addition to elementary instruction in the sciences, to watch over the moral conduct and habits of their pupils, not only in school, but going to and from it, they should suffer no immorality or impropriety of conduct to pass without suitable notice and discipline therefor.

Resolved, That we will always sustain our teachers, and co-operate with them in all reasonable measures for the maintainence of good order and discipline, and whatever will promote the intellectual and moral improvement of the school.

Resolved, That it is the imperative duty of parents frequently to visit the School, to acquaint themselves with its condition and prospects; also to promote the regular and punctual attendance of scholars, in order to derive the greatest benefit from the school.

Each school district had specific codes of conduct. Above are the bylaws and resolves for School District No. 9 (the North School) from 1881.

Eight

BELLINGHAM 1969

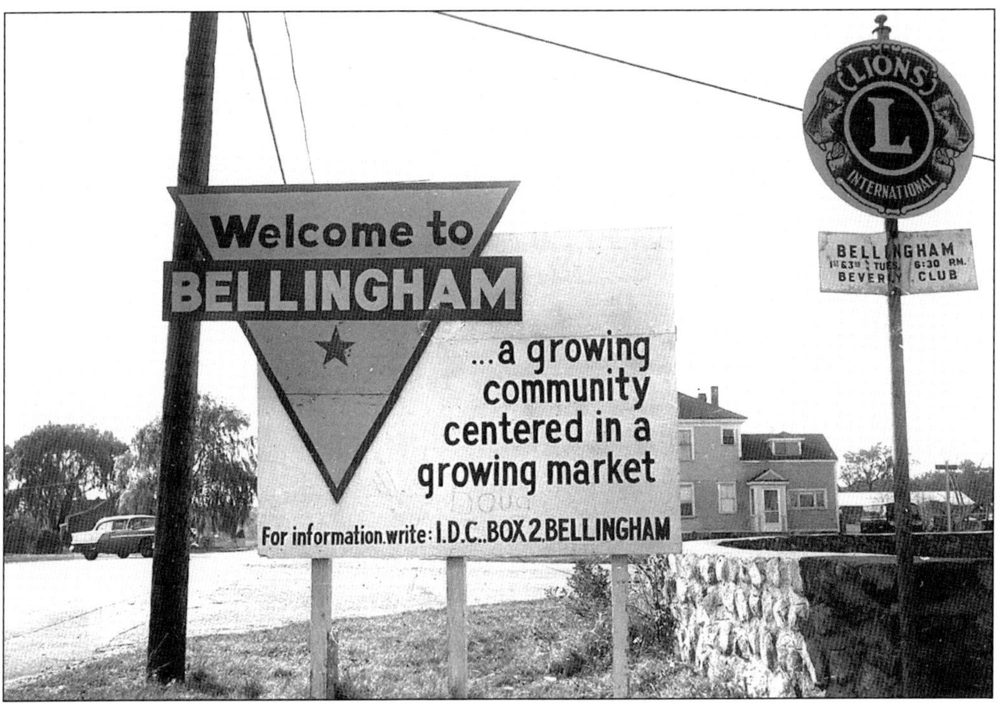

In 1969, the cities of Worcester, Boston, and Providence were considered a "golden triangle." Bellingham, located 30 miles from each city, was in the heart of the triangle. The star on the sign above shows Bellingham's location.

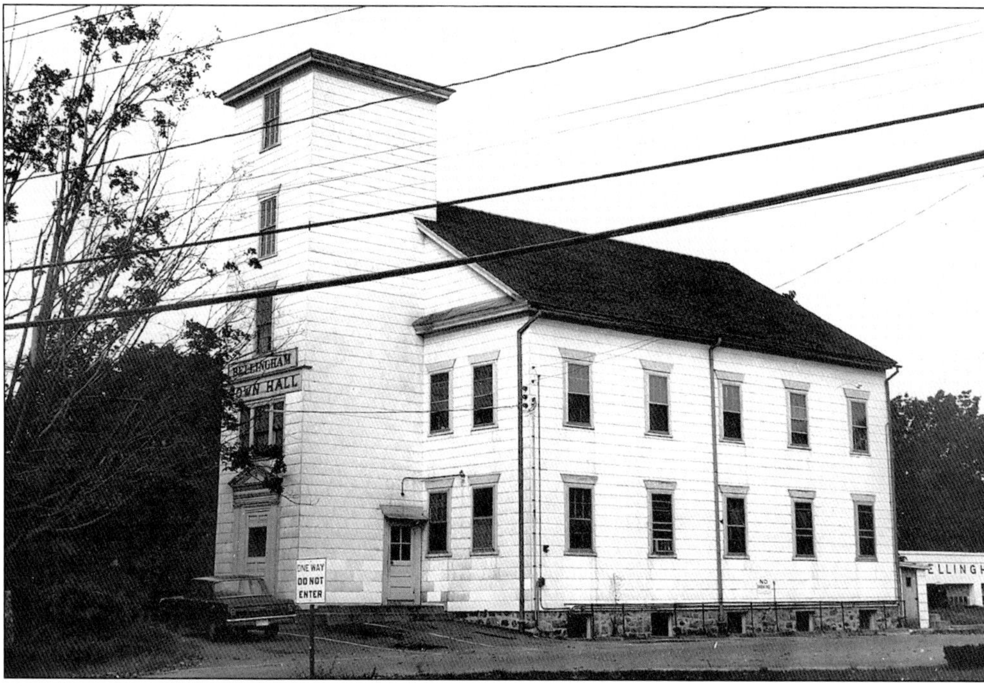

Shown above is the town hall in the spring of 1969, before the landscaping project. Below is how the grounds appeared during the summer of 1969. Ed Denault, below, is shown with his automobile.

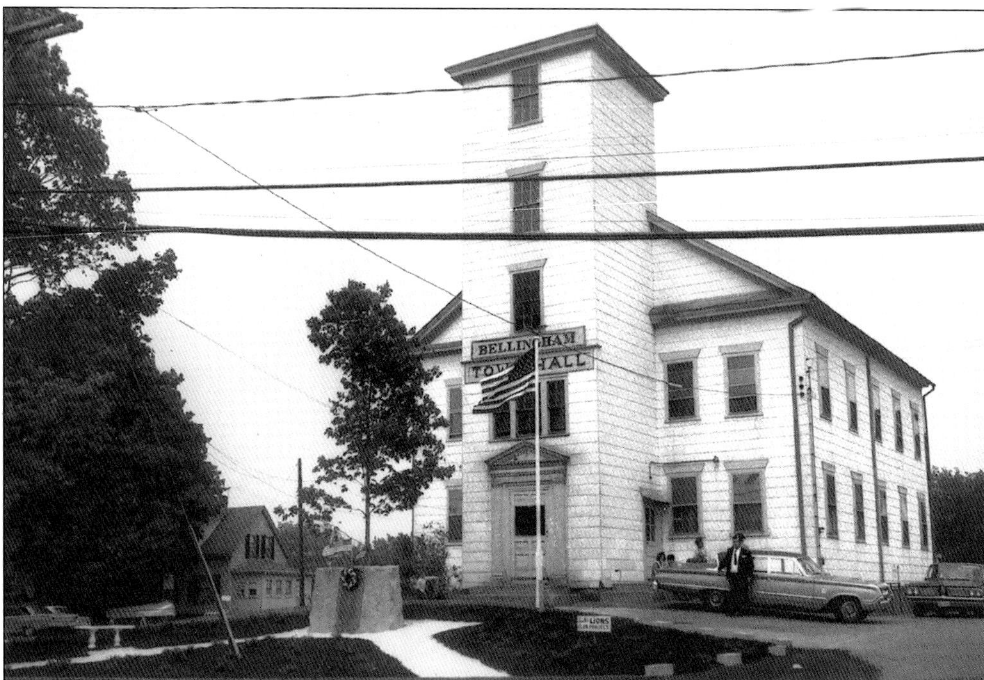

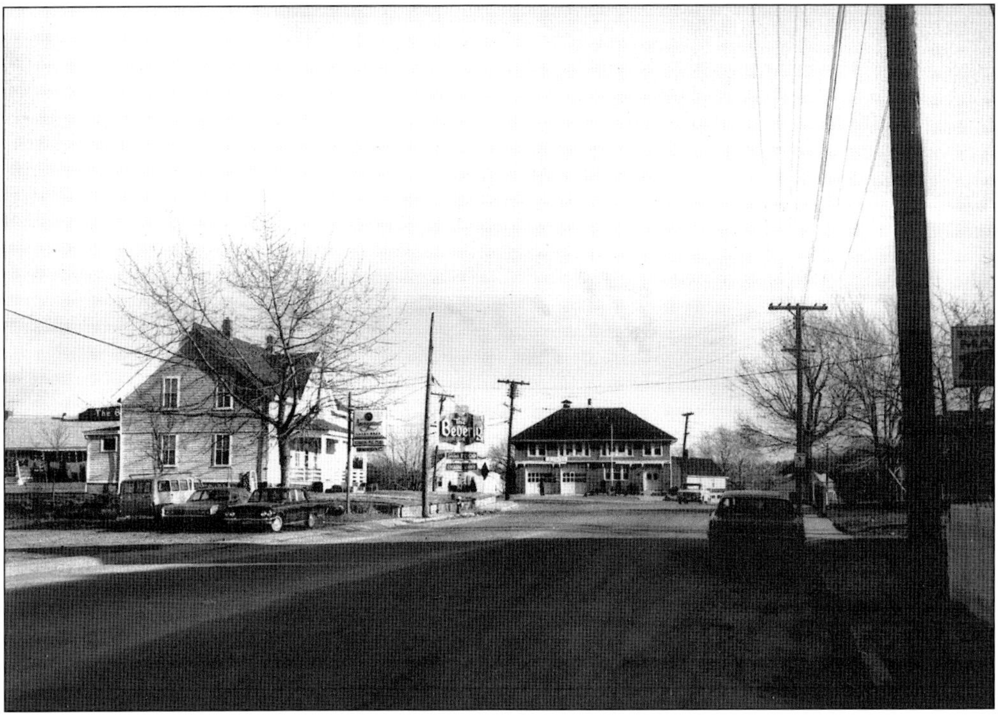

Pictured is Wrentham Street at Crooks Corner.

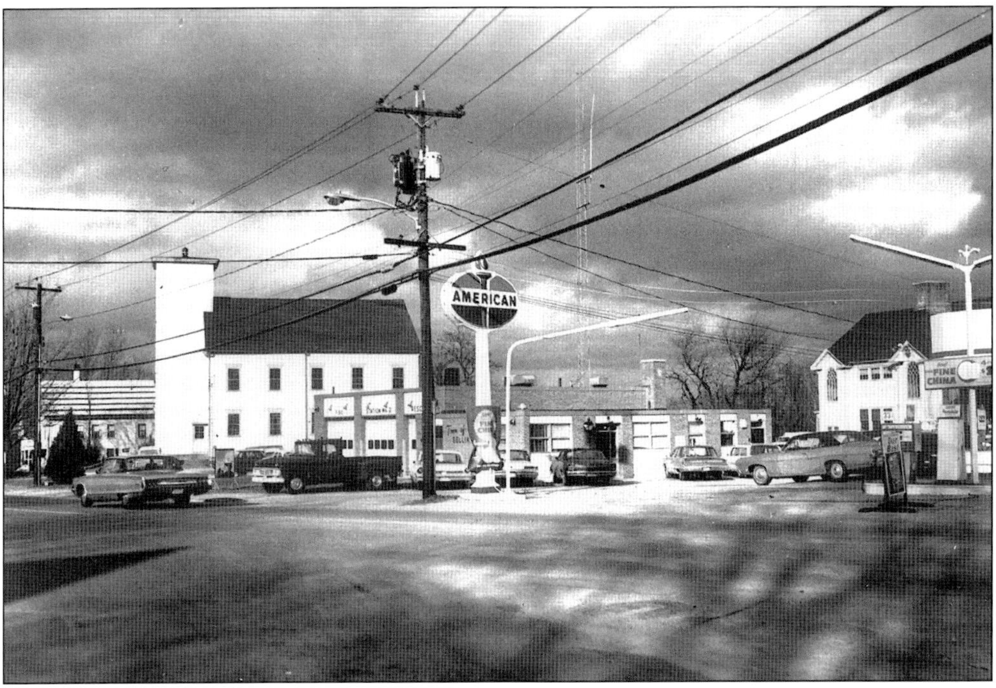

Shown is the town hall complex at Bellingham Center.

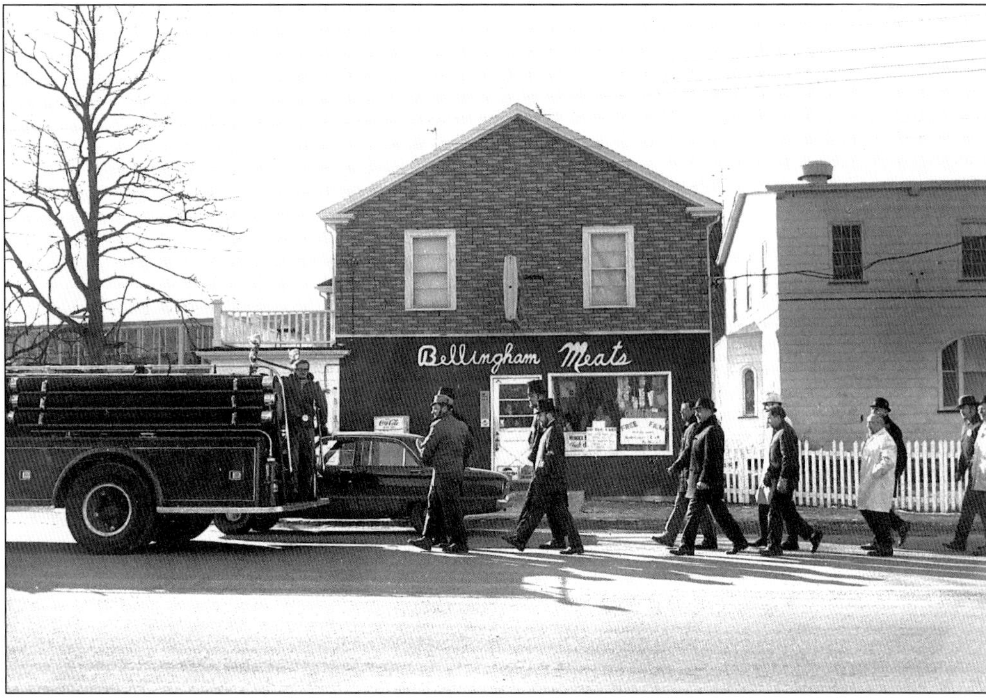

A local bicentennial group, "the brothers of the brush," held a small parade on Wrentham Street. The brothers would bury their razors and not shave for an entire year.

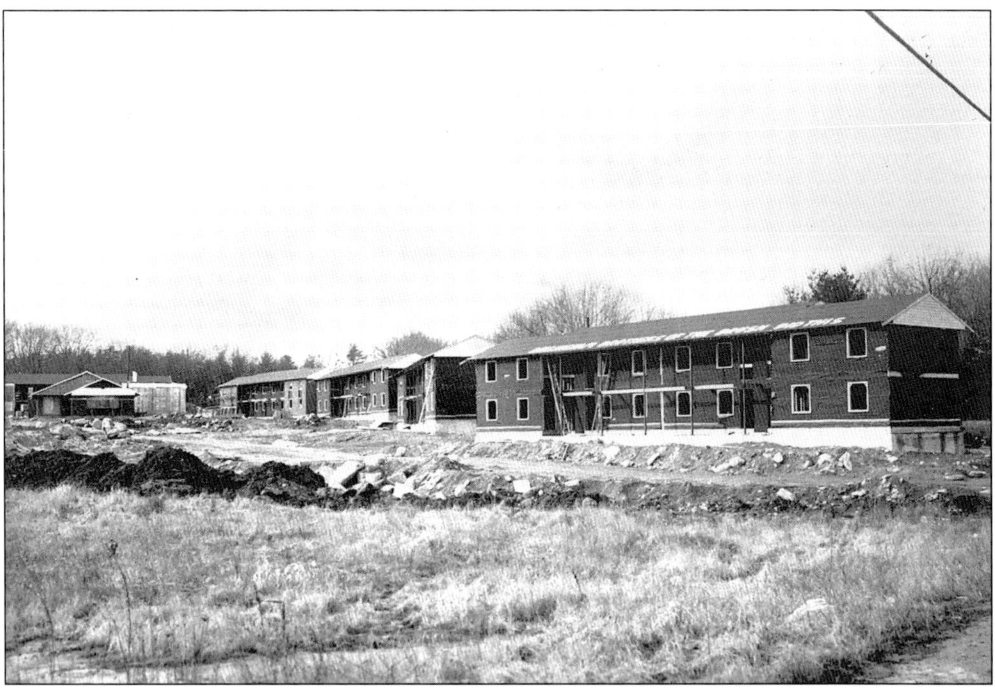

The Depot Court housing project is being built in this picture.

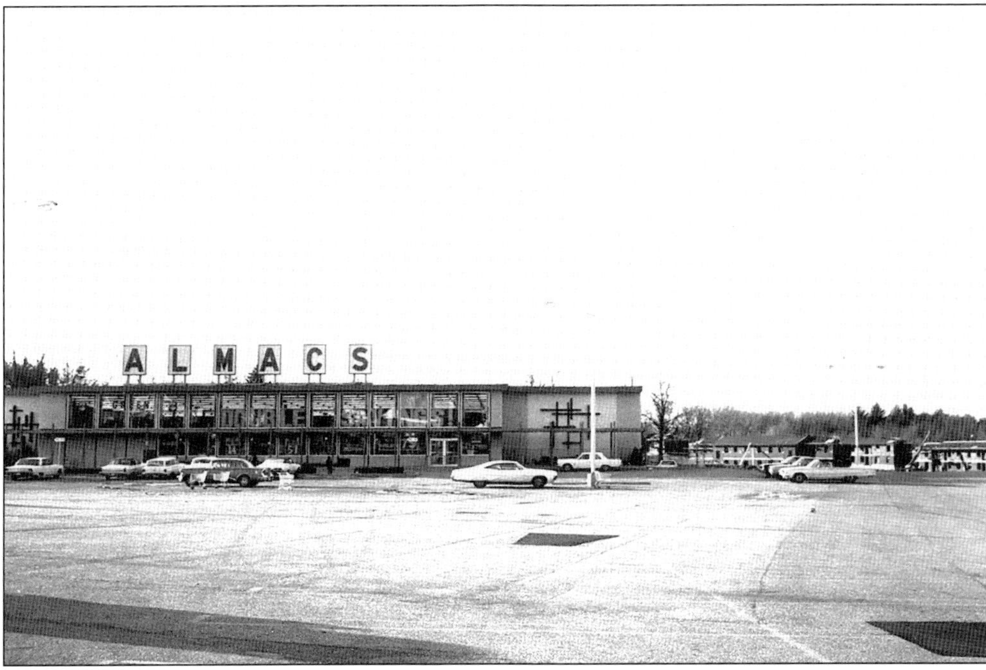

Almacs, at Bellingham Center, is shown here. Note Depot Court in background. Almacs and its parking lot are now the site of the town common.

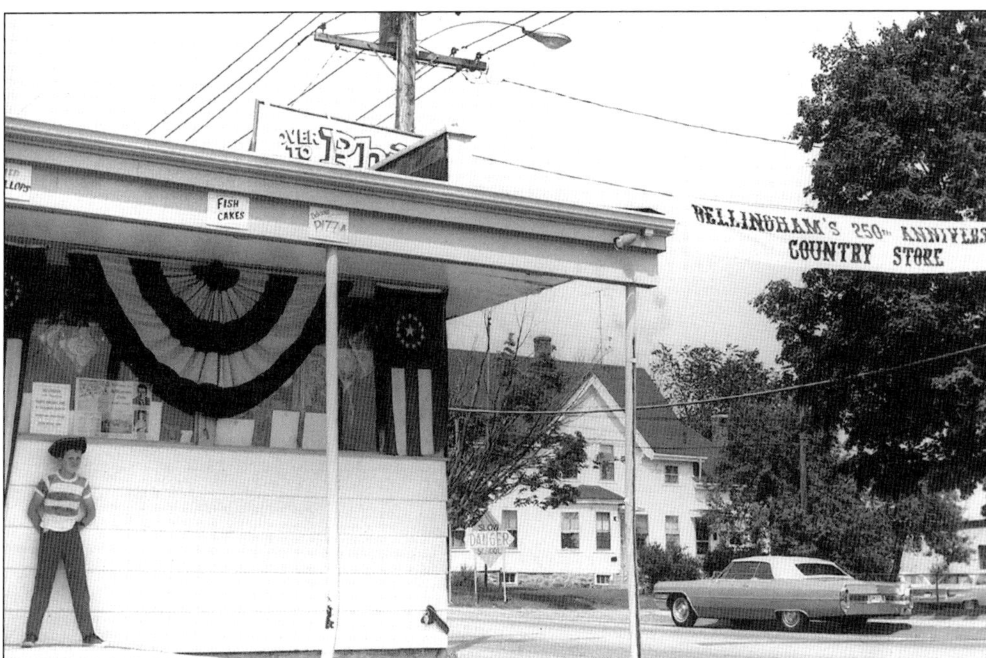

Phil's Fish and Chips on Pulaski Boulevard was also the home of the bicentennial souvenir shop.

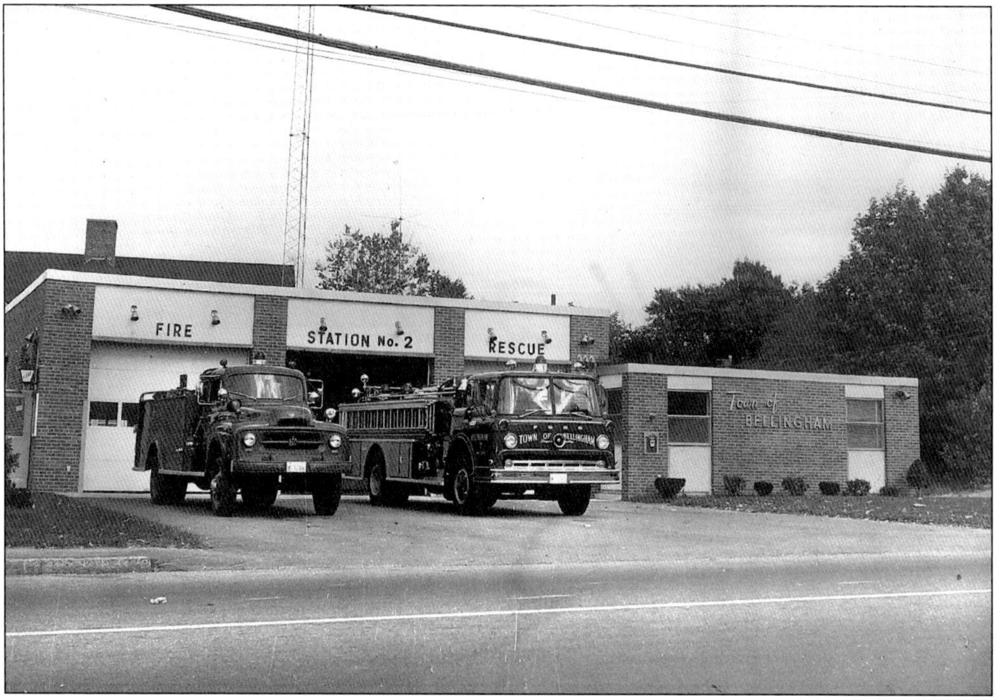

Shown is the combination police and fire station, No. 2, at the Bellingham Center town complex.

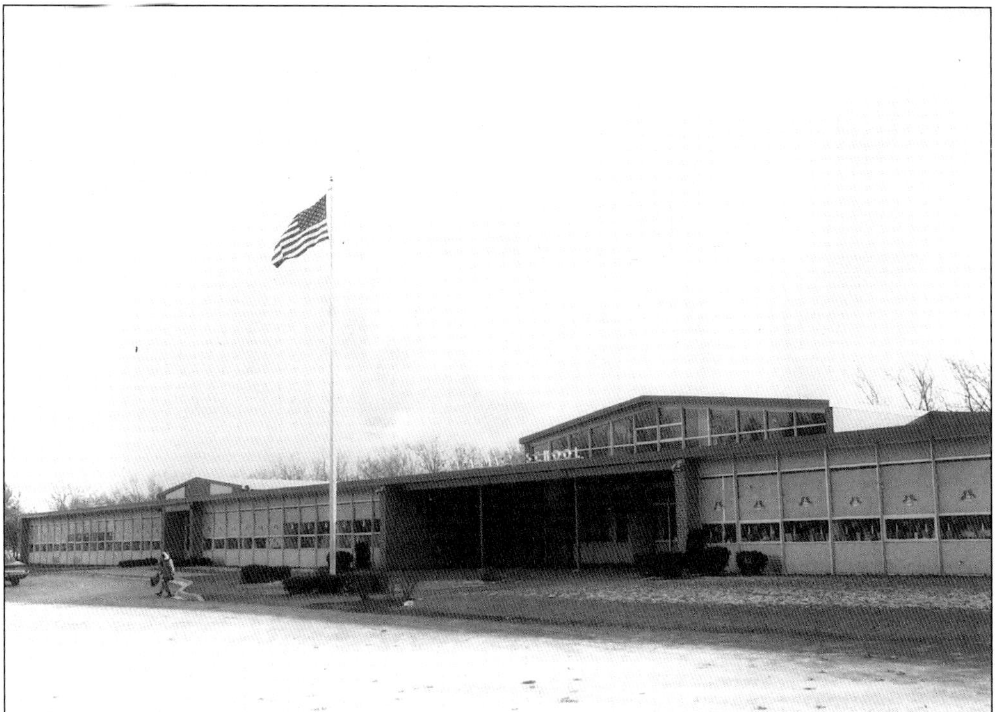

Shown is the Clara Macy School on Monique Drive.

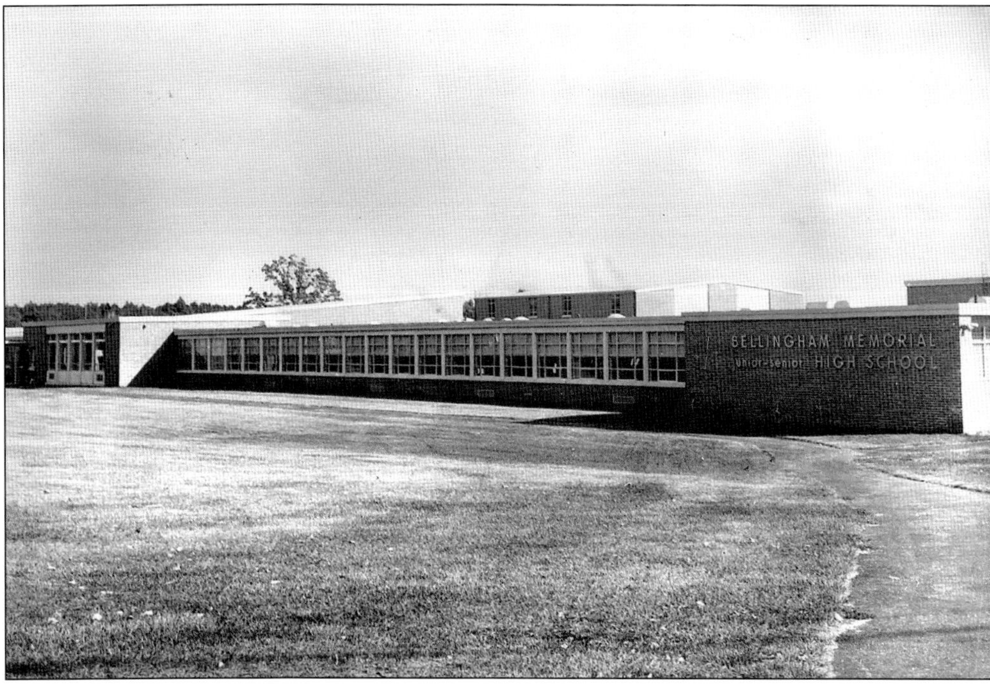

Shown is the former Bellingham Memorial Junior-Senior High School located on Blackstone Street and South Main Street.

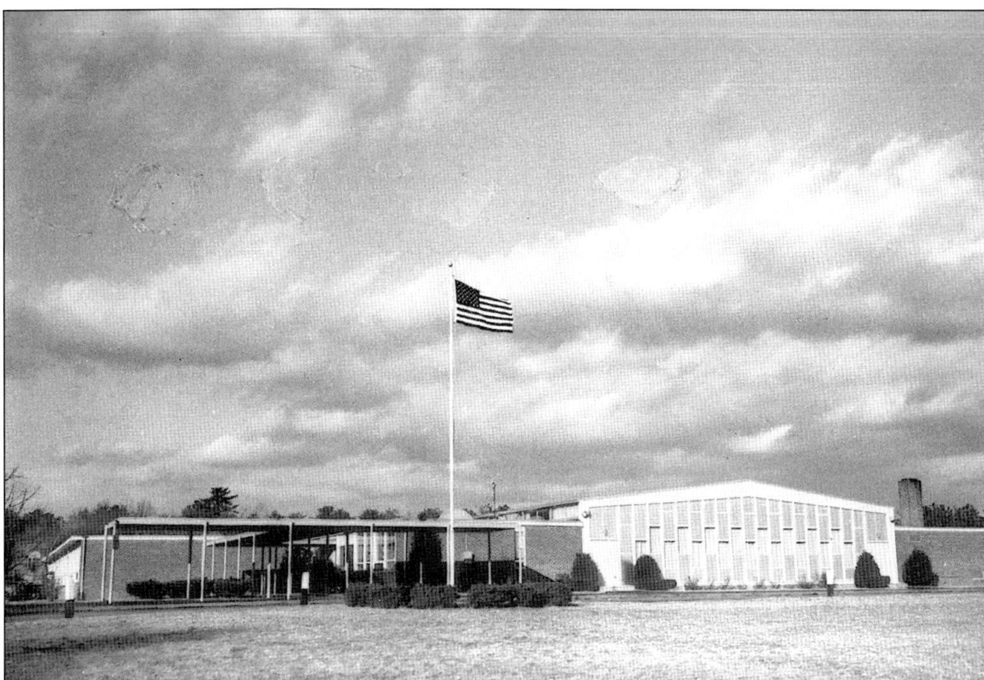
The Pinecrest School on Harpin Street is pictured here.

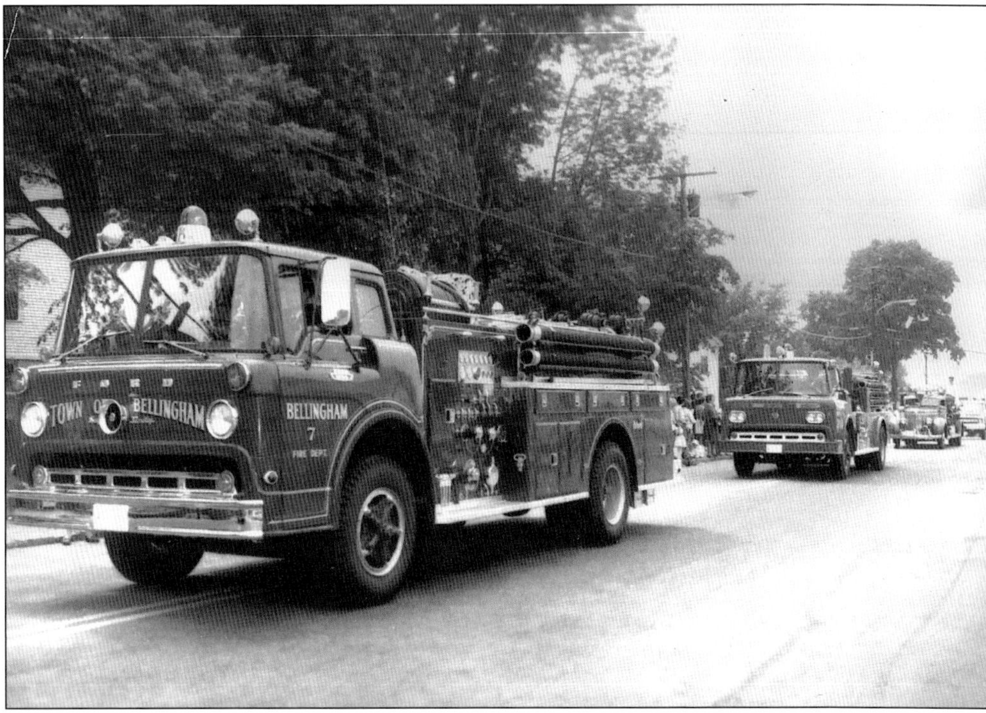

Bellingham residents celebrate Memorial Day in 1969 with a parade at Bellingham Center.

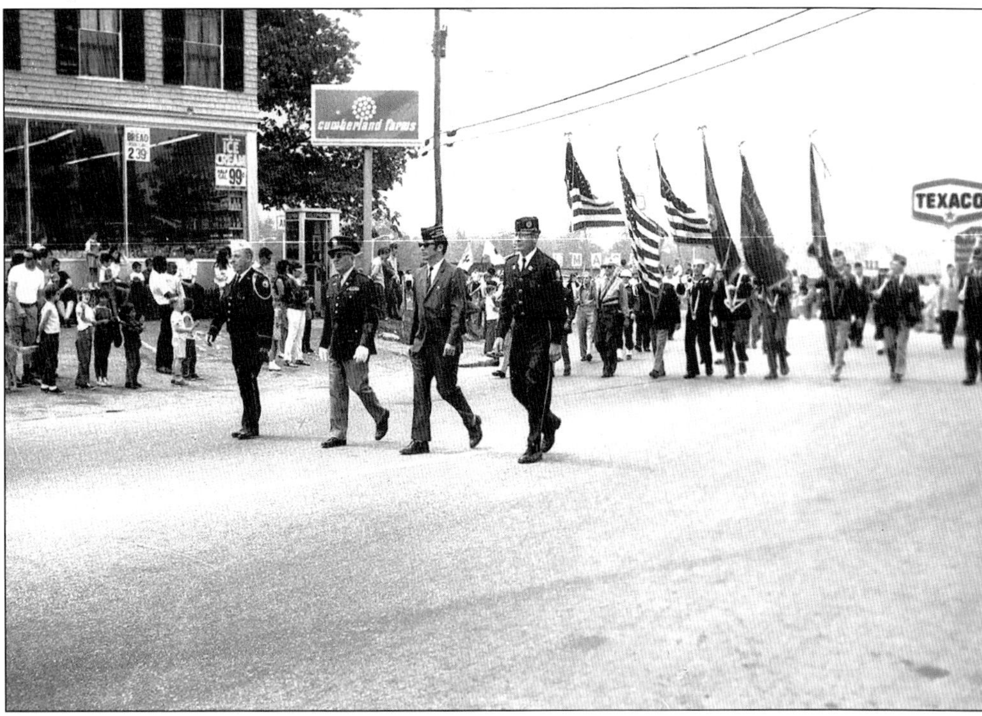